SHAPESHIFTING INTO HIGHER CONSCIOUSNESS

Llyn Roberts is a muse for the Earth. Her words sing from the knowing of her soles, engaging a rhythm that endures from the wisdom of ancient times. Llyn's teachings are grounded, strong and centered. They reach deeply into the human soul igniting a passion that offers new life to our relationship with the land.
Mick Dodge, *The Barefoot Sensei*

Shapeshifting Into Higher Consciousness is a living breathing experience of the power within each of us to radiate the creativity of life itself. It is not about shapeshifting. It IS shapeshifting. As I read, practicing even briefly the potent exercises so clearly described, I felt myself shifting to the highest essence of my being, empowered by the Light within the whole of creation. The practices seem innate, natural, and spontaneous. A palpable field of resonance is evoked. You can live the fullness of life, healing, love and creativity through the guidance given so gently and wisely in this book. It is the work of a master shapeshifter and embodiment of the evolving world, already radiant in our midst.
Barbara Marx Hubbard, Co-founder The Foundation for Conscious Evolution

Authentic and powerful. When this book finds its way into your life you will have found what you are looking for. It is a primal guide that will open your heart, ignite your spirit and reconnect you with the conscious world. There you can find, and experience peace, happiness, joy, and the innate magic of life.
Clinton Ober, Best selling co-author of *Earthing*

Llyn Roberts has written another amazing and powerful book that empowers us all to reclaim our most deeply held values. Shapeshifting Into Higher Consciousness *will inspire everyone who reads it to use our personal and collective will to bring forth an environmentally sustainable, spiritually fulfilling, and socially just human presence on this planet. I recommend the book and its message to everyone who is committed to participating in the great transformation of our time; it is a brilliant piece of work.*

Lynne Twist, Author of *The Soul of Money* and Co-Founder The Pachamama Alliance

This book will take you step by step into higher consciousness; it shines the light on our fullest human potential during this crucial time of evolution on earth. It is true that we each have Divine purpose and that we can channel our heartfelt longings into reality. Llyn's work will help you rediscover this magic and use your innate powers to create a better world.

James Twyman, Best-selling author and Peace Troubadour

At times of crisis like we face today we have the opportunity to rise to a higher consciousness. Llyn Roberts offers the tools, the wisdom, and the stories that will make it possible for all who dare to dream their reality differently. She offers us the keys to shapeshift into our personal and collective destinies. I've waited for a book like this for a long time. It is a must-read for anyone who wants to be part of the great transformation ahead!

Alberto Villoldo Ph.D., Best-selling author of *Shaman, Healer, Sage* and *Courageous Dreaming*

Shapeshifting Into Higher Consciousness

Heal and Transform Yourself
and Our World with Ancient
Shamanic and Modern Methods

Shapeshifting Into Higher Consciousness

Heal and Transform Yourself
and Our World with Ancient
Shamanic and Modern Methods

Llyn Roberts

BOOKS

Winchester, UK
Washington, USA

First published by O-Books, 2011
O-Books is an imprint of John Hunt Publishing Ltd., Laurel House, Station Approach,
Alresford, Hants, SO24 9JH, UK
office1@o-books.net
www.o-books.com

For distributor details and how to order please visit the 'Ordering' section on our website.

Text copyright: Llyn Roberts 2010

ISBN: 978 1 84694 843 5

A CIP catalogue record for this book is available from the British Library.

Design: Stuart Davies

Printed in the UK by CPI Antony Rowe
Printed in the USA by Offset Paperback Mfrs, Inc

We operate a distinctive and ethical publishing philosophy in all
areas of our business, from our global network of authors to
production and worldwide distribution.

CONTENTS

Aimlessly Wander
Walk Like a Shuar
Retrieve Physical Huacas
The Siberian Mark Exercise
The Whole Earth is a Vortex
Dream Harmony on Earth

Empowerment: Arutum, Windhorse and Khiimori
Retrieve Empowerment Huacas
Awaken to Higher Purpose
Live and Journey Fluidly
Journey to the Reflecting Pool, About Scrying
The Wisdom of Heart and Body
Time, Space and Dreaming
Siberian Chalimar (Prayer Tie) Ceremony

The Luminous You across Lifetimes
Revive the Core Self:
Quechua Tree Method, Tibetan Practices
Remold the Everyday Self:
Emotions ~ Unleash the Real You,
Shapeshift into Light in Daily Life
Awaken to Luminosity with Others:
View Other's Essence, Read and
Retrieve Essence

Wild and Womanly Ways
Reclaim the Deep Feminine:

AUTHOR'S NOTE

This book stands on its own. But if you are new to shamanism or spirituality, or to understanding that we and our world are interconnected and energetic in nature, reading *Shamanic Reiki: Expanded Ways of Working with Universal Life Force Energy* (Roberts & Levy), will offer a helpful foundation.

The chapters of *Shapeshifting into Higher Consciousness* are not ordered in an exclusively linear manner. Therefore, although later reading is to great extent founded upon earlier chapters, you may also find the reverse to be true. As each chapter weaves a world unto itself, this book is best read when you are relaxed, open, and can give your full attention to it. Allow the content to seep into you beyond the words. You may read it in entirety first, then go back to incorporate the practices. Or you may spend a month or more immersing within the messages and experiences of each chapter. You will get the most out of this book if you engage it intimately and creatively. Open to whatever your experience is and regard what you read and practice as a template. If something does not resonate for you, let it spur you to explore the topic more deeply. You may ask yourself: "What do I really think and feel about this?", "How can I understand it from my own perspective?", or "What does my personal experience say; how does this apply to my own life?"

The material presented here is currently taught in *Shapeshifting* programs and on sacred expeditions offered jointly by myself and John Perkins. It appears here in an easy-to-grasp format with detailed descriptions so you can bring *Shapeshifting* into daily life and/or deepen the experiences of your workshop or sacred journey.

The exercises in this book are comfortably adapted to guide individuals or groups and you can also practice them by yourself. Following these approaches can be helpful if performing the exercises alone: 1) read the entire exercise, implementing one step at a time until you master it; 2) record each step on a recorder at a pace that allows plenty of time for each segment; 3) review the exercise until you thoroughly grasp the steps, and write notes or jot down the italicized introductions (or the main steps) for easy reference when doing the practice. The exercises in this book make its message practical and immediate, encouraging new ways to be.

As I am its author these writings favor my personal orientation to John Perkins's and my work.

As you explore this book, open to the living energy of these writings as *Higher Consciousness* is evoked in the process. Power, wisdom and energy are awakened through the reading so pay attention to how you feel, and to what unfolds in life, as you travel through these pages. What is your experience? Note insights, dreams. Attend to how you feel, what you become aware of. Open to synchronicity. Engage the vibrant forces all around us, all the time, and with which we are one.

I appreciate the journey you engage through the reading of this book and trust its benefit will radiate well beyond you. During these profound times of change, let us each embrace the wholeness that is our human birthright. Together, let us dream and create a better world.

This material is offered for informational purposes only; its user must accept full responsibility for applying the information that is presented in this book. Energetic practices and alternative, spiritual, and/or shamanic systems are commonly viewed as compliments to modern medical and psychological modalities. Spiritual, energy and shamanic practitioners are not authorized to diagnose or treat psychological or medical illnesses. For situations requiring clinical expertise or intervention, clients, as well as practitioners, are advised to seek the advice of a licensed professional.

INTRODUCTION

By New York Times Best Selling Author, John Perkins

When I first met Llyn Roberts early in 1997, I was immediately impressed by her work as a healer, teacher and psychotherapist influenced by spiritual teachers from a variety of cultures. I was especially taken by her deep connection to the earth and by the wisdom she had gained from a commitment to expanding her personal horizons.

She had grown up in a provincial New Hampshire community – as had I. For both of us, this background generated a yearning to explore exotic lands, cultures, and ideas, to get to know people and places that had been portrayed to us as "remote," "unusual," even "bizarre" and "dangerous." In our early twenties we both headed out into the world. She traveled to India, I to South America.

Many years later, our paths crossed. We first met at a workshop I was facilitating in Cambridge MA, shortly after the publication of my book *Shapeshifting*. It was apparent that there was a bond uniting us, the sort that is interwoven through past lives. I invited her to assist me on a trip I was leading to the Amazon and Andes organized by Dream Change, a nonprofit I had founded in the early 1990s.

I was not surprised when she proved to be much more than an assistant. Her knowledge of indigenous people and her compassion for trip participants made my job easy.

It did not take long for Llyn to become a trip leader herself and to take Dream Change to new levels; she organized and facilitated tours to visit indigenous shamans in Siberia, the Asian Steppes, Maya lands of Central America, and she formed an alliance with Andean shamans that resulted in powerful apprenticeship programs. Several years later she took over the directorship of Dream Change.

For many years I had talked about the Legend of the Eagle and the Condor (see page 00). This ancient prophecy that traces its Amazonian/Andean roots back at least 2000 years states that we are now entering a time that carries the potential for the heart and mind, the scientific and the intuitive, the male and female, to unite. As that happens, human beings will be empowered to soar to new levels of consciousness. This prophecy says, however, that this powerful transformation will not happen automatically; we the people must take actions to facilitate it. I realized that I needed to help manifest this prophecy in a very concrete way. I needed to take action. As a workshop facilitator, I needed to find a woman who could balance out my male energy. I knew that woman was Llyn.

For many years now Llyn and I have co-facilitated shapeshifting workshops. These range from evening ceremonies with Kuna and Embera elders on the banks of the Panama Canal to sixteen day apprenticeship programs in Upstate New York. We have witnessed amazing transformations in this process. We have seen people shift into the energy fields of animal spirit guides, overcome diseases and addictions, break through psychological barriers, understand their missions in life, and open themselves to their deepest powers.

Part of our own shared mission is to facilitate the entry into this new epoch that has been foretold since ancient times by the Quechua, the Maya, the Hopi, and the people of the Asian Steppes, Himalayas, African Serengeti, and so many other cultures. The common theme throughout all of these legends is the idea that we are poised at the brink of a transformative time unlike any history has ever witnessed. We humans have the opportunity to leave behind societies characterized by greed and exploitation and create new ones that are based on compassion and sustainability. The prophecies encourage us to create a world children around the planet will want to inherit. They also tell us that to do so will require a new form of awareness. We must shapeshift to higher consciousness.

Llyn and I have learned from our indigenous teachers and from our experiences as workshop facilitators that the route to higher consciousness is a series of steps. A Quechua shaman provides a step for me; I move to a new level and then offer a step for Llyn; she integrates this with previous steps of her own, ascends to a still higher level and becomes a step for me as well as the people in our workshops; they present themselves as steps for us. It is a continual process, a sort of "piggy-backing to higher consciousness."

My *Shapeshifting* book provided a step that led to this new *Shapeshifting* book by Llyn. This one that you now hold in your hands offers practical ways you can soar to the top of all the steps we have taken so far. It is an eloquent and experiential approach to continuing this piggy-backing ascension.

I encourage you, as you read this book, to be aware of all the sentient beings and all the elements around the universe – the people, plants, animals, stones, mountains, fires, waterways, and spirits – that have contributed to it. They are our allies. Your allies. Please allow them to guide you through these pages. Feel their power and yours. Let your spirit and body vibrate at new levels.

Together we will manifest prophesies, we will shapeshift into higher consciousness.

DEDICATION

I dedicate this work to my children Sayre and Eben, to John Perkins's grandson, Grant, to every child of every species on the earth and beyond, and to the undying spirit of life.

"We must be willing to get rid of the life we've planned, so as to have the life that is waiting for us. The old skin has to be shed before the new one can come." - Joseph Campbell

CHAPTER ONE

SHAPESHIFTING AND HIGHER CONSCIOUSNESS

It is still not uncommon for the words *shaman* and *Shapeshifting* to bring up a fear of black magic or to conjure images of people turning into bats or lizards or "anything unnatural" as Samwise Gamgee put it in J.R.R. Tolkein's classic, *The Fellowship of the Ring.* But in general, contemporary culture is comfortable with, and better understands, the many and subtler benefits of ancient views. The examples are endless and include: the use of traditional medicinal plants whose curative powers have been known to native peoples for centuries; the growing number of shamanic teachers and practitioners among North Americans and Europeans; the world wide recognition of the Dalai Lama as a peace proponent and social leader traversing cultural boundaries; and the growing ease with which Eastern modalities such as Reiki, meditation, acupuncture and yoga are integrated into allopathic medicine and Western wellness paradigms. Today, in the fields of modern psychology, health, medicine, and even in social and business sectors, time honored wisdom permeates the mainstream.

Coinciding with our success in assimilating wisdom ways from diverse original cultures, modern society boasts unprecedented technological leaps. Yet despite this, most of us would agree that the world today exists in a state of chaos. That we are proportionately not in any greater turmoil than other tumultuous eras, to a degree is true. But one fact separates us from our ancestors: we have gone far beyond even industrial age tragedies of poisoning individual water bodies, ruining specialized ecosystems and decimating isolated species to shifting the bionetwork of the earth herself. In so doing, we threaten our own and many species' survival.

As the consequences of wreaking havoc with our host planet play themselves out they look dire. It is at precisely this time that so many of us are searching for hope. We are looking for a way out of this nightmare. But balance will not restore overnight. Humanity has devoted centuries to cultivating societies that see themselves as separate from nature. The deeper solution demands that we live by higher values. We must dive deeply to reshape the consciousness that got us here in the first place. This is a journey to our higher human qualities that help us live from our hearts and minds combined. There is *opportunity* underlying these times of change, which indigenous cultures have long foreseen.

For centuries and through periods of severe persecution, original peoples from Tibet, Latin America, Siberia, North America and other places have protected messages about today. These are prophecies that have remained hidden until recent decades. Diverse cultures predicted this episode of calamity and upheaval. Yet they also saw that it holds tremendous promise for humankind, the opportunities equaling the threats. Some common themes emerge in these prophecies: 1) the times heralding change will be fraught with imbalance, turmoil and polarized factions; 2) the earth is becoming conscious, emanating higher vibrations that shift our awareness; 3) our greater humanness can awaken, integrating heart and mind, spirituality and materialism; 4) the world as we know it, and we - our bodies and consciousness - are transforming; 5) living from the heart in harmony with the earth is essential to survive.

In exploring throughout the pages of this book we will see

how *Shapeshifting* is pivotal to our ability to navigate unprecedented social and environmental change. Contemporary culture has a tendency now to look increasingly for answers in indigenous paradigms. This appears divinely orchestrated as it is within ancient wisdom approaches that we find some of the most optimistic perspectives for our ailing world.

As we step headlong into change it is helpful to remember that life's most valuable initiations, for example the birth of a child, often come with chaos, risk and pain. Knowing an infant will be the fruit of her labor changes a woman's relationship to the pain and pandemonium she endures as her child makes its way into the world. From this vantage, and that of indigenous prophecies, we can choose to see the chaos on our planet - with all its grief and hazards - as a transformational stage. In doing so, we awaken the living intelligence pushing us now to evolve. In doing so, we rouse our natural ability to *Shapeshift*.

More about this Book
Although some see *Shapeshifting* as changing into something you are not now, like becoming a tiger or an elephant that is not the goal of *Shapeshifting* in this book. Neither will these writings offer pat formulas for making the world and your own life trouble free. Instead, you will discover ways to heal and awaken intrinsic human qualities obscured until recent times. In doing so, you will be supported in forging an intimate connection with spirit and the natural world. This is most important during these times of change. We will explore time-tested methods based on modern and ancient principles. These have transformed illness, changed troubling personality traits and life circumstances and can make our world a better place. We and our world are not separate. Healing ourselves also heals our world. In becoming more whole we radiate wholeness to everything around us. We are inspired to live in ways that affirm all life on this planet and coax others to do the same.

If this material is new to you, some of it may seem magical, mysterious or even *extra*ordinary. Whatever your experience, please remember that these concepts are indeed ordinary. They are our birthright, part of the natural fabric of being human. Perhaps more extraordinary is that our innate capacity to heal and transform has lain undeveloped for so long. These attributes have only been historically tapped by spiritual adepts and traditional shamanic peoples.

The perils and promises of our modern day urge us to reclaim who we really are. It is within all of our reach, now more than ever, to do so.

In reading these pages I hope you feel supported in opening to a larger vision of yourself and of life. Being fluid melds heart and mind. It invites nature to heal, guide and nourish us. Previously unchangeable aspects of us, others and the world can transform. In these ways we can dance with the rhythms of these prophesied times. We can open to new ways of knowing and being. As we do, we will discover how to live in harmony with our planet.

But before changing the world, let us explore more of what *Shapeshifting* and *Higher Consciousness* are about so we can understand how to apply it to daily life.

What is *Shapeshifting*?
Described in the simplest of terms, *Shapeshifting* is about changing from one state to another. It is innate to us all and the calling card of nature and life. Everyone has experienced nature's *Shapeshifting*. Do you remember lying down on the grass as a child and gazing at the endlessly morphing clouds in the sky? Or watching a winter stream manifest ever changing worlds of ice and snow through the long, cold months? Or standing outside feeling soft breezes waft against your skin, only to feel the breeze suddenly shift to penetrating gusts?

We, and the world within which we live, are ever-changing and evolving. When we take the time to really see and immerse ourselves in the natural world around us - the winds, trees, animals, stones, skies - we discover that everything is constantly moving. The seasons and skies alter in color and weather patterns. The air can transform from an oppressive stillness on a hot summer's night into a gentle breeze that gulls glide on at the ocean's edge. Then again it can morph into powerful hurricanes that destroy homes and trees. Even stones appearing unyielding will over time deteriorate. They crack, change color and crumble into sand. We are part of this natural life circle. Human beings also continuously morph from one state to another. Our body changes dramatically through the course of a lifetime from birth to death. Medical science says our cells and organs continuously reconfigure. We can see this when we get a cold or a virus and recover from it. Or even if we develop life threatening dis-eases we can have spontaneous remissions, rendering hopeless prognoses not so solid. Our emotions also wax and wane. Yet unlike the moon they can do so with lightning speed. Our thoughts, too, incessantly shift, rise and fall, affecting physiology, emotion and perception.

Here is a mundane example of the shifting nature of body, perceptions and feelings. Try going grocery shopping sometime before you have had a chance to eat. You will be more focused on food and may pile more of it in your cart than your refrigerator can handle. Then if you stop for lunch on the way home, by the time you unpack everything you will wonder why you bought so much. Such is our shifting nature and inseparability of body, emotions and mind.

Being an energy practitioner well before I worked with indigenous shamanic healers, I witnessed physical *Shapeshifts* routinely. Eye conditions were remedied after one session, back problems that no medical or chiropractic intervention could cure were reversed in one treatment, women receiving energy work simultaneous to radiation treatments for breast cancer treatment suffered no skin burns, ear infections in infants disappeared never to return, and so on. This is not to say that every session resulted in spontaneous healing. And it does not discount the often complex, compelling circumstances of illness, or its opportunities. But in beholding many afflictions transform effortlessly, I wondered why we view miracles so exceptionally.

Whether changing weather patterns, shifting moods or mutable physical afflictions - it is easy to see that we and everything in our world are quite fluid. The ecstasy of life is to reconfigure. Sometimes it is a little disconcerting to recognize this is the key to *Shapeshifting* and to affirming all life on this planet. As a young person meditating for the first time I found the practice unsettling. I did not realize how busy my mind was. Or how my identity was held intact by loosely strung together internal dialogue. It was shocking to sit labeling each thought as "thinking". My thoughts simply came and went. My mind was (I was!) fickle and did not have continuous form. This was uncomfortable until I started resting more in the gaps in between. I began to focus less on the thoughts themselves. This practice has helped me embrace the magic of each moment. Then I could relax more into the ever changing flow of life.

Shapeshifting is an inherent aspect of the dance of life and of our own nature. *Shapeshifting* helps us live in the gaps. Throughout this book we will explore how to use it consciously. It can help us change perspectives, reality, and experience greater wholeness.

More About *Shapeshifting*

We have seen how the notion of *Shapeshifting* is supported by observing everything in our universe as already malleable, and how our bodies, intentions and experience are intertwined. The second quality helping us transform ourselves the world around us is oneness. Everything is connected and shares the same source.

From time immemorial aboriginal peoples across the planet have experienced life as interwoven and alive. Reality is a responsive fabric. Children grew up in such cultures knowing they were inseparable from: the waters, stones, trees, birds, winds, other people, animals, stars, past and future generations. They were taught to communicate with the intelligence of life. In this way they nurtured health and happiness for humans and the natural world. Nature nourished them physically: through the clothing and shelter it provided them, the plants and animals they ate, the winds that purified their environment, the air that infused each breath they took, the waters that soothed and cleansed them as well as quenched their thirst, the fires that cooked their food and its heat, as well as the sun's, that warmed them and radiated light. Nature was more than a resource. The trees, plants, earth, waters, animals, stones, celestial bodies and rivers were a sacred living web. There was a sentient mesh that connected people with all of life.

This concept is demonstrated in the movie, *I Heart Huckabees*. In it, Dustin Hoffman holds a white blanket representing the unified fabric of the universe. Then Hoffman pops his fist up under the blanket in several different places. One bump of his fist in the blanket after the next shows the individuated aspects of our world – himself here, another person there, the Eiffel Tower, a hamburger, Vivian his wife, a disease, a museum, and so on. Each item had its own form and location (each protrusion of Hoffman's fist) on the fabric. Yet each was, in essence, the one blanket. Everything is connected. All is one.

Traditional peoples know that everything is interconnected. All is infused with energy and power from the same source. This enables a hunter in the Amazon to merge with the qualities of a jaguar for stealth and swiftness desired to catch his prey. It makes it possible for a healer in the high Andes to embody an active volcano, *Shapeshifting* into the sacred mountains of his region and engulfing clients in fire to incinerate illness. A Buginese sailor in

Indonesia can blend with the consciousness of a frigate bird and fly across the ocean to chart his ship's course. A Siberian shamanic elder can don her feathered headdress and soar like an eagle into non-physical spiritual realms. There she can gather power, energy and insight to help villagers recover from cultural oppression. The notion of oneness is integral to the hunter, healer, navigator or community leader. They can access power from other realities and adopt perceptions of other life forms. Hence these people are intermediaries to the spiritual forces of the web of life they tap into. They actively participate with the cosmos and nature. The shaman utilizes wisdom, power and energy that filter through the senses, intuition, and longing.

A Siberian woman I worked with long ago expressed it beautifully: "Don't be passive, let the unique energy be shared by feeling yourself as one whole. What someone teaches or could tell you isn't as essential as what you feel and experience. Absorb wisdom and energy through your skin, mind and soul."

With practice and commitment we each can open as conduits to natural forces. This ability is innate to us all. To consciously *Shapeshift* we direct intention to alter energy and form. Energy includes thoughts and emotions. As well, it includes the underlying spiritual blueprint or subtle force-field of anything material. Form is anything we perceive as solid or physical; for example, our bodies, buildings, cars, the earth and the elements. Yet form can also be institutions, governments, behaviors, organized religions. It can be any structure constellating itself in a defined way. In journeying through these pages you will see form and energy as inseparable.

Directing intention to alter energy and form means more than thinking we want to change. It means more than thinking about what we want to change. Like the shamans mentioned above, it requires us to engage body, heart and imagination. We must take on the qualities of what we desire or want to be. Have you ever wanted something so intently you could smell or even taste it?

Have you ever been so sure in your heart or gut that something would happen and although it seemed impossible, it in fact did happen? This is part of the magic of *Shapeshifting*. In aligning the whole of who we are to another form or idea we emulate its essence. We encourage its potential. Whether animal, plant, concept, behavior, a healthy body, new life rhythm or a global shift; what is focused on makes it possible.

This concept is in use by athletes who visualize athletic performance which *Shapeshifts* the body and increases their competitive edge. Studies show that lying down to actively imagine can be effective in conditioning the body. This tells us amazing things about our imagination. This is not so different from the way Einstein and others have throughout history used imagination in a method coined as a *Thought Experiment* to explore unresolved theories. You will find many such accounts in Martin Cohen's book *Wittgenstein's Beetle and Other Classic Thought Experiments*. We might ask why we so readily admire un-orthodox approaches of great scientists, artists and so on, yet are slow to integrate such wisdom into daily life.

Everything in our world is continuously shifting, part of one fabric and arising from the same source. This opens us to the realm of the *Shapeshifter*. In knowing that *Shapeshifting* is possible, we can engage body, heart and imagination to shape what we focus on. Now let us look at what motivates the kind of transformation explored in this book.

About *Higher Consciousness*

Ultimately, the best person to begin describing *Higher Consciousness* is you. If you were to think about the transcendent qualities of the people in your life or across history, what would they be? Your list would likely include people who rose above personal interest to benefit others or the world. You may perceive the higher power of life as God, Source or Light. You may call this Spirit, Energy or the Creative Intelligence. You may know it as

Grace, or in another way. But, however you perceive the higher power, how do you experience it? How do you know its influence in daily life?

Here, we will simply describe *Higher Consciousness* as that state within which we know oneness with the higher power of life. Day-to-day persona is inseparable from this limitless, spiritual self. Our universal qualities comprise, yet also radiate beyond, our bodies and personalities. The spiritual reality interfaces every aspect of us and our world.

Yet we do not always experience this. *Higher Consciousness* is about remembering what is intrinsic, yet also greater than us - whatever words we may use. This state can increase intuition and connect us with life forms and realities beyond our own. It spurs us to live from our hearts and souls, in deeper relationship with the world around us. Transcendent perspective acknowledges everything as one weave: love and potential.

Ways to realize life's transcendent qualities comprise cultures traversing the globe. Connecting with the divine comes naturally for some while others cultivate it through yoga, meditation, prayer, compassionate service, chants or religious rituals, or shamanic trance. Practically, we may glimpse *Higher Consciousness* when standing at the ocean's edge as the winds whip our face and waves crash at our feet. We may taste vaster intelligence when struggling to make an important decision, then suddenly knowing what to do. While tending our garden or looking into a child's eyes we may perceive the essence of these beings. Try to remember when an ordinary moment appeared vivid or translucent. Were colors brighter, smells more aromatic, sounds intense and touch heightened? Your body may have felt lighter, expanded. Time may have stopped, your heart cracked open. You may have felt it in the middle of a forest, or in summoning strength through sleepless nights to nurse a fevered child. Or in recognizing your enemy was human and vulnerable like you. Transcendent experiences cut through illusion. They dissolve ego and open our hearts.

Access and *Apply Higher Consciousness*

Most of the examples above cite spontaneous expansive states. But ancient cultures found the sun a potent icon to access *Higher Consciousness*. Without the sun, life on this planet would not exist and its symbolic significance spans diverse cultures. Agrarian societies honored the sun's cycles. Sites marking the longest sunlit day of the year are found from North America to Siberia. Sun gods reigned in Egypt, Mesopotamia and Greece. Ancient Incas believed they originated from the sun god, Wiracocha - strikingly similar to the Tibetan Buddhist sun deity, Vairochana, also linked to ancient Indian solar wheels. Toltecs believed that the sun awakens higher knowing. Hindus use sunlight to balance hormonal and nervous systems, and open the pineal gland to *Higher Consciousness*. There is no doubt that sunlight rejuvenates us physically and mentally. It represents the force of life itself, the higher power.

Imaging that we are the sun, or *Shapeshifting* into the sun, offers expanded views for modern dilemmas. The exercise below outlines an easy way to try this:

1) Sit or lie comfortably and close your eyes.

Take some deep breaths and do some gentle stretching, then relax. Let your mouth drop open slightly, relaxing jaw and hips. Allow your shoulders to drop away from your ears. Take time to settle, letting the breath fully come into your body, allowing preoccupations to drop, and relaxing more completely with each breath out.

2) Now in this restful state, take a few moments to contemplate an issue that is difficult for you.

This could be a problem with a neighbor or co-worker, uncertainty about going back to school, fear about the state of the world, difficulty with one of your children, what route to take for a physical illness, concern about politics or the environment, worry about your bills, or anything that troubles you.

3) As you reflect on this item, notice your feelings and thoughts.

Are you afraid, angry, or worried? Do you feel angst or confusion? Do you feel numbed or have unnamable feelings? Take your time. Also notice what part of your body are you aware of as you feel these feelings.

Next, what are your thoughts? What bothers and tugs at you most about this issue? How does it affect you? Be honest.

Notice thoughts and feelings without judging or doing anything about them. It is good to speak these aloud if you are drawn. Accept and see them for what they are.

4) Now, gently dissolve this focus and completely let the problem go.

Let shoulders drop relaxed and take a few deep cleansing breaths. Gently stretch again or playfully roll on the floor. Try to completely forget about this problem for the moment. Imagine you have put it in a paper bag and placed it outside the door so you do not have to think about it at all right now. Muse that you can come back to deal with it at another time or when this session is over.

5) Next, sit or lie down again and when relaxed and comfortable, visualize or feel as if you are lying on a warm, sunlit beach.

Or create or remember whatever alternative pleasant scene works for you. Feel or imagine the texture of sand, grass or earth beneath you. Notice whatever sounds there are such as birds chirping, insects flying and buzzing, waves crashing. Pay attention to the smells, the sensation of breezes against your body, or whatever you experience. Open your senses in this imaginary space. As you do, imagine or feel the warmth of the sun soaking into and relaxing your body. Really feel and know this is happening, not worrying about how you experience it. Become comfortable as the sun's glow fills, warms, illumines, and soothes you.

6) As you rest in this relaxing place, wherever it is, focus on this light source, the sun that is beaming down on you.

Envision the golden droplets of light sprinkling down upon

your skin as coming directly from Source, Spirit, God, or whatever you call the higher power. Take your time. Feel energy, light and love. Allow unconditional well being to pour into you. This light touches you beyond personality to your essence. It embraces and nurtures you without judging you – it suffuses those aspects which you like, accept and are in touch with. It equally envelopes those aspects you hide, feel ashamed of, are numbed, in pain, or that you deny. Feel and believe that the warm, glowing light of the sun loves and penetrates you unconditionally.

7) *As the higher power infuses you, go deeper now to feel its light permeate your whole being. Feel you are becoming this light:*

Allow it to merge with cells, muscles, bones, organs, tissues and tendons. Let it swirl inseparably from heart and emotions. Invite light to suffuse your head, thoughts and mind. Take all the time you need. Feel oneness with this energy source, the sun. Breathe light and energy in and out. Taste it. Feel it. Become it. *Shapeshift.* Relax.

You may feel embraced and nurtured. You may feel expanded and at peace. You may feel energy or vibration.

What do you feel? Stay present. Open your heart. Enjoy. Bathe in, and become one with, the light that suffuses you in whatever way you experience it. There are no rules: no right, wrong, or better ways to do this.

8) *When you feel completely filled with, and are basking in light, gently call the issue back to you.*

Take a moment to look at the problem again, but from this spacious place. Have a gentle touch. Feel or sense the dilemma more than thinking about it. Take plenty of time to observe it carefully and from all angles, however this occurs. Intend it. Consciousness in this space is different. Time in this space does not exist. Relax. You may perceive differently. Fresh angles may appear. See from the eyes of your heart, viewing this issue and all connected to it from a higher vantage. See or feel it from this deeper perspective. Be with this experience for awhile then let the focus relax.

9) Now completely let go of the issue you were focusing on and take some deep, cleansing breaths.

Let it all go. Again, take a few deep, refreshing breaths. Slowly wiggle your toes and fingers, gently coming back into the room or wherever you are. Take time and gently stretch. When you are ready, open your eyes.

People often like to sit quietly after this practice, but sense what is right for you. See what percolates. Then you might want to take notes on the experience before moving on to something else. Insights gained in expanded states, similar to dreams, can evaporate like a morning mist. Sitting in filtered sunlight in the early morning or as the sun is setting can be powerful. Or try it under a full moon. Bask in the moon's glow or in the sunlight. Plants transform light energy from the sun into physical energy (ultimately providing the oxygen that sustains us). So it is that sunlight can transmute the mundane to higher knowing. Regular practice makes it easy to do this exercise anytime and anywhere. You can summon expanded perspective on the spot and for any issue.

If the sun is not shining or the exercise did not work for you, let it inspire you to create one that does. Or travel in imagination to a time when you felt exalted or infused with love and power. What feels to you like the transcendent force of life? Make this a visceral experience, not just a mental exercise – really feel it, as if it is really happening. Light, love and expansion must permeate you.

For some, music or art opens this connection. One woman could access *Higher Consciousness* by envisioning herself sitting at the piano playing her favorite piece of music (or by actually doing it). In becoming one with the music she enters what is best described as "a state of grace". This can shine a broader light not only on troubling issues, but on life in general. Others open to Source by feeling their love for a pet, child or a friend. Some do so through time in nature, or in being silent. There are many ways. Taking even a moment to ponder such things can make us feel good. Try it. In traveling these pages we will explore many methods that open our hearts and connect us to essence, soul, wholeness, or whatever name we choose. We will engage the world expansively.

Be Genuine

Hopefully the above practice helped you feel one with the source of life. And that what was troubling you shifted the second time around. Whatever you felt is valid and right for you. Do not judge it. Again, with time and practice, opening this way becomes easy to do on the spot. It supports a richer relationship to everyday circumstances. Always first be honest about the feelings that seize you. Honor what is there, not holding back or trying to change anything. Do not try to make things more acceptable. Be real. This helps our censoring aspects relax. When freed up, we connect from a deeper place and open to broader perspectives.

Being human, none of us are perfect. And we are conditioned by the values of others and our cultures. This shaping can make us lose touch with ourselves and mask our intrinsic intelligence. Spiritual dogmas also mold us. Many confuse enlightenment with having prescribed thoughts, feelings, or doing what is "right" according to religious paradigms. Placing priests, gurus, shamans, or others on pedestals can make us forget our own wisdom. It also encourages us to project unrealistic expectations onto others. Throughout this text we will see that being genuine is what gains us access to the transcendent.

One man used the above practice to focus on a tough relationship with a colleague. This woman and he pushed each other's buttons. Ordinary meetings could turn into lengthy ordeals. These two clashed in values, personality and methods, differences exacerbated by their dysfunctional organization.

Through the exercise *Access and Apply Higher Consciousness*, this man first admitted how he felt. Not only did he not like this colleague, she enraged him. Though embarrassing, this was his truth. In allowing these feelings, it was not long before this person began to feel sad: sad about not finding the higher road, and deeply sad at what this took from him and his work. Later in the exercise from the vantage of *Higher Consciousness*, this worker's revulsion softened. He recognized his colleague's many qualities. He felt his appreciation for her as a unique human being and understood her negativity was driven by insecurity. He also saw how his own wounds had caused him to react to her so strongly. In glimpsing this, waves of compassion washed through this man. These insights set him on a healing path and freed him from relating with this colleague in a destructive way. Instead, he focused his energy to improve the organization. This brought out his gifts instead of his neurosis.

Go deeply into and own what you really feel. This supports us to see and act more clearly. Let go of self-judgment and honor your truth. You will be liberated to release old patterns and engage freshly. The above practice helps us become more genuine, compassionate, and clear. In merging with the higher power we meld the spiritual with the mundane and can find whole perspectives for everyday circumstance. Perceiving through *Higher Consciousness* opens our hearts so we can find our way through chaotic times.

Why Shapeshift into *Higher Consciousness?*

Why *Shapeshift into Higher Consciousness?* Because in doing so, we have everything to gain. Because we owe it to ourselves to wake up, live from higher values and create a world worth living in. Because we are one with a vast, intelligent universe that has boundless energy to create. Because *Higher Consciousness* is who and what we are. These opportune times urge us to embrace our divinity and, so, bring heaven to earth.

In prophecies held for millennium by the Quechua peoples, descended from the Incas in South America, this time of change is called *Pachacuti*. In this *Pachacuti*, the legend is that the 'Eagle and Condor' will fly together in the same sky. This predicts an era of unprecedented strife and turmoil pressuring two separated aspects of human psyche, the heart and mind, to come together.

Representing the honed powers of mind with its prowess for a bountiful nest, the Eagle symbolizes prosperity and mental acuity. It embodies more masculine North American traits of materialism and abundance. The Condor is a spiritual and more feminine archetype for the heart and feelings. It symbolizes earth-oriented values of South American cultures. In this *Pachacuti*, the prophecy of the Eagle and Condor flying together invites the people of North and South America to unite. It coaxes the heart and mind of each individual to act as one. Earth dwellers can live abundantly, yet also - compassionately and interdependently - with each other and our planet.

The end result sounds wonderful, indeed. But what if on our way through this *Pachacuti*, we become immobilized? What about the strife and turmoil heralding its promised beauty and light? Most of us are living that turmoil for at least part of our day, week or month. Finances, health, family or global concerns can overwhelm us. Recognizing the suffering that occurs every day can devastate us. What are we to do during those times when chaos simply looks and feels like chaos, and turmoil has no other taste than turmoil? Remembering that we are evolving can bolster and open us to higher perspectives. Seeing and acting clearly is not easy during challenging times. But in our moments of despair we can wake up and open our hearts. We can engage consciously.

The Tibetan Buddhist term, *Bardo*, literally means "between two shores." *Bardo* is commonly known as the period following death after consciousness leaves the body. This is prior to reincarnating and taking on a new life. *Bardo* is the transition from death to re-birth. Yet, it also describes the gap between moments or events; the intermediary period as something changes from one form to another. One experience, or reality, has died or ended. The next moment, or event, has not yet come into being. *Bardo* is a rich interlude. It is a realm of potential where we can cleanse the old and create anew. Our ability to do so is shaped by past momentum, future longing, and our ability to be present. In this gap, awareness can magnetize or repel; we can draw to us or push away from any number of possible outcomes. Imagine leaving familiar lands to cross an ocean expanse, like early explorers. You are between two shores. You have abandoned what is recognizable, you navigate into the unknown. The journey may feel perilous, one that you are not sure you will survive. You pass many lands along the way. One scenario has you grasping at the first solid piece of land you come upon. You are driven by the grief of what is lost, the terror of dying, and the uncertainty of what is to come. The gap, the journey, is unbearable. Another scenario finds you passing by alluring lands yet that do not resonate. You trust and employ your heart and senses. You intuit the right direction, navigating beyond fear and seduction.

It can be helpful to look at these prophesied times of change from the perspective of *Bardo*. Especially as the Quechua word, *Pachacuti*, means "Transformer of the Worlds." Prophecies from original peoples the world over tell us that the world is changing. The world is not ending, but the world as we know it is ending. Old ways of knowing, living, and being are coming to a close. We have embarked from familiar shores and are ourselves mid-stream. None of us are sure of what lies ahead. Uncertainty and rough waters characterize the passage. It may feel as if we have nothing to hang onto. Old fears, habits and longings, surface and intensify. How we experience, interpret, and respond to what is happening can make all the difference.

There is the story of long-time Buddhist practitioner and

actor, Richard Gere, sitting serenely on a movie set in Hollywood, unfettered by the commotion swirling around him. Another story tells of a Nova Scotian student who asked an indigenous elder for advice on the safest place to live during these times of change on Planet Earth. The paraphrased reply was: "Where you will be is less important than who you are."

Our perspective, our consciousness makes all the difference. A higher vantage is energizing. It helps us *Shapeshift* fear into clarity, calamity into opportunity. In relaxing and letting old forms die, we see dissolution as an evolutionary stage. New, life affirming ways await us. Our hearts, bodies, and souls yearn for connection. Our children, communities, and societies clamor for wholeness. We can ride this momentum into change. In seizing the opportunity of this *Bardo* we can *Shapeshift* into healthier ways. But how do we do this?

The next chapter explores some of the foundational practices that can help us *Shapeshift into Higher Consciousness* and live in greater balance.

"We and the cosmos are one. The cosmos is a vast body, of which we are still parts." – D.H. Lawrence

CHAPTER TWO

SHAPESHIFTING INTO HIGHER BALANCE

No matter who we are or where we live, most humans desire to be healthy and happy. Yet, suffering appears to be the hallmark of life on Planet Earth. Sakyamuni Buddha taught that suffering, the first noble truth of human existence, arises from attachment and desire. This ancient message applies to modern times as our greatest imbalances stem from overly material values. The results now threaten our families, ecosystems, and global community. As just a couple of examples: pollution related breathing problems plague record numbers and global toxins and human induced weather changes affect all of us, including once remote tribes. Many of these previously sustainable forest-based peoples have lost traditional ways, their ancestral lands ruined by oil interests. Beyond these, none of us escape worry about nuclear destruction, pandemics, and the effects of global warming. Such stressors, unique to our era, know no geographical border. They are brought on by people and, in turn, affect every life form on this planet.

How can we foster well being for us and all life? How can we come into greater balance? In these precarious times we need a different set of tools to be healthy and balanced; one that recognizes that we are not separate from anything, or anyone, on this planet. True happiness comes in living from higher values and this is the only way that we can *Shapeshift* through these times.

This chapter focuses on ways to *Shapeshift* into balance and wholeness. It is up to us to create clarity or pain. In this *Bardo*, this opportune gap, let us forge good ways to live. There is abundant support available now to help us find our way through unprecedented events. All that is needed to tap into this support is the willingness to define ourselves freshly.

Earth and Heaven

Remember times when you have felt disharmonious or out of balance. Maybe you did not sleep well or you drank or ate too much. We each have unique parameters for what feels good and what does not. But it is important now to expand our notions of balance. A more vital definition of equilibrium includes a connection to our body, nature and the larger world. Such integral bonds are ignored in fast-paced societies, yet, they are the ground for sane civilization. Do you live in your body? Do you feel grounded in nature; present, yet, expansive? Seemingly simple, most people have little real experience of these feelings. Without higher balance relationships and health can be negatively affected. The reality we perceive and create can get skewed. With the way things shift rapidly now it is necessary to redefine who we are and how we live. It is important to get clear about where we want to go and to set ourselves on that path.

When I was in my early twenties I had spent time in college, working and traveling. I paused to reflect. I had experienced a lot and gained some hard lessons which pushed me to ask essential questions: "Who did I aspire to be? What did my heart and soul long for?" In getting my priorities straight, I was able to embark on a clearer course.

Take a moment to contemplate your own deeper wishes. You may have a list of things you want to buy, how you want to live, who you want to be with. But, go deeper than this. Who do you want to be? What makes you feel connected, whole? What makes life feel satisfying, rich and meaningful? Our authentic and deeper self can get lost in heavily marketed societies. Distraction and superficiality mask our higher potential. But in setting upon the right direction we can find our way back. Once we decide to become more embodied then how do we do it? How can we attain higher balance and live from more whole values? Increasingly, people look to ancient wisdom ways to answer these questions.

Earth and Sustenance

Shamanistic orientations are inherently balancing and expanding; they prod our greater humanness. Of primary importance for indigenous people is rapport with their body and the earth; relationships which nourish the individual and fuel shamanic power. These intimate liaisons that channel the forces to heal make right relationship to nature, a given.

A native teacher I traveled with for two weeks in Hakassia, Siberia dedicated herself to healing individuals in her community and reviving their earth-honoring ceremonies. Sharing a room with this shaman woman frequently, I observed her fundamental relationship to her body and the elements. Upon awakening at day break every morning this shaman woman she sat up in bed to meditate on the rising sun. After that she would massage her whole body. If we happened to be staying near a stream or river, which was often the case, the *Shamanka* (female shaman) would go outside to make offerings at the water's edge. Then she would walk into the water and sit down so it rose to the level of her chest. Fully immersed in the swift current, the elder again rubbed her body. I did not join her in the river, but imagined the dip exhilarating as the November temperatures hovered between fifteen above and fifteen below zero.

Shamans draw on the elements for vibrancy and strength. They rely on nature for support. Respect is inherent as daily life is interwoven with the earth.

Those of us in modern cultures, particularly city dwellers, can benefit from such vital connections our indigenous sisters and brothers enjoy from birth. Most of us admit to feeling separate from our bodies and the earth. Think of the time spent in trains, cars, planes and in buildings. Remember how much of your day is spent working on computer or talking on the cell phone. If not balancing these with a strong association with the natural world, these activities can be weakening. They foster wrong views about our relationship to the earth. We can forget our interdependency with, even the fact that we live upon, the earth. Shamans see this as a split in our energy field which cutting us off from our body and breath and nature's replenishing forces.

Tibetan Buddhism, now flourishing in the West, is also based in a culture that sees itself indivisible from our planet. All indigenous teachings consciously engage our physical reality including the human body and nature. Fragmented Westerners often miss these critical connections. A visiting Buddhist teacher once described a Tibetan's energy body descending into the earth like a carrot, nourished by the earth. The Tibetan's body, like the carrot's leafy green top, was the only visible component above the earth's surface. In looking at North Americans, this teacher saw we had no such link to the earth. To him we appeared cut off at the ankles, our bodies hovering above the ground. It is impossible to create a sane world when our feet do not even touch the earth.

On an absolute level we are always one with the fabric of life. We are woven of the earth, stars, every living, non-living, material and non-material thing. But because of conditioning, habits, or trauma, the life flow and connection with all other life becomes obstructed. Though we may not recognize it for what it is, this makes us feel separate. We are dissociated from self, other, the web of life, spirit, and the earth. We cannot discern our proper place upon the earth, let alone the universe. This dissociation feeds the illusion that we can inflict anything upon nature without consequence. It makes it harder to stay healthy and joyous. Think about how it feels when you are truly "in" life, as opposed to when you are not. Without these wholesome connection humans tend toward mindless habits.

It is noteworthy that addictive substances such as cocaine, alcohol and tobacco come from plants traditionally regarded as sacred. For centuries to this present day, coca leaves are used medicinally and spiritually in South America. Tobacco is one of the four sacred plants of Native Americans, inseparable from the four sacred directions. Tobacco is used in prayer, to make offerings and to cleanse. Tuvan, Siberian shamans ride tobacco smoke to other dimensional realities. Alcohol, often called "spirits", is essential to rituals of Andean, Siberian, Maya and other cultures. Siberian peoples use vodka for cleansing energy. If the person being healed seems "dirty", vodka is dabbed at the base of the skull to cast out negativity. Quechua peoples brew *Trago* alcohol from sugar cane plants. The sugar cane is nurtured by, and holds the energy of, the four sacred elements. The plants gain nutrients from the earth. The waters cleanse and nourish the stalk. The air, the fire of the sun and heat of the earth also infuse the plant. *Trago* is sacred because it is imbued with the power of the elements. This synergy becomes a vehicle for the Fifth Element, spirit. In Quechua this is called *Ushai* (Oo-shy). *Ushai* is transmitted from shaman to client by blowing the alcohol mixture directly onto the body. This heals and cleanses the energy field and protects the shaman by repelling unwanted energy. It also calls in spirits from non-physical reality.

In disregarding sacredness, we fall out of rhythm with nature. We distort what the natural world offers. Instead of relating to plants in ways that affirm life, we indulge imbalances that destroy it. In reclaiming our bond with the earth we connect with what is sacred. In living fully in our earthly bodies, we heal and become grounded. In doing so, we begin to perceive freshly. There is, within all of us, the desire to live in harmony with our planet. The knowledge of how to do this comes more easily when we are awake.

We can unite with the earth and balance our energy: 1) by caring for and living fully in our bodies and in the environments we create, 2) through intention, ceremony, offerings and practices, 3) spending time in nature, 4) lying upon the earth and breathing into her, opening the life flow between us 5) working for ecological and earth-honoring causes, 5) enjoying nature's beauty by experiencing the rain, snow, wind, fire, being in the forest, by the ocean, gazing at the trees or night sky, or whatever inspires, 6) tending to our garden, plants and animals, and a variety of other ways.

Heaven and Potential

In reconnecting with the earth we also open to realms magnificent beyond imagining. When Joni Mitchell sat down and sang at her piano about the legendary Woodstock, NY Music and Arts Festival she hit a chord for thousands. Her lyrics were powerful then and still are. We do have to get ourselves back to the garden. But are we stardust, are we golden? Are we billion year old carbon? The song, *Woodstock*, was written back in 1969. In recent decades scientists have confirmed that the earth and everything upon her is made of stars. These stars died, exploded and alchemically reformed into the elements and metals of planets. They have also determined, contrary to Joni's song, that our planet is four and a half billion year old carbon. If the earth has a pulse and rhythm as shamans claim, they interplay with cosmic rhythms. This suggests that galaxies, stars, planetary bodies, space, and the universe are also aspects of us. These are also parts most of us have cut ourselves off from.

Shamanic peoples the world over sustain life by revering the earth. They also cultivate celestial ties. Pre-Buddhist Tibetan "sky dancer" deities and "sky gazing" practices link with space. Aboriginal groups, including those in Australia, trace ancestry to the stars. Both Cherokee and Amazonian Ur-eu-wau-wau tribes hail from the Pleiades. The healing work and divination of Tuvan, Siberian "sky" or "celestial" shamans is guided by the moon and the stars. Tradition says each Tuvan child is guided by a star from birth. Tribal peoples of diverse original cultures perform ceremony and practices to connect with, and show reverence to, the earth. Similarly, they access energy and wisdom from the "star people". They even *Shapeshift* into the consciousness of sky deities and stellar brothers and sisters.

Maintaining an internal balance of heaven and earth is also relevant to practical aspects of modern life. Too much heaven and not enough earth may cast our head into the clouds. We all know folks who are appear devout, psychic, sensitive, and aware of non-physical realms; yet, they do not seem grounded. A young couple practicing Tibetan Buddhism visited the Abbot of a monastery in upstate New York. They described to the Abbot their dream to move from their home in Chicago to live near the temple. Did the teacher approve their vision, should they move? Their eyes glowed when the serene man said "Oh, yes, you could move here." Yet their enthusiasm soon dipped: "But how would you support yourselves?" the Lama continued, "You'd have to get a job. Work is hard to come by here." Visions must be honored and sometimes followed, but with discernment. We can manifest our dreams, but best to keep our feet on the ground in doing so. In forsaking earthly matters, we can end up in a mess.

Alternately, with too little heaven we may not perceive the lighter, magical aspects of life. The internal blend of heaven and earth is distinct for each of us. Yet we will not realize our potential unless both are active and balanced.

The practice below found in varying forms across cultures, balances the earthly and heavenly qualities within us. This way we can live every moment from our center, be present and feel more whole. As this well being is self existing it is independent to what we own, what we do, what our title or social status is, or any external condition.

Take your time with this exercise. Feel and enjoy the energies moving through you, whether vivid or subtle.

Shapeshift into Earth and Cosmos

This practice is ideal to do outside, standing barefoot on the earth, but doing it inside is fine, too. In fact, it can be done anywhere and at anytime. If you have physical restrictions feel free to sit in a chair, or just do the exercise as fully as you are able to while standing.

1) Find a place to stand in or outside. Close your eyes and place your hands over your heart. Take a few deep, refreshing breaths. Allow thoughts and emotions to settle. Feel your warm hands over your heart. Take time to feel this warmth, the beat of your heart, or other sensations that may arise.

Earthly and celestial energies converge in the center of the human energy system, the heart. We can express the combined qualities of heaven and earth through the vehicle of our open heart.

2) Rub your feet for a moment against the grass or ground where you stand. Or rub them into the carpet or floor. What are the sensations? Enjoy and have fun with this. Really feel it.

3) Open to your connection with the earth. Even when inside a building, beneath its foundation is the earth.

Travel in your mind's eye through the earth's root systems and sedimentary layers. Remember her underground caverns and hidden river systems. Travel with your imagination through the layers of the earth's crust and mantle to her magnetic core. If you do not see it, just sense it. Enjoy the feeling of it. Feeling is more important than seeing. Remember that the earth can nurture, ground, and support you. Feel your feet and base of your spine open to the earth's energy and sustenance.

4) Take some deep, cleansing breaths. Feel how solid you are as you stand upon the earth.

Savor these feelings. Feel how good it is to be in a human

body. Take another nice, deep breath feeling the wholesomeness of connecting with the earth and your body in this way. The earth is you.

5) *Maintain your connection with body and earth. Simultaneously, become aware of the space around you.*

If practicing in a group, begin by feeling the spaces between the people in the room. Worlds exist in these spaces in between. Allow your awareness to rest in space. Relax the focus on objects and people. If you are outside, note the space of air and sky. Sense the gaps between buildings, trees or other land formations.

6) *Travel out now with your imagination into these spaces.*

Imagine touching the blue sky above the trees. If you are in a building imagine what lies beyond the bounds of the room; travel with your awareness out through the walls and ceiling, into the space outside.

Beyond this, feel stars and planetary bodies. Sense the universal gasses. Remain rooted in your body upon the earth. At the same time travel out in imagination as far as you feel comfortable. Sense the vastness; these heavenly qualities are also you.

From your distant vantage now, envision the earth. She is beautiful, yet, just a small orb in the midst of infinite space and galaxies. Open to mystery and magic by imagining that you are also this space. Sense the universe that longs to come alive in you.

7) *Now allow the focus on space to dissolve. Take a deep, refreshing breath. Take another deep, cleansing breath. Then bend forward, extend your arms to the floor and reach toward the earth. Imagine you have energetic fingertips which can reach through the earth's many layers to her magnetic center. Feel your connection to this pulsing energy. Sense the healing forces the earth generates. Allow these to flood into your energetic and physical hands.*

You may see energy yet sensing it is just as valid. Some of us have keen inner vision, others sense, feel, or intuit. Some folks hear or even smell what is normally undetectable to the physical senses. Do not worry or feel disappointed if you do not see psychically. Most important is to open your heart and body, and to trust.

8) On the next in-breath, breathe healing energy up from the earth's many layers and into your body, all the way up to your heart.

Bring it up with your hands and through the through the soles of your feet. Let it rise up through your legs. Sweep vital forces with your hands, up through your legs and torso. Then on that same in-breath, anchor earth energy into your heart. You will be fully standing, hands over your heart. Feel this river of energy pool in your heart as this breath in peaks. .

9) Now standing and holding hands over heart, gaze skyward. Propel hands and arms toward the heavens. As you do, send earth energy up and out from your heart. On the very next out breath, propel these out from your heart, through your throat, head and out your crown.

Feel, sense, and know these luminous forces are traveling out to cosmic spaces. Make a forceful SHOO! sound to propel them. Complete the out-breath as you thrust your hands and arms fully upward to the heavens.

10) Now, with hands extended above you and face gazing up, immerse your energy fingertips in the heavens. Stay present, feel your body and the earth. At the same time expand your awareness out toward the cosmos.

Imagine and feel. Sense the quasars and planetary bodies. Feel the stars and galaxies. Remember your connection to these distant realms. You are made of the earth, yet you are also the stars. Become one with these. Open to your heavenly qualities.

Sense the luminous fields of pure, healing energy. Collect and retrieve these healing forces with your energetic hands and fingers. They will saturate with light.

11) On the next in-breath, pull these energies down from the skies and in through your crown. Pass them through head and throat, anchoring them into your heart.

You may also feel showered by light. Place your hands on your heart as this in-breath comes to completion. Feel the starry forces mixing with the earth energies in your heart. The heart is where heaven and earth meet. Grounded and open hearted humans can express these energies out into the world through compassionate action.

12) With hands still upon your heart, feel the blend of earth and cosmic forces. On the next out-breath pass stellar energy down through your body and into the earth.

Guide these forces with your hands from your heart down through torso, legs, out through the soles of your feet into the earth. As you do, make a forceful SHOO! sound. Arms should be fully extended and body bent towards the earth again. Feel healing beams permeate every layer of earth to her magnetic core.

Now you are again ready to retrieve and collect earth energies as described in #8, and on from there. This exercise is ideally repeated in its entirety six to twelve times.

More on Shapeshifting into Earth and Cosmos

In practicing *Shapeshift into Earth and Cosmos,* remember that a separate and complete breath accompanies each step after making the first connection with earth, ie: in-breath collecting earth energies, out- breath sending them into the heavens, in-breath retrieving stellar energies, out-breath sending them into the earth, and so on. Find a comfortable breathing rhythm with the pace of your own breathing. A suggestion for instructing groups is to describe then show them the practice first, guide the group through two or three cycles of it, and then invite people to do it on their own. From here, six or more cycles of the practice done at each individual's breathing pace is ideal.

Make your breath a dynamic force. Bring vigor to the SHOO!

sound in thrusting energy into the heavens and the earth. Sound is vibration and it strengthens the breath, so do not hold back. Your breath provides the force that drives energy through your body and beyond it. In combining breath, movement and sound we can break up energetic blockages in the body. We clear mental and emotional cobwebs and encourage vitality throughout the body. Enjoy and fully engage your movement, voice, and breath.

As you close this practice, pause for a moment. Notice how you feel before moving on. Take a deep breath and ask yourself: How do I feel? Is this different than before I began? How does my body feel; are there tingling sensations or an intangible feeling of vibrancy? What do I feel? What is the quality of mind; are my thoughts more spacious and settled? Note the sensations and how good it is to be in a human body. Enjoy the sensations.

By now you have a taste of what it means to be present and living fully in your body. It is something you have to experience to know. Many times we think we are living fully in our bodies when we are not. As healthy as jogging or working out at the gym hooked up to an I-Pod may appear, it does not automatically translate to embodiment. Depending on the approach, exercise can make us more aware, open hearted, and fuse mind and body. But oftentimes it just separates us further. What is your experience? Anyone can *Shapeshift* their physical form, yet sometimes we are driven to perfectionism. If this is the case we may be cutting off our breath, closing our heart and staying stuck in our head. This can translate to rigidity. We can *Shapeshift* our bodies into perfect physical specimens, but we have to ask ourselves, "Am I engaged with the flow of life all around me? Am I present, open hearted?" It is wise to look more closely at how health and balance are interpreted in modern times.

Folks come more fully into their bodies through the practice of *Shapeshifting into Earth and Cosmos*. They say they feel energized, balanced, and awake. People express feeling expansive and open hearted, yet at the same time grounded. This describes s shift into more vibrant energy patterns. See how you feel. Enjoy whatever you sense whether incredible or ordinary.

If guiding a group through this practice, ask the members to stay silent a bit after completion. Invite them to focus on the spaces in between people and objects in the room. Suggest they gently rest their awareness on, and sense what they perceive in, the spaces in between things. Something palpable is often felt which can defy labeling. Descriptions have included "luminosity", a "presence" and a "larger intelligence." People depict this presence as integral to each individual, yet something that exudes beyond them. Do you or group members sense a buzz, hum, or a charge in the air? Is there a sparkle in the room? Doing the practice alone evokes a similar awareness. This will help you to appreciate moments of silence and attune to the gaps in life, where you will find richness. Magic and possibility are everywhere, all around us, we just need to slow down and open enough to perceive them. Space is the nesting ground of creativity and the portal to *Higher Consciousness.*

As beneficial as it is to do such practices, we can *Shapeshift* on the spot. You are one with the earth. Simultaneously, you are vast, limitless. It is ideal to prompt yourself to remember this throughout your day and know it within your core. We can be grounded and expansive anytime and anywhere.

Alternately, here is a way to do this practice when you cannot do it physically. Recall from Chapter One the value of intention and imagination. Sense or see in your mind's eye a tree, a central symbol in shamanic cosmology. Trees have intricate root systems penetrating deep into the earth. A tree pulls water and nutrients from the ground passing through the trunk as sap, which is mostly water. Finally, the tree disperses water into the air through its branches and leaves. Ten apple trees can release up to four tons of water a day. The tree absorbs and takes in energy from the earth, then releases this earth energy into atmospheric spaces. Envisage doing the same. Imagine passing vital forces from the earth through your own body. Feel the earth's energy as it moves through you. *Shapeshift* into - be the earth.

Similarly, trees use solar energy to make sugars from carbon dioxide in the air. They are also showered with extraterrestrial forces like star and sunlight. These penetrate each leaf, branch, passing down through the trunk, roots, and propel into the earth. Trees are magnificent channels of earthly and cosmic substances. We can be the same. Feel healing forces shower you from starry spaces. Breathe them down from the heavens, into your heart and then through your own trunk (torso). Then send these healing energies with your next breath out, deeply into the earth. Feel the internal and external balance of earth and cosmos.

Ground in the Infinite

In the exercise, *Shapeshift into Earth and Cosmos*, we breathe into, and know oneness with, the earth. Alternately, we merge with space and infinity. Because of this, *Shapeshifting* helps us live in the gaps. Magic lives in the spaces in between. Potential lies in the gaps between objects and people. Mystery abides between in and out breaths, even in the spaces between thoughts. Enchantment fills the hollow between words. This potential is always there, we just need to open to gain rapport with our infinite aspects.

Being versatile with space is supportive. It is not uncommon, these days more than ever, for what seems solid and reliable to unexpectedly collapse. Many of us or our neighbors know the grief of losing our savings or home. Terror grips when we lose our job and we become depressed in witnessing the violence that escalates in our cities. Thinking about how things will play out environmentally or worrying about the next global catastrophe causes us to panic or suppress our fears through mindless distraction. Familiar reference points are disappearing as Life on Planet Earth radically shifts. Prophecies say she, and we, are dying to old ways. We are dying, and being cleansed, to start anew.

A woman at one of our workshops in California arrived distraught after losing her retirement in the stock market. She felt betrayed to have her future shift overnight and spewed that resentment onto others. It is hard for us when things happen beyond our control, contrary to our plans and wishes. Life can be difficult. It is not enough to say "We create our own reality so why don't you create a life that's smooth and easy?" The challenges we meet in life can strengthen us and there is often a purpose to events beyond what we comprehend. It is also frequently the case, chiefly so in this time period, for things to come to a head pushing us to rapidly transform. Positive change is stimulated when, through our struggles, we embrace life's shifting patterns. Just as a fever heats up a child's body to burn impurities, adversity (as well as the planet itself), is heating up. The rub and resistance is becoming severe. Yet similarly to how fevers are often observed by mothers to instigate developmental and behavioral boosts in children, we can interpret the intensification in our lives, and globally, as a sign that new heights beckon. In doing so, we can let go of outdated patterns and create a new world.

Reclaiming our connection to space, and to the universe, gives our heart and soul a place to rest as we move through all this shifting. It helps us stay clear and make friends with uncertainty. Resting in the infinite, regardless of what dissolves, helps us find our way. We discover that being conscious is not a New Age concept that makes us impervious to pain. Instead, it is the ability to be present with whatever is occurring. As we do this, we can remember the vastness of space to ignite our fortitude and trust. In feeling the power of the universe we can *Shapeshift* into our own greatness and remember that anything is possible. We can open to grace. This is principally important during the times within which we now live.

I have a copy of a 1992 interview in which Michael Toms, host of *New Dimensions Radio*, is speaking with the Benedictine monk, Father Bede Griffiths. Father Bede said he thought civilization as we know it could very well come to an end during this era. As civilizations have come and gone before Father Bede Griffiths thought it entirely probable that we could meet the same fate. Yet, he claimed hope for humanity. Things do look pretty bad in careening toward tragedy. But the powers of the universe, what Father Bede called "God", make anything possible. This was also proclaimed by a Maya elder I worked with. The paraphrased words: "It doesn't matter how hopeless things appear. The problems of the world may seem complex beyond solving. But in remembering magic, all things are possible."

Shapeshifting into Earth and Cosmos expands and grounds us. Then, in attuning to the spaces in between and to universal energy, we open possibility. We remember that we are divine. The next exercise helps us integrate this.

Breathe Presence and Light

Breathe Presence

1) Do some gentle stretching, then, sit comfortably. Take a few deep, cleansing breaths. Adjust your posture then take another nice, relaxing breath.

As you sit, make sure your back is well supported and your feet are touching the ground or earth. Letting your lips part slightly will relax jaw and hips. Allow shoulders to drop away from the ears. Try scrunching the shoulders up to your ears first, hold for a moment, then drop them back down. This eases tension.

Have an upright posture, sitting up straight, but not holding rigidly. Your spine should be straight but flexible. Imagine the breath able to travel the length of your spine. Earthly and heavenly energies (which you have already opened to) should travel up and down your spine freely. Allow your belly muscles and lower back relax. Your belly should expand with each breath in. Imagine a soft, golden balloon filling here with each breath in, then deflating with each breath out.

Take a few more deep refreshing breaths.

2) *Allow your hands to rest comfortably on your lap. Now take a few moments to scan body, mind and emotions. Do not reject or try to change anything.*

What is the quality of your mind? Are your thoughts spacious or incessant?

How do you feel? Is there something definable; sadness, anger, joy? Or a there a feeling you cannot discern? Where in your body would you say this emotion lives; in your heart, gut, head, genitals?

How does your body feel? Are you comfortable or is there pain in any part of your body? Does your breath flow freely? Do you feel in tune, connected with every physical part of you? Or are there areas that feel blocked, tense or numbed? Simply notice.

Do not judge what you notice. All of who you are is welcomed in this moment. You do not have to change or rearrange a thing. In simply becoming aware things do often spontaneously shift. Yet all you have to do is notice. What expresses you in this moment? Just be aware.

In doing so, invite yourself fully here. Welcome what you perceive as the "good" and also the "bad" parts of you; likewise, regard whatever is considered to be in "illness" equally to what you consider to be in "health".

Welcome also, aspects of your personality you do not like, equally to those you do like. What are those?

As well, embrace those aspects of your body you feel good about, and those you do not. What do you like about your body and what do you not like? Take note of these, as if detached. See freshly, as if for the first time and without judgment. Take a nice, deep breath.

The above is related to acknowledging your feelings in the *Being Genuine* section from Chapter One. Think of it this way: you will not get anywhere on a road trip until you first climb into your car. In the same vein, we get to higher places by first climbing fully into who we are.

Take another full, refreshing breath. Know that every part of you is welcomed. Accept whatever your experience.

3) Recheck your posture then continue breathing normally. Simply feel and enjoy the movement of the breath in your body.

Our firm, yet flexible spine supports breath and energy moving fluidly throughout the body. This sustains us in opening our heart to the world and others; and allows us to stay present with what we encounter. Imagine a soft, open heart, supported by a firm but flexible spine.

Breathe at a normal pace and pay attention to the feeling of the breath moving through your body. Feel the air coming in through your nostrils, mouth, or both. Feel the sensations of it on your lips. Feel it caress your nostrils and glide into your lungs and belly. Feel the gentle rise and fall of your chest with each inhalation and feel yourself relax further with each exhalation. Enjoy the sensations of the breath. Focus on and really feel them.

Air infuses us with life force and oxygenates our cells and blood. Breath is the vehicle for spirit, how spirit imbues life into the physical body. The breath is a rhythm we can always come back to. No matter what is happening around us we can return to the rhythm of our breathing. When we are lost, we can find our way back. Conscious breathing can help us feel centered regardless of circumstance.

As you breathe, feel and luxuriate in the sensations. Infuse and nurture every physical as well as non-physical part of you with vibrant energy.

4) Now, as you breathe pay attention to the gaps between the breaths. Rest a light awareness on these, allowing a gentle transition between in-breath and out-breath.

Begin by noticing these transitions, gently resting your awareness on the gaps. A fluid rhythm connects you with these inside and outside spaces. All are you, permeated by life force energy. Take a few moments to place a gentle awareness on these transitions, continuing to feel the sensations of your breath. Then, relax your focus. Let the practice go.

5) *Take a deep, cleansing and refreshing breath. Take one more deep and relaxing breath.*

Breathe Light

This light breathing exercise is found in varying forms in Eastern traditions. It is a great vehicle for personal healing and to merge with *Higher Consciousness* and is ideally practiced immediately after the above exercise.

Read the instructions below and when you are ready you can do them at your own pace. Allow a few minutes for the practice which you can extend to longer periods as you feel comfortable.

1) *On each out-breath let go of anything that is ready to go.*

This can be physical tension, a specific worry, pain, or whatever. You do not have to think about it, just have the intention of letting go of what you don't need. Release what is not serving you, simply know this is happening. Breathe what you are letting go of out into space, not worrying about where it is going. Know that what you release is instantaneously recycled into replenishing energy.

2) *Continue to expel that same breath. As you breathe that breath out, travel to distant cosmic spaces.*

Expand through awareness and out with your breath to the far reaches of the universe. Or travel to the distant horizon. Alternately, breathing into the earth is a good alternative. In working with universal light forces remember our discussion about star and celestial forces; the earth is light, too.

In breathing consciousness out, maintain awareness of your body and the room. The goal is not to eject out of the body in this practice. To the contrary we remain fully embodied and expand awareness out. This practice is about becoming present and opening to who we truly are. We can *Shapeshift* into, and awaken, our intrinsic love and light.

When you breathe out to the universe, feel it. Sense the radiant, luminous forces. You may see these as a shimmering, golden white light. You may see nothing at all. If that is the case, simply feel or know they are there. Your feelings and intentions are most important.

3) On the very next breath in, breathe this light all the way back to you.

Sense, see, or feel light traveling from vast expanses of spaces. Feel luminous energy coming into you through your nostrils and mouth. Allow shimmering energy to penetrate every pore of your body, 360 degrees around you.

As you take this breath in fully, feel the sparkle enter you. There may be heightened sensation, a vibration, tingling. Or you may feel nothing at all. Just know that light shines into every cell, muscle, tendon and ligament. Feel it illumine organs, bones and every physical part of you. As well, this light radiates through your mind and mental faculties. Feel it filling your heart, bathing your emotions. Allow it to suffuse you. Light shimmers and quakes through every part of you.

4) On the very next out breath, begin the practice again.

When complete with this exercise, let the practice dissolve. Let everything go and come back to a normal pace of breathing. Take a couple of deep, refreshing breaths. When you feel ready, open your eyes.

More on Light Breathing

After several moments of breathing this way, you may feel saturated by light. Feel the light and energy that support your body now. Sense if light also begins to radiate from and around you. If so, feel this increase with each breath. As your body fills with light, imagine that each cell is pulsating with this light. As well, this light touches every psychological aspect of you equally: what you accept about yourself as well as what you hide or may see as "bad". It embraces all of who you are unconditionally.

In this practice, we extend to the heavens (or into the earth, or out to the horizon) to fill with light. This is the divine life pulse that infuses all things. Ultimately, we are never separate from this light. It is us. Such practices help us to remember and awaken the light within.

Once you have established good rapport with this practice, try adding a dimension. As you breathe light, note areas that need attention. What part of your body calls? Do you have tension or pain? Is there something you could not let go of in releasing the breath out? Place your hands on your body in these places. See where you are drawn. As you breathe light, let it concentrate or collect in the area where your hands rest. Let the light pool here as you breathe fully into that place. Feel the luminous forces loosen, soothe and heal the spot on your body where your hands rest.

Share Your Vibration

When practicing the above exercises with a group, upon completion of *Breathing Light* this simple ritual below is a wonderful way to establish an authentic ground of sharing.

Assuming that you are sitting in a circle in a group, ask each person to, one at a time, offer what best describes them in that moment. This can be a word, a sound or a gesture. Most important is to stay in the moment and offer from the heart. We ask that each person take only a moment to do this, that they move quickly around the circle. As we work with large groups, I pass a microphone from person to person. But a special stone, stick, or other object can be used instead. We also offer our own vibration.

In expressing through sound, people can say a word, hum, laugh or whistle. They can chant a syllable, croon or whatever. It is uplifting to see what inspires and often it is unlike anything they have done since they were children.

We use the word *vibration* because words, sound and movement are energy. In his book, *Mantra: Sacred Words of Power,* Thomas Ashley-Farrand emphasizes using the power of words to change our lives and activate creative energy. He explains that mantras and seed syllables convey meaning beyond their sounds as they are conductors. They vibrate the subtle energy field of the human body and affect physiology. Sound is utilized in many healing forms because it harmonizes the body's tissues and cells. As human beings are 70% water, sound readily vibrates through the body's fluids. Everything in existence is a vibration of energy pulsating at varying speeds which displays the patterns we know as reality. Similar to shamanism, this perspective recognizes all life as sentient. Nothing is inanimate.

In gesturing, some do subtle motions with their hands, bow, or look at everyone in the circle. Others act flamboyantly: rolling on the floor or kicking a foot into the air. Silliness is welcomed and makes spirituality earthy. As each offers, group members open their heart to that person. The circle celebrates each person's unique vibration. We hold space for every individual, whatever their expression.

Words like "spacious," "beauty," "harmony", and "light" are commonly heard when doing this exercise. These are words that make us feel good. But just as welcomed are words like "hurt," "confused," "stuck" or "angry." Some might take objection because they say that only positive, uplifting words are beneficial. These are the only ones they want to open to. This is a good point and the basis for a lot of New Age manifestation techniques. It is true that perpetuating negative messages can keep us pessimistic. Words and thoughts can *Shapeshift* us. But first, we honor what is. These practices can bubble to the surface emotions we may need to feel and/or release. When done with the right intention and with compassion, authentic sharing liberates instead of binds us. It is healing to have others witness who we really are. It is not healthy to get stuck or habituated to pain yet voicing what we really feel is often the first step out of that pain. In doing so, we meet and bring our wounded aspects to light. A circle of people with loving intention can open their hearts to honor anything members may share. There is a power in naming and, ultimately, everything is sacred.

Express genuinely in *Sharing Your Vibration*; you must offer your real expression. Otherwise it is not your vibration. For those not drawn to voicing or sharing demonstratively, here is an option: hold your hands over your heart feeling the texture of the moment. Silently offer this to the group. Then pass the microphone or sacred object on to the next person.

If practicing alone, *Sharing Your Vibration* is just as valid. It is a productive way to transition from the practices that come before it. This practice reminds us that deep sharing can happen in ways beyond what we are accustomed to. We all know that body language accounts for a huge percentage of the dialogue between people. Even this scratches the surface of what is possible. In consciously sharing our vibration we open to each other on essential levels.

Closing Note to Chapter Two

John Perkins and I have heard from countless people whose lives have been transformed by *Shapeshifting* processes. After an intensive program in New York one participant headed out to work with Katrina hurricane victims. The woman hoped the 8 days with us would bolster her ability to face those who had been caught in the wake of disaster. We received an email from this person, who was a nurse, a month later. The practices in this chapter sustained her in confronting tragedy. She was able to stay present in the midst of turmoil. This woman drew from a higher place to benefit those she came to support.

Another person who attended the same program several years later worked to create holistic health centers for young people. Yet, as it was typical for the communities he worked with to initially resist outside ideas, this man felt anxious before meeting local leaders. In the course of the shamanic program he determined to *Shapeshift* this unease, as it did not serve his goals. Instead of rushing into meetings at the last minute he committed to arrive early in order to have time alone in the conference room. The facilitator said he would use methods from our workshop to prepare to speak with people. His goal was to help his clients feel at ease and to more effectively communicate his ideas.

In pursuing health and happiness, we will all benefit by acknowledging that higher balance includes connecting to our heart, body and the earth. A more integrated way to know ourselves also celebrates oneness with the universe. In these ways we can be fully present, live sustainably with our planet and remember our limitless potential. When our hearts are full and our bodies pulse with light, imbalance will shift. Who knows what is possible as heart and mind become one?

The new ways that are calling encourage that we live by more whole values. Compassionate spiritual presences can support us in doing this and they are accessible now more than ever. In the next chapter we will explore how to retrieve, and *Shapeshift* with, spirit allies called *Huacas*.

"The soul should always stand ajar, ready to welcome the ecstatic experience." - Emily Dickinson

CHAPTER THREE

SHAPESHIFTING WITH SPIRIT HUACAS

A trademark of shamanism, whether in Siberia, the Amazon Basin, or anywhere else, is the shaman's relationship to spirit allies and compassionate helpers. Whether we view these figures as archetypal, real or imaginary, spirit influences are prime intermediary figures between the shaman and the non-physical world. Many North Americans are familiar with spirit guides being animals. Animals predominate in American Indian and many shamanic traditions. Yet spirit allies can take many forms and even change appearance. Spirit allies commonly have personalities, attributes, and powers. We access these via intention, prayer, drumming, ritual, or meditation. But you do not have to be a shaman or indigenous person to believe in otherworldly helpers. Every spiritual tradition on the planet from Tibetan Buddhism to Christianity espouses guidance from the ethers. These may be called totems, saints, rishis, devas, deities and nature spirits. Likewise, there are angels and archangels, goddesses, dakinis and dralas, light beings and so on.

This was evidenced by an interesting man I worked with. A Columban Father in his early seventies, Peter was one of a small number of missionaries stationed in Japan for several decades. Fascinated by Eastern ways, during the time he lived in Japan Peter studied Reiki and frequented centuries old ceremonies. As Columbans encourage a personal bond to spirit, energy work and local rites found a comfortable place in the clergyman's religious framework. This made for an uncomplicated bridge into shamanism. When journeying to spirit allies for the first time, this man was delighted to meet his favorite archangel. Shamanic methods made for more intimate relationships Peter had revered since childhood.

Access to beings from on high is not reserved for those of superior spiritual ranking, sensitivity, or from by-gone eras. Yet, aside from the times we devote to prayer, practice or ceremony - whether in synagogue, church or fire circle - contemporary cultures have appeared cut off from non-physical partners. Except for the cinema, books or the arts, spirit has seemed absent from daily reality boxes. But these realms are moving to the forefront. They are shifting notions of us and our world. Are experiences with other worlds increasing? Or are they just being talked about more? In the movie trilogy, *The Lord of the Rings,* there is a scene where Frodo and Samwise Gamgee are watching the Elves leave Middle Earth. The poignant portrayal represents the exile of magic. Enchantment was no longer abided by the human heart, so lighter beings receded from view. We could imagine that, now, the mysteries are being called back; veils obscuring lighter worlds are thinning. During this evolutionary cycle of humankind, lighter beings return to Middle Earth.

These experiences are becoming part of ordinary reality. When a good friend's mother was in her last year of life she began seeing a man and woman next to her. The eighty-six year old woman was at first frightened by the apparitions, worrying about what they intended. Each day the man moved closer to where she lay in bed. This alarmed the frail lady. But these spirits always smiled. Though they never spoke, neither did they do her harm. She began to relax and even to enjoy their company. As the days progressed more spirits arrived. These, and the first two, were continuously present in the woman's final weeks. My friend's mother passed from this life into the next with the help of loving allies.

We are now in a similar state of transition, moving from one way of knowing to another; from a form of death to new life. Like the non-physical partners aiding my friend's mother, spirits can mid-wife our passage. Allies of all traditions, including those not fitting into neat categories, are conscious energy. These realms connect us to source and can benefit us, now, more than ever. Linking to a resourceful spirit world is supportive. It broadens what we deem possible.

So are such spirit forces real? If you have not already discovered this for yourself, there are countless books on the shelves describing real life spirit encounters. Stories of other world experiences and details about how to work with allies, is popular these days. In addition to the many shamanic sources, *Spirit Guides & Angel Guardians* by Richard Webster is a great primer for working with allies appearing in human form. In her book, *Soul Companions,* Karen Sawyer presents over 40 modern teachers contacted by a diverse array of spirits. (My own story is included in this book.) Yes, these spirit forces are real. But not in how we normally think of reality. The spirit realms are fluid, malleable. Our experience of them is affected by our intention and state of being. There is much conjecture about non-material forces which can heal, protect and awaken us; many in unorthodox ways. Most important is that: 1) we are not alone, 2) opening our views can bolster us in changing times, 3) spirit allies can help us to heal and they can enlighten us.

This chapter introduces spiritual allies called *Huacas* (wakas), explored in this book for their ability to help us *Shapeshift.* "*Huaca*" is a Quechua word loosely translated as "sacred item". *Huacas* can appear in any shape, which is often surprising for people used to spirit guides only being humans or animals. *Huacas* can be energy forms as we will present here. Yet, they can also be physical objects found in this reality. For instance, non-physical partners which guide a shaman's work, yet are only seen through spiritual vision, are called *Huacas*. Ancient Inca stones, plant bundles and feathers that adorn a Quechua

Andean's altar are also called *Huacas*. We will explore more about finding and working with physical *Huacas* in the next chapter. For now, let us discover how to forge a relationship with non-material, or *Spirit Huacas*.

Open to Spirit Huacas

Shamanism offers expedient ways to open to spiritual forces. The primary one is through shamanic journeying. A journey is a voyage into other worlds, a sojourn into what we call non-ordinary or alternate reality. These realities parallel our walk-a-day life. Yet, as with the magical realms of the Elves in *The Lord of the Rings*, the invisible domains are not usually apparent unless they are welcomed. We access the non-ordinary through imagining. Just as in a child's day dream, we relax linear focus so the creative elements come alive. We all day dreamed as children, so this is not new or foreign. But most of us have been habituated out of dreaming arts by societies that over-value rational thinking; an imbalance that results in dissociation. The way out of fragmentation is to open our hearts. Exciting solutions appear when we engage more fully. First, we must ease outdated ways and loosen an overly material center of attention. This leaves room for what lies beyond the mind; that which is gleaned through sense, longing and imagination. Shamans perceive from body and heart.

How much of your life is spent consciously dreaming? If you cannot recall, then it is not enough. This lost skill keeps us fluid and vital. Mindful imagining connects us with power, wisdom and energy otherwise beyond reach. Conscious dreaming is an open state of being that channels larger intelligence, so why not have it inspire everything we do? These spheres are needed now more than ever; they illumine and empower options otherwise unseen. When writing, I welcome fertile domains by looking up from the computer for a moment to stare off into space. Or I break from writing to take a walk in the forest or by the bay.

Whatever is stuck gets unraveled in this way. New pieces of the book may also trickle in. It is delightful when ideas seem to float in from nowhere. I have seen Thomas Edison's day bed situated near his laboratory, where he took afternoon naps. Many of his inventions are said to have been inspired on that mattress. The Spanish painter, Dali, napped while sitting in an armchair holding a spoon. When Dali relaxed enough the spoon dropped, waking him to fresh dream imagery. This fed the creation of his celebrated work.

Just closing your eyes and lying down will shift Beta brain waves that dominate the waking state to Alpha brain patterns. Alpha waves are characterized by the relaxed alertness associated with the creative process. Hypnotic rhythms produced by sound as in drumming, some musical pieces, rainfall, and even our own breathing, can induce a deeper state, as can meditation. Theta brain waves prevail at these times. These normally only occur in adults who are almost asleep, as in the tactics of Thomas Edison and Salvador Dali. Yet, noteworthy is that they are also measured in wide awake children who are day dreaming. In relaxing our attention, we invite magic. Ingenious things appear. This is related to "heavenly" forces and tending the "spaces in between," both detailed in Chapter Two.

Having an intellectual framework that supports sojourns into the imagination is a fruitful first step. Now let us employ the dream realm to retrieve a *Spirit Huaca*.

Retrieve Spirit Huacas

1) *Sit or lie down where you will not be disturbed. Close your eyes and relax.*

If indoors, you may want to play soothing music or put on a drumming CD. Relax. This will subdue the censoring aspects of mind. If you prefer quiet, do some gentle stretching before you sit or lie down. Take a deep, refreshing breath. Relax. If outside, enjoy the sensual experience of what is around you. What do you hear, smell, taste and feel?

2) Now, from this relaxed state, imagine a place that evokes healing, comfort and safety - your "Sacred Place".

This can be a place that you know in this reality or one that arises from imagination. Whatever it is, this place should be a haven; it must be sacred and feel healing. It can be a cabin, room or tent imbued with sacred objects, flowers, or incense; a bed of fresh pine needles underneath a canopy of evergreens; a luxurious patch of white sand at the ocean's edge; a sanctuary of your creation filled with spiritual icons; or any number of places. Whatever it is, you should feel protected and nurtured here. This space, and all within it, should be healing and sacred.

Engage your *Sacred Place* viscerally. Use your senses to see it and feel it. Imagine the details and make being there an intimate experience. As you do, keep coming back to the feelings of sacredness and healing. Notice how safe and nurtured you are. Feel this in your body; breathe these qualities in and out. Ultimately, your *Sacred Place* lives within you. Identify the place in your body where your *Sacred Place* might live. Is it your heart, abdomen, solar plexus?

After establishing your *Sacred Place*, you can begin any journey here. Its qualities envelope you, inducing a productive, gentle experience. You can return to your *Sacred Place* at the journey's end. This aids your transition between ordinary and non-ordinary worlds. Experience in alternate reality is enhanced, as is your ability to resume a fully alert state. The soothing effects of your *Sacred Place* can also be evoked at any place and time just by taking a deep breath.

3) From within your Sacred Place, now, silently state your intention to retrieve a Shapeshifting Huaca. You can do this by simply saying "I would like to retrieve a Shapeshifting Huaca."

4) Open to the journey space in whatever way it appears to you and relax.

You have set the intention to retrieve a *Shapeshifting Huaca*.

There is nothing else you need to do. Relax and allow spirit and your imagination to take you where they will. Your experience will be directed by the arrow of your intention.

Relaxing the mind is the best way to have a fruitful journey. A journey is not something you have to think yourself through. It happens of its own accord. On the other hand, people sometimes confuse themselves, wondering if they are just fabricating what occurs. Simply trust and notice what happens or appears. Do not judge or dissect it.

Remember that we all have different ways to perceive. Some of us see very well in alternate reality, while others do not. Some folks get a feeling sense, while others intuit their journey. Whatever happens in this space is right for you and however it unfolds is valid.

Also, do not worry about which reality you are navigating. Some shamanic orientations describe complex spiritual topographies with upper, middle and lower worlds. For our purposes here, we are opening to imaginal realms however they appear. This is the place that bridges the connection to spirit and creativity.

5) When something appears, ask it if it is your Shapeshifting Huaca. If it is not, ask this form to take you to your Shapeshifting Huaca.

Keep in mind that these energies can appear quickly. In workshops, they often arrive on the first drum beats. Think of these forms as already part of you, but which you have not been aware of until now. These *Huacas* have been waiting for you to become conscious of them. They desire to assist you.

When you perceive something, ask if this is your *Shapeshifting Huaca*: "Are you my *Shapeshifting* Huaca?". *Huacas* can come in mystical forms such as balls of light, magic wands, ancient symbols, stones or crystals. On the other hand, they may appear ordinary like a red shoe, a shovel, an image of a lake, or an orange. *Shapeshifting Huacas* can also show up in human form or as animals. Be open to what appears.

Welcome the answer in any way it comes. After asking whether this is your *Shapeshifting Huaca* you may sense or intuitively know the answer. You may actually hear it spoken "yes" or "no". You may see it written on a piece of paper in your mind's eye. Whatever way the answer arrives, determine if this is the *Huaca* you have solicited. Trust. If the answer is "no", ask this form to take you to your *Shapeshifting Huaca*.

In doing so, when another form comes, go through the same process.

6) When you have found your Shapeshifting Huaca, imagine it just above your heart. Reach up and pull this energy into your heart.

Imagine your *Shapeshifting Huaca* floating just above the area of your heart. This will be in front of you if you are sitting up and above you if you are lying down. Feel the energy of this form above your heart, sense its essence. Feel or see it in as much detail as you can. When ready, reach toward your *Shapeshifting Huaca* and with both hands slowly pull it into your heart. As you imagine moving it into your heart, feel this *Huaca* coming into you. Sense its power, energy and wisdom. Rest your hands upon your heart for a few moments, breathing into, and enlivening, your connection with this form.

7) Now, rest your hands on top of your head to counterbalance the energy.

When the connection in your heart feels complete, rest both hands palm down on the top of your head. Take a couple of refreshing breaths. As you breathe, feel the energy from your hands radiate through your body from the head down. This will balance the *Huaca* energy that has just been awakened in your heart.

8) Return to your Sacred Place and transition back to ordinary reality.

When you feel ready, relax your arms and return to your *Sacred Place*. Feel the comforting qualities here and take a deep cleansing breath. Make the transition back into ordinary reality.

When ready, you can open your eyes. This is a nice time to do some gentle stretching. After, you may like to take some notes on the experience while it is still fresh.

(Note: The practices in Chapter Two are great for balancing the mental, emotional, physical and spiritual bodies. As they are grounding and expanding, doing these exercises before journeying can be beneficial. They will synchronize body/mind and liberate your imagination.)

Retrieve Spirit Huacas for Others

You can also retrieve *Huacas* for others. Amending the above, lie down next to the person you are retrieving for. Make sure you and your partner are touching at the shoulder, hip and ankles. Alternately, you can sit back to back, or side to side. Just make sure there is physical contact between you and the other person as you need intimate rapport with his or her energy field to retrieve the *Huaca*. If working with a group, make sure partners only touch each other physically and no one else in the room. This contains the focus so partners do not pick up on another's journey. Also, make sure each partner knows the first name of the person they are retrieving for.

Follow steps 1 and 2 above, after which your partner will continue to experience their *Sacred Place* while you journey for their *Huaca*. At this juncture, simply follow these guidelines:

3) State your intention to retrieve a Shapeshifting Huaca for your partner.

This is the declaration of your journey for your partner. This is important as your intention guides the journey's unfolding. If your partner's name is Daniel, then you may state silently to yourself "I would like to retrieve a *Shapeshifting Huaca* for Daniel". Then you can relax and allow spirit and your imagination to take you where they will, on your partner's behalf.

4) Open to the journey space in whatever way it appears to you and relax.

There are more detailed notes that you can review for this section on the journey itself outlined above in step 4.

5) When something appears, ask it if it is your partner's Shapeshifting Huaca. If it is not, ask this form to take you to your partner's Shapeshifting Huaca.

When meeting a *Huaca* in the journey space, confirm whether this is your partner's *Huaca*. In making this confirmation, you must again use your partner's name. For example: "Are you Daniel's *Shapeshifting Huaca*?" Per above, welcome the answer in any way it comes.

After asking whether this is your partner's *Shapeshifting Huaca* you may sense, or intuitively know the answer. You may hear it spoken "yes" or "no". You may see it written in your mind's eye. Whatever way the answer comes, determine if this is the *Huaca* you have solicited. Trust. If the answer is "no", then ask it to take you to your partner's *Shapeshifting Huaca*.

In doing so, when another form comes, go through the same process.

6) When you have found your Shapeshifting Huaca, imagine it just above your heart. Reach up and with both hands pull this energy into your heart.

When you are certain you have found your partner's *Shapeshifting Huaca*, imagine it floating just above the area of your heart. This will be in front of you if you are sitting up and above you if you are lying down. Really feel the energy of this form above your heart, sense its essence. Feel or see it in as much detail as you can. When ready, reach toward your partner's *Shapeshifting Huaca* and slowly pull it into your heart. As you move it into your heart, feel this *Huaca's* essence.

The main difference, now, is that you will be aware that this *Huaca* is not yours. As wonderful or powerful as it may be, you are retrieving on your partner's behalf. Rest your hands upon your heart for a few moments.

7) Next, transmit the Shapeshifting Huaca from your heart into your partner's heart by breathing it into them.

Sit up if you are lying down. Or move in front of your partner if you are sitting next to or back to back. Bend toward your partner and place your two hands cupped over the heart area, yet with an opening at the top of your joined hands. Feel the energy of their *Shapeshifting Huaca* pulse in your own heart. Then when the time feels right, blow this energy from your heart into your partner's heart. Blow through the hole at the top of your cupped hands, directly into the heart area. You will feel or imagine the *Huaca* rising up and out of your own heart and through the vehicle of your breath, being transmitted into the heart of your partner.

After the *Huaca* is in place within your partner's heart, hold a hand there for a moment. Take a nice, deep breath.

8) Counter balance this transmission of energy of your partner's Huaca with a breath into your partner's crown.

In this final step ask your partner to sit up if they are not already. Move behind the person so you can reach the top of your partner's head. Follow the same procedure with the breath, yet this time you are not transmitting a *Huaca.* You are simply counter balancing the energy with a breath into the crown.

This completes the retrieval. You, as the retriever, may want to take a few moments in silence to return to your *Sacred Place* and close the experience. Or you may feel complete as is. When both you and your partner are fully present with eyes open, it is time to share. Tell everything that you can remember about this retrieval including sharing in detail with your partner about their *Shapeshifting Huaca.*

In retrieving *Huacas* for yourself or others, remember to accept what comes without judgment. This can sometimes be challenging. Years ago when I was first connecting to shamanism, a young Canadian man did a *Huaca* retrieval for me. The *Spirit Huaca* this person retrieved was the Pepsi logo. I was disappointed. I thought shamanism was loftier than commercial soft drinks and I did not drink soda. I wanted a meaningful *Huaca*. I am embarrassed to say that I ignored the *Huaca* this man retrieved on my behalf. Several weeks later while driving my car, a truck ended up in front of me. In seeing the symbol on its back door my mouth dropped open. It looked like the yin yang, the Eastern symbol of non-duality / wholeness. I was shocked to see that I was looking at the back of a Pepsi truck. The logo on the truck's back door did not have the word "Pepsi" written through it as usual, so now I could see this proverbial icon for what it was. This taught me a powerful lesson about not judging what is received in a shamanic journey.

Alternately, it is common for people to retrieve items that hold immediate and uncanny significance for their partners. Retrievers have no inkling about this before they share the journey. Do not feel shy about what you retrieve for a person as it is always just the right energy; the synchronicity of the *Huaca* may even surprise you.

Ordinary Magic

Although this retrieval method is a compelling way to engage spirit allies you may want to try a more folksy approach. As children, certain environments may have enhanced our day dreaming abilities but, likely we did not need special circumstances to access these realms. Shamans I know do not, either. The parallel worlds are inseparable from everything they do, interfacing all of life. If magic is always present that means we just have to wake up to it.

In working with Andeans in ancient Inca rituals, I am struck by how interwoven are the mundane and mystical. These Quechua peoples channel healing forces by *Shapeshifting* into the volcanic fire of the sacred mountains encircling their valley. The cosmologies supporting their rituals are complex. In each of the three volcanoes resides a master spirit. Additionally, there are goddesses and gods, their entourages adorned with jewels and crystals. All wear ornate clothing, with colors symbolic of each mountain. These visuals only hint at the elaborate relationships, stories, and cosmic connections in which these volcanoes, and the sacred waters of the valley, are steeped. All of this could be pure fantasy. Yet healings occur when these forces are invoked. Having been visited by a master spirit in the flesh, I view these archetypes as real. But juxtaposing splendorous inner vistas, Quechua people are earthy. During healings the shaman's children are close by; chickens and dogs meander in and out. The movement between mystical and commonplace is fluid. A shaman can be deep in trance one moment, laughing and telling jokes the next. Similarly, connecting to the sacred mountains is a daily part of life, whether healing or hanging out the clothes. All shamanic peoples I have known have similar traits. Heaven and earth find balance when physical and spiritual are less separate.

Likewise, I have never seen shamans lie down and put blind-folds over their eyes to journey or perform retrievals like Western practitioners. During shamanic ceremony or while performing healings, they relate to invisible worlds in a folksy manner, as they do in ordinary life. From a shamanic point of view, spirit is always there. It is part of every day's rhythm, just as the corn growing in the fields and the food cooking over the fire. Those of us not oriented this way could benefit by such an outlook.

It is powerful to do retrievals such as the one outlined above and shamanic journeying offers efficient entry to the spirit world. But it is best not to get attached to protocol. We do not need shamanic technique to connect spiritually or to feel spirited. When sitting on the bus, open your perception to the other worlds that co-exist with you. Notice the synchronicities through which spirit whispers to you in everyday life: when meeting someone unexpectedly at the grocery store or hearing a song on the radio that holds special meaning. When at a meeting, invoke spirit to help nudge just the right insight. Recall that splendor interfaces the physical and you will awaken the magic of daily life. Despite how routine or commonplace things may appear, spirit is everywhere, all the time. All we have to do is open our hearts to remember that our world is sacred.

Once we have retrieved a *Shapeshifting Huaca*, what do we do? How do we relate to it? We will explore this next.

Shapeshift into Spirit Huacas

Because they are fabricated of energy, we can connect with *Spirit Huacas* just by intending to do so. An easy way to do this is by taking a shamanic journey. Similar to the first steps of the retrieval process, start by visiting your *Sacred Place*. Then state your intention to get to know your *Shapeshifting Huaca* and open to what comes. Look at your *Spirit Huaca* from all angles, get to know it intimately. Also notice how your body feels in connecting with your *Huaca*. How do you feel emotionally? Does the *Huaca* communicate in words and if not, what is the best way to exchange with it? What does its energy feel like? What are its qualities and how can you work with your *Spirit Huaca*? Get to know your *Huaca* thoroughly in the journey space, in whatever ways inspire.

Another way is to get to know your *Huaca* is to *Shapeshift* into, or merge with, it. You can do this in the journey space by going to your *Sacred Place* then imagining the form above you. See it clearly, in as much detail as you can then invite the *Huaca* to descend into your body. Let it become one with you. You can also imagine it hovering in front of you then feel you are walking into the form. Or, merge with your *Shapeshifting Huaca* without protocol. Know its qualities as your own. Feel its consciousness. Take on its shape and look through its eyes. Feel its world. For instance, if it is a feather, you may feel delicate and light. You may sense wings fluttering or birds flying. You may soar, yourself, over broad vistas. You may feel like you are a feather that is still attached to a bird, or part of a shaman's feathered headdress. Or it may be that you are a Bird Person shaman soaring to other worlds.

People often associate *Shapeshifting* with complete alteration of physical form, such as a person turning into a jaguar. This is just one way to *Shapeshift* and becoming an animal is not our goal here. But as *Shapeshifting* into other physical appearances is a powerful tradition it is important to emphasize that shamans uphold their identity when they don other forms. Similarly, when we merge with our own *Spirit Huacas* we maintain a sense of who we are. Consider trying on your *Huaca's* attributes like a well-fitting set of clothes. In other words, do not lose yourself in the process. When we expand consciousness out with the breath in the practice of *Breathe Presence and Light*, we do not leave this reality behind. To the contrary, we stay present and expand into a larger sense of self. In the same way, when we *Shapeshift* we stay rooted in who we are and broaden this sense of ourselves to include the *Shapeshifting Huaca's* traits. This way, we know these qualities are ultimately our own.

Through our *Huacas* we can experience life in ways we normally do not. We are not separate from the energies we retrieve, or anything that exists, and this is why we can *Shapeshift*. Though they can feel foreign, *Shapeshifting Huacas* are actually one with us. Shamanism is ecstatic because through it, we tap into the pulse of life. This is an up close and personal path that is guided by the body's wisdom and the heart.

When working with *Huacas*, meaning can lie beyond obvious qualities of what is retrieved, and can be multi-layered. For instance, my Pepsi logo turned out to signify more than my partner and I knew; it emulated the yin yang, symbolizing the union of opposites. The year after this revelation another layer unfolded. At a conference a group of us journeyed to retrieve a symbol from star intelligences. I received a perfect circle with a wavy line through it representing transition, a death of old ways and an opening to new. I drew the image on a piece of paper when the journey was over so I could work with it more at home. The next day I realized that this symbol was also my Pepsi logo *Huaca*. The orb similarly looked like the yin yang. But as half of this new circle was not black like it is in the yin yang, I again had not recognized it. I now had another stratum of meaning to explore.

As in the above example, your relationship with your *Huaca* will be unique and likely go beyond what you, or others, may initially construe. Workshop participants often ask us what we can tell them about their *Spirit Huaca*. Nothing we could say holds more value than what they will discover on their own. Relationships with *Huacas*, as is true for meaningful relationships with people, are as powerful as the time and energy we devote to them. A teacher can point the way and facilitate our ability to access expanded worlds, but from here, we each must liaison directly with spiritual forces.

What you need from your *Huaca* and its purpose can shift over time. The *Spirit Huaca* can also change shape, so do not get too invested in yours staying the same. You will know your *Huaca* by its energy signature as each form has its own discernable presence. This is why it is so important to identify how your *Huaca* feels to you beyond what it looks like. John tells about working for years with a spirit guide named Manco, who appeared as a rugged Andean man. Manco's presence was tangible to the extent that John could smell the man's musky scent. One day in meditation John was surprised when he was greeted by a ball of light instead of his beloved ally, Manco. Realizing the spirit had *Shapeshifted* into light, John felt sad about losing the sensual aspects of their connection. But soon he realized why Manco had taken on this new form to offer what he needed most at that time.

It can be helpful to think of *Spirit Huacas* as non-physical keys opening portals to power, energy and information. *Spirit Huacas* are energy, consciousness. This energy comes together to form a specific pattern which influences what we see or intuit when we retrieve them. Yet these are outer forms and not their essence. The outer form can change. A *Huaca's* obvious and hidden attributes are available to us because all is one.

For now, let us explore a practical use for non-material *Huacas*. This exercise introduces how to merge with a *Huaca* to *Shapeshift* powerlessness about global dilemmas, similar to merging into the sun as a symbol for *Higher Consciousness*, detailed in Chapter One. This is presented as a partner exercise, but you can adapt it if desiring to do it alone.

Shapeshift Views of Global Dilemmas

1) Find a place to sit facing another person, your partner. One at a time, you and your partner will share about a tough global issue. Give five minutes for each person.

Try not to censor what you share. Be genuine. Do not try to be politically or even spiritually "correct". Express what you really think and feel about your topic without holding back. How does this predicament affect you? Delve deeper than thought. How do you *feel*? What makes you angry? What makes you afraid or sad? Know that your partner is listening without judging you.

As the one partner shares, the other simply holds the space. Try not to inject your own thoughts and ideas, just let the person share. This is not about taking turns, making things better, or convincing someone that they should feel otherwise. It takes awareness to drop our own agendas and slowing down can help. Take a deep breath. Recognize that you will support your partner best by giving room for, and not judging, what they may say. Feelings just are. They are inarguable and must be honored. You will have your own time to share later.

Make eye contact to help your partner to know you are really listening. Comments such as "I hear you," or "Yes, please say more," or "How do you feel about that?", can also do this. Encourage the person to feel and express these feelings as best they can. Yet it is optimal to keep your own speaking to a minimum.

Really listen. If you have drifted off, simply come back to listening. Open your heart to what your partner is saying. Sense what they may be feeling. Do not be afraid. Let it touch you. It may provoke feelings of your own. See if you can allow that, let your own feelings come up. If this is uncomfortable, notice the quality of this discomfort. What does it feel like? Can you breathe into, and simply be with, this feeling? Uneasiness for the listener is not a problem, and it is common. Simply breathe with these feelings when they come up and relax into your experience. Commit to becoming more at ease with this space. The practices in this book will help.

Sometimes people cry when they share and this is okay. Allow space for whatever occurs. Listening is a practice, a discipline, and you will become better at it over time. Rest a hand on your partner's knee or forearm if that feels appropriate (be sure to check if physical contact is okay prior to beginning). Tremendous support can flow through simple, non-intrusive body language. The majority of human communication happens non-verbally, anyway. We just are not normally aware of this.

The listening arts are something we could all improve upon. We get so used to thinking and acting at a fast clip, immersing in our own thoughts when others are speaking, waiting for the next gap to interject our ideas. This is the norm for many of us. In listening empathically, we hold another in sacred space. In doing so, we make room for magic. As we hold sacred space for our partner and rest our own thoughts and projections, our awareness creates a conscious container. This is a skill of heart which deepens with practice.

When the first person has shared for approximately five minutes, partners should bring sharing to a close in whatever way feels right. Sometimes people like to hug, or hold hands or simply say "Thank you". Not everyone is comfortable with physical contact.

When both feel ready, it is time for the other person to share. Follow step number 1 again, but this time the roles are switched.

2) After you and your partner have shared about a global issue, find a comfortable place to sit or lie down. Now, each of you can separately journey to your Sacred Place. When ready, merge with your Shapeshifting Huaca.

Make sure you are not touching your partner, nor should you be in physical contact with anyone else in the room. Take your time. Immerse in the healing qualities of your *Sacred Place*. Feel comfort, safety and sacredness. Engage your senses.

When ready, *Shapeshift* into your *Spirit* or *Shapeshifting Huaca*. Use any of the ways described above, see what feels right in this moment; feel its energy, look as if through your *Huaca's* eyes, feel its consciousness. Try on the traits of your *Huaca* as if a well fitting set of clothes. Take time to immerse in its qualities.

3) When fully one with your Huaca, bring up the global issue you spoke about. Look at it thoroughly, this time from your Huaca's perspective. Take your time, look at every angle.

See this dilemma through your *Spirit Huaca's* eyes. How does it feel? In looking at every angle of this global issue, what is your *Huaca's* perspective? What do you notice? Is this different than what you felt or noticed before? Take all the time you need.

4) Bring your Huaca journey to a close and return to your Sacred Place. Take time to transition. When ready, sit up and open your eyes.

Take a few nice breaths as you rest in your *Sacred Place* and slowly begin to wiggle your toes and fingers. Take plenty of time to transition, coming fully back into the room.

5) Return to your partner and share this journey experience, one at a time. When finished, thank your partner in whatever way inspires.

Articulate as much as you can remember about what is was like to view this global issue from your *Shapeshifting Huaca's* perspective. When both have shared, thank your partner and close the experience in whatever way feels right.

Global Dilemma Journey Stories

We have guided countless people through this process at holistic educational centers, environmental conferences and community gatherings. There is a tremendous amount occurring in the world that we feel powerless to affect. It is rare to find a productive setting where we can express how we feel about these things. Sharing is vital and makes people feel connected. When this is followed by the *Shapeshifting* practice of looking at the predicament through a *Spapeshifting Huaca's* eyes, the results are surprising. Most prevalent is a renewed sense of hope.

One woman's heart ached about the war in Iraq, where her son and many other young people were stationed. This woman's *Spirit Huaca* showed her how to extend love to her son at a distance, helping her to view energy as a tangible field of influence. She could affect people by directing her love to them. With her inner vision, this mother saw positive energy surrounding American troupes, including her son. This looked to her like a pink cloud of light. Seeing the actual energy made this insight very real. This made all the difference and brought tremendous relief. Someone pointed out that the land, air, waters and animals were also degraded by war. As well, humans on both sides of the battlefield were confused and in pain; the larger situation could also benefit by this energy. Despite being thousands of miles away, this mother now enveloped her son in love. This gave her a positive focus, something worthy to do instead of just feeling helpless. The result was that she felt closer to her son and her anguish lightened.

In a workshop the following year another woman shared an almost identical experience. After sending energy to her son and his company in Iraq these men described a tangible sense of being watched over. Her son, who had previously scoffed about his mom's energy work, now encouraged her to "Keep doing whatever you're doing".

Another person, an activist, shared how sad he was about the loss of animal species and the environmental destruction on our planet. More than sad, this man felt hopeless and angry. These species were gone forever and there was no turning back the clock. The rate of glacial melting and deforestation made the future bleak, desperate. To him, it was impossible to reverse things in time to prevent wide-spread catastrophe and so much damage was already done.

This person's *Shapeshifting Huaca* was a tree. When he *Shapeshifted* into the tree he felt calmer than he had in a very long time. As a tree this man was rooted in the earth, he and his planet inseparable. This was reassuring and made him realize how fragmented he had felt. He, as a tree, weathered the seasons and human-induced hardship. This person felt his branches bend under violent winds and snap with ice storms. He saw his trunk become scarred by bear claws and deer antlers. His growth had been stunted by pollution. Yet the tree was intact, he survived. That the tree withstood adversity made this gentleman remember the earth's endurance. This was a comfort. He then saw the evolution of the earth through his tree eyes. Life took countless shapes; forms came and went, but the force of life itself was vibrant no matter the outer shell. This was the same life force that streamed sap through his trunk and nutrients through his leaves. His tree body perpetually *Shapeshifted;* even upon death the tree would feed microorganisms, spawn new trees. This did not make this man feel less sad about species disappearing from our planet. But the tree's perspective sparked hope and it anchored him. He felt more present and in touch with life's resilience. *Shapeshifting* into a tree renewed this person's spirit. It inspired him to continue his work and to open to what is possible.

Shapeshifting Huacas allowed this man and woman a deeper view of reality. Seeing from the *Huaca's* perspective lifted their morale. This practice can also be used by communities tackling tough local issues. It is bonding for a group to journey about shared issues and typical to have common experiences. The deeper perspectives *Huacas* offer can help situations that people are split on, in turmoil over, or do not know what to do about. Fresh angles are routinely uncovered. This is just one of the many ways to work with *Huacas,* more of which we will explore throughout this book.

Spirit Huacas are supportive because they connect us with spirit, and nature's intelligence. Next we will look at how to align more deeply with the wisdom and life force of nature.

"The best and most beautiful things in the world cannot be seen or even touched. They must be felt with the heart."- Helen Keller

CHAPTER FOUR

SHAPESHIFTING WITH NATURE

At the beginning of this book we learned that the ability to *Shapeshift* is grounded in the continuously reconfiguring spirit of life and the notion of oneness. We have noted that although oneness with the natural world is innate to indigenous cultures, imbalances result when societies lose this perspective. Equilibrium can be restored by embracing more whole values and by coming back into rhythm with our heart, our body, and our planet. We have discovered ways to open to, and balance, earthly and heavenly energies. Now we will explore how to directly align with nature and the elements. Bonding with the natural world is fundamental to being human and supports the approaches in this book. In this chapter, we venture more deeply into this liaison.

Of the Aboriginal groups I have worked with, the Maya, whose prophesies are in the public eye due to the popularization of the Mayan Calendar, are masters of cosmic awareness. In the early part of this century a plethora of literature has been circulated about 2012 and the Mayan Calendar. Yet, often less focused upon is the Maya's deep attunement with the earth. The lands of ancient Guatemala have endured earthquakes and volcanic eruptions spanning centuries. Because of this, when visiting sacred sites and walking through the jungle of Tikal, Maya Elders ask that we pay as much attention to the pyramids that are submerged, as those we see. There are also hidden spiritual structures beneath Lake Atitlan. These, we learn, influence human consciousness and affect the waters. We are told that boating late in the afternoon can be treacherous as the lake's energy field activates, its vortex causing the winds to pick up making the waters choppy.

This level of resonance to the earth's unseen energies characterizes all shamanic groups. Yet, the Maya uniquely view the earth as a living body with a spinal column not unlike our own. From the perspective, along this spine of the earth are mountains reminiscent of vertebrae and energy centers like the chakras of the human body. According to the Maya peoples we have worked with, as the earth has a spinal column, it also has a heart. Attuning to the earth's heart harmonizes us and brings us into balance with our planet.

These times of monumental change urge that we heal our fragmentation with nature. Every native group we know espouses that we are one with every beat and pulse of the earth. Yet, we of the modern world have all but lost this wisdom. In Siberia, where the word shaman originated from "saman", Tuvan shamans drum to attune to the rhythms of the earth and universe. The drumming rituals of many Aboriginal peoples more than symbolize union with the heartbeat of the earth and universe. Research proves that drumming reconnects us with our deeper selves by inducing relaxing Alpha and Theta patterns in the brain. These restorative brain waves are undetectable in close to half the US population. It is imperative now, more than ever, to remember and honor interconnection with life. This supports us through changing times and encourages a healthier foundation for living together on this planet. In resonating with the heartbeat of the earth, we align with the life force that pulses through everything, and each of us. Throughout this chapter, drawing from myriad traditions, we focus on ways to do this.

Harmonize with the Earth

Before going further, one might question the wisdom of aligning with the heart of a planet which seems unpredictable and unstable now, more than ever. Unprecedented fires, earthquakes, hurricanes, volcanic eruptions, tsunamis and weather changes appear the norm. Public radio and major television news channels refer to the "severe storm cycle" concurrent with a "global axis shift." That the earth's magnetic fields can shift location has been scientifically debated until this millennium. Axis shifts are chronicled throughout indigenous lore and are part of Mayan and other predictions for this time. We might desire that the earth be static and unwavering, yet she is alive and evolving. Indigenous prophesies tell us the earth is *Shapeshifting*, as are we. In joining with the consciousness of our Mother Planet, they say we can make peace with, even shape, her changing rhythms. Aligning with our planet makes us feel more trusting and fluid. Oneness with the earth brings us into oneness with ourselves, which can ease our movement through perilous times.

Resonance with the earth tangibly benefits animals who can detect subtle changes in the earth. Rabbits and deer have been known to flee the area of an upcoming earthquake epicenter. Elephants have been observed to run to higher ground and low nesting birds fly to higher sites when tsunamis are approaching. Untapped by most, this sensitivity to slight precursors of change that animals display is also a human facility. It is our nature to sense delicate shifts in the earth. Largely unappreciated, people have predicted terrestrial events years in advance and across great distances. In 2003, following visions of massive storms engulfing Florida, I suggested to friends that they sell their home and leave the state. My friends took me seriously, yet they had endured 25 years of hurricanes in Florida, so, how bad could it be? What ensued was the Sunshine State's worst hurricane season in recent history. Similarly, in 2008, I spent two months on an island in the Puget Sound. One June afternoon when gazing out to the bay, a wind suddenly squalled. The air gusted through my window and as it touched my face, I knew the Southeast would see rough hurricanes that year. Thousands of miles from those regions and months from prime hurricane season, how could I know that?

We think animals perceive faint shifts in the earth because of heightened faculties. They have a honed sense of sight, smell, touch, taste and hearing. But, beyond the evident, instincts are at play which we cannot interpret. These come from an animal's inborn attunement with nature. Humans, too, can awaken this. In their predictions for this time period, alive for centuries, the sages and Elders of diverse cultures say the human species is ripe for a leap of consciousness. As we confront our survival, chaos may be a catalyst for us to awaken. In ancient Tibet, "extraordinary" capacities like precognition, telepathy, healing, yogic control over physiological systems, were accepted conditions of human nature awakened by conscious focus. Although such qualities have been rarely displayed by individuals throughout the history we are acculturated to, humanness includes such natural abilities, as well as gifts not yet tapped. Our higher aptitude now pressures to surface.

Similar to animals, increasing our sensitivity to the earth activates dormant abilities. This explains why many shamanic peoples are adept at predicting, even shifting the weather. This topic is beautifully portrayed by Nan Corbin with David Corbin in their book, *Weather Shamanism*. There are countless anecdotes across cultures describing people impacting the weather. I have seen Eurasians stop the rain, part the clouds, and produce rainbows before my eyes. The shamans say that when they work with the elements through ceremony they make people and their surroundings one again. This reconnection makes it easier to get nature to cooperate. Abilities like these are not reserved for tribal peoples. In *Shapeshifting* workshops, the weather appears responsive to our rituals. In invoking the element of air, the wind can kick up out of nowhere. Unusual cloud formations manifest during ceremony or the rain may suddenly cease and the sun, shine, despite the weather forecast. Apprentices joining rural intensives often witness extremes; from high winds, to downpours or snowstorms that miraculously clear as our work progresses. The weather appears synchronous to our gatherings and this could just be coincidence. But what is coincidence but a convergence of events? From a shamanic point of view, this describes oneness.

Our experience, and what shamanic people the world over teach, is that we are inseparable from the elements. We can attune to stone, tree, sky, wind, water. In experiencing oneness we gain wisdom, energy, and power. As with animals which pick up on subtle signals from the earth, humans can also know things otherwise impossible to know. Attuning this way is energizing. It stirs a fresh outlook of us and our world. As with Tuvan shamans who harmonize with nature's patterns to unite people and environments, we can also attune to: the consciousness that rides on the tail of the winds; the weather spirits who whirl like dervishes in tornadoes; the power that ignites volcanic eruptions and earthquakes; the energy that howls like a wolf through blizzards and tropical storms.

By tuning into the earth, knowing her heart as our own, and awakening to nature's pulses, we resonate with forces that push us now to evolve and grow. The time is ripe time to expose our own latent talents and, so, rouse the confidence to find our way through changing times. It may be very wise now to harmonize with the earth, her changing momentum and weather patterns, and honor her topography instead of manipulating lands and waters to human fancy. It is up to us to wake up and choose new ways to live.

Other than what is outlined above and the practices introduced in Chapter Two, how do we harmonize with the earth? How do we join our heart with the earth's heart? Easing the tendency to separate from the natural world will prove our greatest asset for navigating unparalleled times. Let us explore concrete ways to open to the land, spirits, and the elements.

Aimlessly Wander

Years ago I spent a total of six months at a Tibetan Buddhist center in the Rocky Mountains. During my stay there I practiced meditation for prolonged periods and did other rigorous spiritual practices. Emerging from such sessions could be disorienting, but an exercise was introduced to transition from intensified states. This was to wander aimlessly over the land, a powerful discipline in itself.

In translating the practice of *Aimless Wandering* to our work I invite people to meander out on the land with no agenda. I ask that they stay present and notice where they are naturally drawn. They are invited to let the energies of the land call to them; to rest the mind; open the heart and senses; to feel their oneness. Wandering is something children are quite adept at, yet which adults often lose all notion of. The word "aimless" seems to conjure negative connotations. Think about the last time you indulged aimless curiosity. When did you last surrender to the excitement of aimless adventure? Aimlessness, coupled with being mindful, opens our heart and body to expanded reality. It helps us engage the wonder and beauty of the world. In being receptive, we can remember the magic of every moment.

Walk the land with your senses engaged and your heart open (preferably with bare feet). Feel the breezes, warmth or coolness and each foot you place upon the earth. Step gently, pressing your weight upon the ball of the foot first like all earth-honoring peoples do as opposed to the heel pounding approach of nature-dominating cultures. Smell the scents and taste the air. Look carefully at the details all around you. Feel your body intently and in consonance with nature sensing which direction calls. Drop thoughts of doing or accomplishing. Invite delight by not thinking about where you are headed, just sense and feel it. Slow down. Allow your mind to relax. Bid body and heart to lead. Listen to nature's call and step in cadence with her rhythms. In slowing down and attuning to the land we pick up on things we might otherwise miss. Intuition sharpens and our inner guidance clarifies. *Aimless Wandering*, or walking mindfully, is sensual and joyous. It gets us out of our heads and into our bodies and hearts.

I hiked with a group of apprentices on a mountain in New Hampshire years ago. Though people usually do *Aimless Wandering* alone, we did so in a group. We walked in silence together much of the time, opening our hearts and senses. We listened to birds, rain and the rustle of leaves. We smelled the damp earth and the wetness of the drizzle. We felt the breezes and coolness on our faces. Deeper, we opened to nature's pulses. Soon the group detected what they thought were the territory's invisible gateways. Trees or stones called to us as the energetic doorways of the forest. We did ceremony in these places in appreciation of the forest and asked permission to enter its territory. Other locations invited unique experiences. A woman identified a hollowed out tree trunk as a vehicle for other worldly travel. Each adult took turns climbing into this cavernous tree, now a time travel machine. Journeying is a potent practice, yet journeying inside a tree trunk was amazing. Later, we reached a white birch grove whose trees lined either side of the trail. This looked like a *Bridge of Light*, so that is the name the group gave it. Someone photographed the *Bridge of Light* and another person led ceremony for us in the grove.

Tree trunk time travel, energetic portals and *Bridges of Light*? One could say this was merely play and if this was all it was, it would be well worth the while. But *Aimless Wandering* his a practice that heightens perception. Having a light heart and a child's curiosity is the surest way to rejuvenate and unlock nature mysteries. This is beautifully displayed by Andean Quechua peoples I have worked with who claim the best way to draw good spirits and good health, is to feel joy. Tibetans, also, tell us that being present and opening our hearts to nature's beauty enlivens and attracts protective spirits called *Dralas*.

Further up the trail several of us sensed the group was ready for a cleansing from a body of water. We could feel the water calling us to it which was interesting as no one could even hear even the trickle of a stream. After wandering for awhile further, we heard what we had been waiting for. I led the group off the trail and as we walked through the woods together, the sound of rushing water drew closer. It was not long before we came upon a cascading waterfall. Thrilled, we offered flower petals to the water, expressed our gratitude then dipped our toes into the frosty pool. Later, some of us, assisted by the others, sat on the mossy rocks to hang our heads (briefly) under the tumbling falls. The pristine waters were exhilarating. Wandering aimlessly, despite being on a trail, transformed us. In opening our hearts, nature came alive.

A week after the hike the woman who had taken the photographs emailed them to everyone in the group. She asked that we pay special notice to the *Bridge of Light*. In looking at the photo, I again admired the sinewy white trunks banking the trail. Yet, now in the bridge's center appeared a ball of light. A perfect, luminous sphere hung in the air amidst the trees. The form could have been a water spot appearing on the camera lens except that nothing like it was seen on any of the group's other photos.

Colleagues of ours at *Earth Train*, in association with the Berklee College of Music in Boston, use similar methods to open folks to nature's enchantment. As part of their *Junglewood* program, they have taken groups of students into the Panamanian jungle. With the assistance of local indigenous people, time is initially spent honoring the forest then everyone connects silently. The youth are asked to tune in to the jungle. They are invited to feel with their bodies and hearts, the spirit of nature. As they do this, they are instructed to listen for the forest's invisible rhythms. Then, like the shamans who drum to attune to nature, eventually everyone in the group participates with these tempos through music. The rainforest supplies the instruments: empty logs and stones are drums, twigs and rocks are clicked together, water is splashed. The program's director, Grammy award winning jazz pianist, Danilo Perez, encourages his students to gyrate and make sounds.

Reconnecting with nature is child's play. Perez claims that when we resonate with the rhythms of the natural world through music, we rejuvenate and become real human beings. Being in sync with nature, he says, brings us back to ourselves. It awakens our higher human values.

Walk Like a Shuar

Resonance with the land is innate to indigenous people and less common to most of us, though we have just lost touch with it. Awareness approaches like the Buddhist one of *Aimless Wandering*, and those such as *Junglewood*, help reestablish these connections. They remind us that the natural world is magical and one with us. The best way to navigate changing times is to evolve. A similar way to resonate with nature is what John Perkins calls *Walking Like a Shuar* or *Walking Without Looking at Your Feet*.

Traditionally the Amazonian Shuar are a fierce warrior culture known as one of the few tribes in the Americas to have gone undefeated. They are also healers, cultivators and hunters. We have taken hundreds of North Americans and Europeans deep into the Amazon Basin to experience life in Shuar territory and to be healed by their shamans. In these life-shifting journeys what strikes most is the Shuar's intimacy with nature. It is hard to separate mystical from physical, ultimately there is no division. Just as the jungle literally breathes oxygen for the planet so too does it breathe spiritual forces.

The Shuar are one with the teacher plants which guide their community and empower shamans to heal. Shuar women are one with land and water goddesses that spin out of the river and up from the earth to nurture their gardens. In tending these plants the women sing captivating melodies, enticing the plants to grow and the goddesses to keep them healthy. Whether rainforest, bird, rock, anaconda or waterfall; all are sacred and alive to the Shuar.

In gliding down the Amazon in a dugout canoe, Shuar men steer the boat through rapids with long wooden poles. All the while they stand, one in the back and one in the front of the boat, balanced and at ease. Every movement is harmonious with boat and current. This relaxed state of alertness is also observed in men and boys as they hunt.

Walking Like a Shuar describes the hunter's wandering. Shuar hunters seldom look at their feet as they walk. As in the walking style of all indigenous peoples, their bare feet commune with each patch of earth they touch. There is no need to glance down as the body knows where to step and when. Senses are acute and as the man feels his every move, he also reads every sign in the forest. The Shuar will observe, listen, smell and taste. He will feel the direction of the sun and the temperature of a waft of air, the leaves massaging his skin as he moves. Just as the women sing to please and nourish their plants, the hunter listens for the songs of the animals and the forest. Physical and subtle senses are awake, indivisible. This man looks at everything around him and moves without a sound. He may *Shapeshift* into a tree for invisibility or emulates a jaguar's stealth. In seeking a bird for prey, he is aware of each species cycle; during mating and nesting seasons they must be left alone. This ensures there will be more birds to feed his family the next year. He also notices change in the forest, even individual plants on trails he's walked since a child. One plant can inform this hunter about the larger scale of balance. Shuar identity is about relationship. Sense of self includes community and all the cycles, seasons, life forms and interrelationships of the forest.

Shuar men and women are fully present in their bodies, their senses keen. In *Walking Like a Shuar* we can also become fully present. We can use our heart and senses to guide us. This makes real that we are in relationship with everything around us. Experiencing inseparability with nature heals us and prods us to act responsibly with regard to the environment.

Retrieve Physical Huacas

The above practices prompt a direct experience with the natural world. Try them and see what you experience. In doing so, you may discover a *Physical Huaca*. Material *Huacas* are much like the *Spirit Huacas* of the last chapter in that, they like to find you. As you wander, or walk the land, a stone, leaf, or detached patch of moss may call out. A feather may light your path. A broken twig may catch your eye. Nature is always communicating with us we just have to pay attention.

If something calls out or tugs at you, ask if this is your *Physical Huaca*. As in the journey space, trust the answer in whatever form: a feeling, a word, or simply a "knowing". If you sense that this *Huaca* is yours, or to be used as an aid for your healing work, pick it up. Thank the land by depositing some loose tobacco, flower petals or bread in its place. You might be inspired to bring your *Huaca* home and find a special place for your sacred item to rest. This could be upon an altar if you have one or on a special shelf. Its energy should be clear but if you sense the need, set your *Huaca* in the sun for a day to energize it. If it is a stone, clean it physically then soak it in sea salt water to cleanse its energy.

Connect with your *Physical Huaca* by journeying to it, similar to how we get to know *Spirit Huacas*. You can refer back to Chapter Three for a refresher on how to journey and merge with *Huacas*. Being tangible, material *Huacas* offer an added dimension as we can also get to know them physically. Explore your *Huaca* visually; look at it carefully and with curiosity.

Notice each detail, pay attention to its color, texture and shape. Engage all of your senses. Smell your *Huaca* and touch it. Even taste it if it is an item that allows for this and you have cleaned it well.

Do not forget to feel your *Physical Huaca's* temperature. For example, if it is a stone does it feel cool or warm in your hand? Does it feel cool on some areas of its surface and warm on others? What is the sensation when you place your stone against your cheek, or after holding it in your hand? Notice also what the stone's or object's shape reminds you of. Observe what sentiment arises as you hold or look at it. How do you feel? Where in your body do you feel this? Do associations pop up for you? You may want to dialogue in the way a prominent sound healer and shaman friend of mine, Zacciah Blackburn, does when attuning to the land: listen with the heart and offer a response from the mind. Then listen with your mind and, in turn, respond from your heart.

Huacas can even show up in our dreams and many people like to sleep with them. Place your sacred objects under the pillow, hold them in your hands, or rest them on parts of your body. If in need of a healing, they can draw congested energy and also rejuvenate areas they rest upon. *Huacas* can balance you and they open intuition. If drawn to sleeping with your sacred items, see what parts of your body call. Intuit, or ask, where your *Huacas* would like to rest. I have slept with stone *Huacas* for years. I start out by holding them in my hands or placing them on my forehead, heart or abdomen. As they inevitably roll off in the middle of the night, you may end up with rocks in your bed. But sleeping with material spirit allies is intimate. Their influence seeps into us through our energy field and allows us to open to the *Huacas* own spirit or essence. I often have dreams of swallowing my stones, indicating the oneness we attain. You can accomplish the same thing by taking the time to journey with your *Physical Huacas*.

As with *Spirit Huacas*, sacred physical objects are also energetic keys. All *Huacas* are imbued with specific characteristics, each has a unique essence. They channel energy from the earth, cosmos, and the elements. Yet contrary to what many think, shamans tell us it is not so much the power of a *Huaca* that is significant, but what occurs as we relate to it. We are not separate from our *Huacas* and their powers. These are ultimately our own. A *Huaca's* deeper gift is to awaken our own forgotten qualities. Opening our heart is all that is needed to do this, and to be able to see these spiritual aptitudes for what they are.

Some time ago I met a biologist living in Alaska. He was intimate with the land, living in a tent despite 40 degree below zero temperatures. This seemed a spiritual existence to me, yet this person claimed to have no inclination toward such things and was now curious. I suggested he reflect on environmental systems, something he could relate to. This scientist saw the natural world as interrelated and interactive. This included the life forms observed with the naked eye, yet also microorganisms that he, as a biologist, used an instrument to see. Spirit and energy are similarly invisible aspects of reality; they interface all physical systems, microscopic as well as observable. In the case of spirit or energy, the tool used to discern what is unseen is not a microscope, but the heart.

The same is true for discerning spiritual qualities of *Huacas*. Take time with sacred objects and open your heart to them. In doing so, you will understand more about your *Huaca*. You will also understand more about yourself. The *Huaca's* spiritual aspects may present in unorthodox ways. Remember how the Pepsi logo finally caught my attention.

To obtain a *Physical Huaca* for healing work, simply set this intention when you walk the land. Determine at this time whether this will be a *Huaca* for self-healing, or for use in healing work with others. There are many suggestions for employing *Huacas* for healing purposes in the book, *Shamanic Reiki* (Roberts and Levy). If you discover a *Physical Huaca* but you are unsure about its purpose, journey to it. You can also place your *Huaca* on your body when journeying to understand why it has come to you and what its gifts are. This makes these qualities tangible within you. Feel its qualities and power, breathe them in.

After using tangible *Huacas* for any purpose, they should be cleansed and reenergized. To do this rest them in the sun on a window sill or outside for a day. You can also put them out for the full moon or under a star-lit canopy. If a stone or crystal, try burying it in the earth for 24 hours. Alternately, soak stones in sea salt water for the same amount of time or smudge them with incense, sage or cedar. Using the Reiki symbols is also efficient to cleanse and energize sacred objects. Just draw the Reiki symbols over the object. You can also draw them in the air or visualize the symbols, then blow this energy into your *Huaca*.

We will work with *Physical Huacas* and *Spirit Huacas* throughout this book. For now, the exercise below is a great complement to *Aimless Wandering* and *Walking Like a Shuar*. Engage your *Spirit* and *Physical Huacas* in whatever way calls to you as you follow the instructions below.

The Siberian Mark Exercise is another method of deepening your connection to the land and spirits. If you have not already been found by a *Physical Huaca*, one will likely discover you after doing this practice.

The Siberian Mark Exercise

As you *Aimlessly Wander*, or *Walk Like a Shuar*, you may find a place in nature that calls to you. Follow your heart, see where you are drawn. When we go for a picnic we look for just the right place to spread our blanket. We want to feel good where we sit and eat. Finding your place in nature is a similar, yet more conscious act. Your intention is to awaken a relationship with the land, so this is more than just looking for a good place. There can be many reasons for our resonance with a particular place, yet we do not need to understand what they are. The important thing is to feel and honor the connection.

When you arrive at a place that calls, as my apprentices and I found the waterfall, greet the place respectfully. One way is to make an offering to the spirits of the land. Different traditions use varying items. Native Americans proffer tobacco or cornmeal, the Andean Quechua use flower petals, *Trago* (sacred alcohol), coins and food. In Siberia shamans feed the land and spirits with salami, bread, milk and vodka. What you give is not as important as the attitude with which you do so, which should embody reverence. You can even offer silence, a meditation, your tears or gift the place with a conscious and radiant smile. You can dance, pray or sing. As you give in a sacred way, whatever form this takes, open to the beauty of this spot. Notice its physical details and as you do, observe how you feel. Allow love and appreciation to rise in you. Let your heart and body flood with feeling. I am easily brought to tears appreciating nature; do not be afraid to be passionate about nature's majesty. Appreciation is the gateway to expanded perception; it creates a bridge through which we can participate with living energy. Our gratitude is also giving back to the earth, acknowledging all she bestows to us. Remember how it feels to love another person, and to feel the other person's love coming back to you. Opening to the earth is similar. When your heart is full, silently or aloud, ask permission to be here. Express longing to commune with this spot. When you feel ready and welcomed, you may want to try the *Siberian Mark Exercise*.

There are two ways to do this exercise. One is to kneel on the ground with your palms and knees against the earth. Your forehead will also be touching the earth. The other approach is that if you are connecting with a vibrant tree or a large rock instead of the earth itself, you can stand as opposed to kneeling. In this case, you would face the tree or stone and place your palms and forehead against the bark or the stone's surface. Either way, close your eyes and permit cozy contact with nature. This is not the time to worry about the wet grass, getting mud on your pants, or soggy hair from the rain. Being in the elements is energizing; it is healthy for us. Be aware if you are kneeling near a poisonous plant, a fire ant mound, or other such thing. Be alert, as the Shuar are, to the many life forms we share this world with. If you carry *Physical Huacas*, place them on the earth nearby. Try to sense where your *Physical Huacas* would like to be placed or ask them where they would like to be as you commune with this spot. You may also be drawn to invoking the presence of your *Spirit Huaca*, or merging with it before you connect. See what feels right.

In doing the *Siberian Mark Exercise*, empathize with the tree, stone, or earth. Feel your forehead flush to the earth or tree. Sniff the sweet aroma of the grass beneath you and take in the musky scent of the soil. Trace the tree's bark with your fingers, the rough or smooth surface of the stone. As well, notice its temperature. Immerse in its sensual aspects. Touch. Stay with your bodily experience and open your heart. As you do, open to nature's invisible rhythms. Feel her pulse, sense her cadence. When distracted, just come back: breathe, feel, and be. Smell, sense, and hear. Feel, open, and taste. Keep coming back. Most significant is to connect with the spirit of what you commune with. Even regarding hallucinogenic plants, a shaman's interest is the plant's essence, not its chemical constituents. Meeting the plant's spirit is always the goal, ingesting them is just one way to do this.

We call this a "mark" exercise, because in being present with nature, the tree, the stone, or the earth may offer something back. This might be received in non-ordinary reality. We may see something through our inner vision. Alternately, we may sense or intuit a mark. Or we might feel something inexplicable or receive a sign in ordinary reality like a thunder clap, a bird's trill, or a warm waft of air. Stay open to what comes.

I was first introduced to the *Siberian Mark Exercise* when

traveling across expanses of the Asian steppe (prairie) from Kyzyl, Tuva to Mongolia with a Tuvan *Shamanka*. The purpose was to offer ceremony and healings to remote communities. As with all the shamanic groups, Tuvans see the energy of trees, fields, waters and winds. Everything is alive. They do not have to get out of the car, lie down, and blind fold their eyes to discern these forces. Shamanic perception is always open, so spiritual reality would be hard to miss. Yet, they do get out of the car to honor the spiritual aspects of the land and deepen their connection to these. The steppe in this region is grassland interspersed with stretches of taiga (evergreen forest). This is bordered by rivers and mountains. From June through August the temperatures can rise to over one hundred degrees and the forest's ground cover is lush. Shrines called *Obaas* dot the landscape where the topography and, the shamans say, the spirits, change. We make offerings here, at the energetic gateways of the land. You would not walk into a neighbor's home without knocking or knowing that you are welcomed. Similarly, shamans will not enter a spirit's territory without appeasing them and asking permission. This also deepens their connection to that which is unseen.

In stopping at one of these locations, I walked over to a small teepee like structure, an *Obaa* this woman built with her own hands. When her father was alive he also spent time on this land. The *Shamanka* asked me to crawl inside the *Obaa*, kneel upon the earth, and place my forehead to the ground. I stayed there for a long time. The shaman woman finally said, "The earth will give you a mark". I worried that nothing would appear to me, but soon I did see a horse. The horse became a clear figure in my mind and I enjoyed watching it gallop. After some time, the horse disappeared and in its place formed a circle of twinkling stars. When this also faded, I knew that it was time to emerge from the *Obaa*. After I came out the *Shamanka*, who was waiting for me, asked what I saw. When I shared my images she smiled.

She said, "Today begins the holiday of horses and tonight we do a ceremony to the stars." I had received a clear mark from the earth. Weeks later I learned of a deeper association: this woman's father was a horse thief and her mother was a celestial *Shamanka*.

There are not any time constraints for *The Siberian Mark Exercise*, except to keep communing until you feel one with the earth, tree or stone. When resonant with the land, it may be time to close. Sense what is right. If you did not receive a mark, do not worry; this is perhaps just not the time. Feeling oneness, sensing the heart and spirit of the earth, is most important. Trust when you feel complete. It is not very often these days that I receive anything tangible when doing the *Siberian Mark Exercise*. But as the practice has deepened through the years, my exchange with the land is profound. Take time transitioning and thank the spot you have connected with. This may be a location that you stay at for awhile to journey to your *Huacas* or to do other work. This practice is a splendid way to begin or close a ceremony, or to greet and commune with any location.

The Siberian Mark Exercise is one way to resonate with the environment; there are many approaches. As in relating to *Huacas*, opening to nature is a visceral talent. Trust the land, the spirits, and the elements to open to you, and teach, you. Years ago I sat with a group on a grassy knoll at the backside of a volcano high in the Andes. A Quechua *Iachak* (shaman) stood knee deep in mineralized waters gushing from a cave. Eight people, accompanied by other shamans, had died attempting initiation at this place in the last decade. The Quechua man crooned a haunting melody, charming the waters, inducting us to its secret cadence. The grotto of asphyxiating gasses only granted safe entry if your heart was open and you were one with the spring.

Aimlessly Wander, Walk Like a Shuar and the *Siberian Mark Exercise* are potent ways to bring us into harmony with the earth. Through them we reconnect with the land and energize our body and awaken our spirit. In addition to practicing these exercises, keep their essence alive throughout your day. You cannot always make physical offerings or prostrate, but you can be aware and feel one with nature whether in the city or countryside. Offer your attention and sentiment. Open to the sun's warmth, the rain's wetness, the breeze's caress. If you cannot walk aimlessly, you can still appreciate the trees, the skies and the winds. Once connected, let instinct guide you deeper than the physical; engage the pulse of life itself. You will feel complete, whole. Rejoining with nature fills us spiritually and heals our relationship with the earth.

Earth resonance also alerts us to tangible, internal and external relationships. For instance, environmentally we may freshly appreciate the water we drink, wash our clothes and bathe with. If we have a well, beyond the water that comes from our faucet, we can attune to land and their watersheds and rain cycles, as well as what threatens the health or supply of our water. If in a city, we envision water pipes, processing, filtering systems, and the reservoirs or tanks the water is piped in from. Included is the health of our water and what we inadvertently flush back into our watersheds and ecosystems. From localized ecosystems, awareness can expand to the network of planetary water bodies, as well as the impact of pollutants and water shortages on aquatic species and us. Connecting with nature makes us realize inseparability. It brings our role as the earth's stewards to the forefront.

In connecting with water we can also grasp the role of the water that encompasses our own body: its aid in digestion, nutrient assimilation and blood production; water's role as an electrical conductor for brain function, as a temperature and blood pressure regulator, and more. Scientists claim the human body is made of 50% to 90% water, depending on where you are in the life cycle.

Water comprises and nourishes us. Shamanic peoples we have worked say the water in us is inseparable from the waters of the earth: oceans, rivers, streams and lakes. They also claim that beyond physical value, applying water to the body clears discordant subtle energy. We are the elements. So much so that Tibetans view the process of death as the collapsing of each of the elements within us and the states of existence they support; first earth, then water, then fire, then air. This is followed by a final dissolution process. As the gross and subtle aspects of the elements dissolve, the forces supporting the life of the body depart. An empty shell (body) is left. Tibetans ceremonially burn or dismember this vessel after death to sever the departing spirit's attachment to the body, and to that life.

The Whole Earth is a Vortex

In closing the above practices you may feel altered. Opening heart and body to the earth expands us. If we are not accustomed to this it can at first slightly disorient, or make us feel "spacey". But this can be pleasant. For instance, you may feel preoccupied with the lustrous green color of the leaves and the grass. You might hear animal sounds and insect prattle you never noticed before. You may detect energy: wave-like sensations in your body, melodies or faint tones you hear with your ears or internally, or pulses that you see release from trees, plants, air and waters. A buzz or radiance might charge the air. Alternately, you may perceive nothing unusual at all, only feel exceptionally good. You may sense abundant life. Trust and enjoy what you feel. Breathe it in. Open your heart and body. Immerse in nature and your spirit will soar.

Contemporary lifestyles habituate us to a fraction of reality. Think of how you block out the refrigerator drone or the whirr of traffic outside your window. We do something comparable with nature. Recall going on a trip for a week, after which you return home. Though nothing has changed, you may see things differently upon arriving back. The blue of the kitchen tiles may freshly catch your eye. You may notice the ceiling fans as if for the first time. You might be shocked at the stacks of paperwork that bury your desk. For better or worse, most of us have habituated attention. This is likewise true of our relationship with the earth.

Fine tuning spiritual focus to perceive more of our world takes getting used to. Disorientation can become exaggerated at sacred sites or vortexes. The energy in these places is intense. This can make it hard to stay grounded, rendering odd accidents not uncommon. On an expedition in Siberia, one man who was not centered tripped on the stairs of a Buddhist temple. Later, he leaned on, and broke, a glass case in a local shop. After trekking in Tikal through the jungle in Guatemala for two days, and upon return to the city, a woman twisted her ankle when she fell off a street curb. Then after hailing a cab to get her back to the hotel, just as the cab door was opened, a car whizzed by and hit it. No one was harmed but a ruckus ensued between the drivers. Such stories are amusing in retrospect, especially since no one was badly hurt. Yet, they urge us to be mindful.

The human system has to adapt to amplified forces, as we do anytime we take in more than we are used to. The details of a new job can overwhelm us until we acclimate to the fresh tasks and environs. Adjusting to nature's energy is similar. We can adapt by slowing down and honoring the tempo, whether connecting with the earth at a sacred site or in a city park.

Power spots and vortexes are abundant in life force. They are energetically vibrant. They are often also physically radiant in the same way a happy, healthy person glows or exudes good energy. Amplified locales are heightened aspects of the larger planetary energy webbing. Because of this, contrary to what many think, we can access this power anytime and anywhere, even in our own backyard. All that is required is our loving attention. The entire earth is a power spot. All upon her are sacred. Everything and everyone harbors natural brilliance. The brilliance of the earth is beautifully intimated by the Quechua word for Mother Earth, *Pachamama*, most accurately translated as: "Mother Earth, Mother Time, and Mother Universe". The luminosity inherent to humans has been called by many names, including: *Buddha Nature, Christ Consciousness*, the *God Within*, the *Higher or Divine Self*, and *Higher Consciousness*. Within everything, and everyone, is radiant essence.

If indigenous forecasters are right, we are at the cusp of a larger view. As we enter this cycle, the exercises in this chapter (and in this book) bridge an expanded way to be. They help us come into rhythm with our own heart, the heartbeat of the earth, and the cosmos. When we resound with the life that pulses through everything, we are inspired to live in healthier ways. In doing so, we will discover that we, and our world, are more than we imagined. Just as it can take time to adjust to nature's energy, these shifts in perception also take adjusting. Something new may appear to be occurring on our planet, yet this is not true. When we turn the light switch on in a dark room, we see things for what they are. Everything in that room has always been there; we just could not see it in the dark. This time period is similar. The human journey has, so far in modern times, been predominantly individuated, cerebral, linear, and material. Yet many of us have the growing sense that we are so much more. To see freshly requires that we open our hearts and engage our bodies. As the light is turned on, we will know ourselves for who we truly are.

Dream Harmony on Earth

This chapter closes with a visualization exercise we have had a lot of success with in varying settings. People describe delight and well being in taking just a few moments to dream beauty and harmony on the earth. Despite how dire things appear it makes sense to imagine as real, what we long for. In introducing this exercise at social and environmental conferences, people feel relieved to get out of their heads. Tremendous energy can go into worrying about, and trying to solve, the world's problems. It is healthy to take time out. And wise for activists of all persuasions to fuel their actions with what the heart deems possible. Uplifted dreams sustain us and they magnetize a hopeful future.

As you engage this exercise, open to your heart's desire. Imagine and feel as clearly as you can, what you really want, personally and globally.

1) In a comfortable seated or standing position, take three deep, refreshing breaths. Let go of tension and allow yourself to really feel each breath.

Let shoulders drop relaxed. Opening your mouth slightly will relax your jaw. Also relax your belly and lower back muscles so the breath flows freely and fully through your whole body. After each deep inhalation, exhale and let go.

Take the next few moments to simply feel the breath moving in and out of your body. Enjoy the rhythm and movement of your body with each breath. This rhythm is something you can always come back to. No matter what is happening around you, in returning to this rhythm you can feel centered. If there are outside hindrances - cars, nature sounds, whatever – include them into the rhythm of your breath. Invite them as part of your experience. There is no need to block anything out.

As you continue feeling the sensations of your breath, know this is a place where you can rest. This is how to rejuvenate. When restlessness or turmoil surrounds, breathe in goodness and relaxation. Breathe in trust and equanimity. Breathe at your own pace in this way until you feel connected and relaxed.

2) Now from this settled place, imagine the majesty and beauty of the natural world. Open to, and really feel, it.

Remember the perfection of nature in all of its expressions - fierce as well as serene. You may call to mind gentle streams and roaring oceans. You may envision soft spring rains or cascading waterfalls. Perhaps you will recall trees, luminous green leaves, and silent mountains; or feel the power of erupting volcanoes, the delicate scent of blooming flowers. Remember the other plants that flourish on the land as well as those in the sea. You may picture endless colorful canvasses of sky. Also, reflect on the earth's living creatures: animals and insects that walk the lands, those that swim the sea or soar upon the winds.

In doing so, however it unfolds, open to the beauty and majesty of the earth. Let this come into your body. Really feel it. Breathe the wonder of the natural world in, and breathe it out. Open your heart. Be touched as you remember the magical world we share. Make this come alive for you. Breathe the living, sentient, qualities of our vibrant planet. Remember that she and we are one. Feel this. Open all of your senses to nature - urban and rural. Feel how this life supports us. Feel how this beauty enlivens and restores. Make this experience as real as you can.

3) Now from this feeling of appreciation for the earth, imagine people living in harmony upon our planet. Feel the goodness of this, take your time.

Imagine humans living sustainably, also with care and respect for each other. Imagine that we are at peace with our communities. We are at peace with everything around us. Feel this deeply: as if it is real now, as if it is already true. Know this as our reality. What does this feel like in your body; your heart? Imagine the details of this harmonious life as vividly as you can. Take your time. Breathe with this possibility, believe it. Anchor this reality in with each and every breath. Feel good, connected. What it would be like if people lived harmoniously with the earth and all its inhabitants?

Notice how you feel, now. Take your time.

4) Lastly, take three deep breaths in and out. With each exhalation breathe out beauty and balance with a HAAAAAAAA sound.

With each exhalation breathe the reality of beauty and balance, out. As you do, intend this breath to infuse the world with harmony. Make this possibility real. Offer this living vision through the vehicle of your breath as a prayer, a wish for humanity. With each breath out, radiate the vibrations of life, beauty, and harmony out into the world. Breathe out ease. Breathe out respect.

As you propel each breath out, make a satisfying HAAAAAAAA sound. Do not hold back. Impel this dream out into the world through your breath. Breathe out love. Breathe possibility.

5) *Take time to transition before moving on. Allow the practice to dissolve, yet stay with the feelings of harmony and beauty. Keep these alive throughout your day.*

(NOTE: If in doing this exercise you are so besieged by the chaos and pain of the world that you cannot get to beauty and harmony, start right there, with what you feel; simply breathe with that. If all you feel is disharmony, honor and breathe with that. Keep breathing. Stay present. You may more deeply feel them, or sense the root of your distress, and in acknowledging them they may transform.)

In Chapter One of this book, it was noted that the imagination can be used as an effective tool for athletic conditioning. Indigenous shamans, as well as modern scientists, tell us that engaging body, heart, and imagination, renders what we envision possible. Curt Butz feels this power of visualizing can help us co-create a foundation for a new future. His book, *The World I Dream Of*, presents the "ideal dream worlds" of over 100 people who have dedicated their lives to global change. The dreamers are scientists including physicist Fred Alan Wolf, green and social activists including grassroots leader Majora Carter, artists, authors, futurists such as astrologer Barbara Hand Clow, and others. Why not imagine harmony and dream an ideal world? The results of imagining beg us to see that reality is dynamic.

Yet dreaming is not the only thing pointing to a less linear, more malleable world. Ground breaking quantum studies prove that photon particles react differently when a person is looking at them than when they are not being observed. The implication is that consciousness impacts reality on the molecular level. Given this, it is not farfetched to muse that dreams can come true, and to use our attention to change the world.

Deep within our hearts, and the earth's heart, is an exquisite reality waiting to be. Remember this world, give energy to it. Dream it into being.

The approaches in this chapter offer powerful ways to attune to the earth. This supports a sustainable mindset and opens us to our greater human potential. We will look next at how to discover and empower our *Higher Purpose.*

"Tell me, what is it you plan to do with your one wild and precious life?"- Mary Oliver

CHAPTER FIVE

DISCOVERING AND EMPOWERING HIGHER PURPOSE

I accompanied John Perkins on a speaking tour coinciding with the release of his shocking best-selling book, *Confessions of an Economic Hit Man*. Interspersing visits to Ivy League institutions such as Columbia and Princeton, we ventured one morning to a small Catholic college just outside New York City. Of 28 Jesuit colleges in the country, St. Peter's is New Jersey's only one. Despite its humble 3,000 students, St. Peter's throbbed with life. Before John's formal talk, we joined some of the undergraduates for lunch. Most were urban commuters holding down jobs to get through school. They spoke ardently about their studies and the many social causes they were devoted to. There was a free-thinking quality to these students and they exuded enthusiasm beyond the usual for college kids. The teachers were just as lively. The main meeting room, with its soft blue walls and centrally placed Crucifix, also was not what you would find on most college campuses. But aside from tangible differences, it was the passion at St. Peter's that caught my attention.

This is not surprising. A Jesuit education is known for its regard of the whole person. It is designed to prepare leaders who are grounded in service and faith, to benefit our diverse, global society. The Jesuit approach recognizes that each individual has a calling or vocation; a special mission in life that is between them and the higher power. The Jesuits, of course, call this Higher Power, God. I have concluded that it is this dedication to

Higher Purpose that kindled the fervor I felt at St. Peter's.

Outside of spiritual figures like Saint Joan of Arc, there are countless stories of people devoting their lives to higher destiny. These proliferate in history, literature, and the arts. Yet until Martin Luther broadened the Christian concept of vocation to include the lay person, only the clergy were sanctioned to hear God's calling. In our modern day, regardless of religious persuasion, it is valuable to consider that we each have a unique and important role to play in life.

There are many aspects to the discovery and fulfillment of *Higher Purpose*. Our mission is not always clear, can come as a surprise, and be fraught with challenge. Drawing again from the epic, *The Lord of the Rings*, the small Hobbit, Frodo Baggins, appeared an unlikely candidate to defeat the Dark Lord, Sauron. Yet Frodo was fated to throw the ring of the Dark Lord into the volcano at Mt. Doom, where it was forged. This was the only place the Ring of Power could be destroyed, the journey there, perilous. Classics such as this, the Danish Medieval legend, *Beowulf*, and others, are well choreographed battles between good and evil; what we might view as higher and lower aspects of being. These struggles highlight tests we all face in life. Such mythical tales likewise mirror that inner travails and triumphs are intrinsic to embracing *Higher Purpose*.

Aside from its challenge, let us return to the passion associated with the pursuit of higher calling, such as I felt from the students and teachers at St. Peter's. Why does passion prevail in seeking our purpose? Think about when you felt this kind of zeal in your own life. What was it like, what were the circumstances? An inner calling historically derives from God, Universal Intelligence, Divine Source, or whatever we prefer to know this as. It transcends selfish interest and despite difficulty or consequence, it resounds to our core. This spiritual core, or essence, called the "Higher Self" in the New Age sector, is synonymous to what is noted in the last chapter as a person's natural "luminosity" or "radiant essence". We express and fine tune our higher, spiritual aspects through our life's purpose. Similarly, in getting closer to our higher nature we discover we have something unique to offer the world; there is a reason why we are here. Regardless of how we arrive, uniting our mortal with our spiritual self is ecstatic. It makes us whole; it ignites the spark of God within.

Whatever our vocation, it must respect all of earthly life. Excepting environmental and animal activists, vocations typically favor human interest. Yet, no matter how good we are at helping people, we cannot forget our planet. Considering the earth should be second nature, as ecological balance is necessary for human survival. But in disconnecting from nature we have lost common sense. Some cases in point are clear cutting forests to maintain oil and beef dependency and restructuring land so our species can live anywhere, regardless of the natural patterns we disrupt. Dominance over nature prevails. Many of us become alerted only when imbalance threatens us personally. Yet, even when our homes wash into the ocean or we recognize global warming, our goals remain self-serving and short-sighted. Honoring our planet would save people a lot of suffering. Even admirable plans, like empowering third world economies or rebuilding homes after disasters, create more pain if not earth-wise.

Whatever our cause, it must take into account fundamental relationships. As our primary bond is with the earth we must protect, and co-create with, our ecology. Doing so opens us to ecstasy. This is how to uncover the distinctive role of humans in the evolution of life on this planet.

That said, let us look at indigenous wisdom approaches to help us discern *Higher Purpose* and to empower it.

Empowerment

Arutum

When John Perkins and I take North Americans and Europeans into the Amazon basin, the forest dwellers invite us to feel the spirit of *Arutum* (Arootum). Shuar members and their children seek this life giving energy from the trees, animals, stars, waters and stones. *Arutum* increases a hunter's perception and a warrior's stamina. It can rouse confidence to face everyday dilemmas or to navigate higher direction. Similar to the Native American *Vision Quest* tradition of fasting and praying alone in the wilderness for life-guiding visions, Shuar transform through *Arutum*.

Nature and her energy are bountiful for the Shuar who live in oxygen rich forests and whose home country of Ecuador hosts some of the greatest diversity of plant life on this planet. Some of these are "dreaming plants" which tribal members ingest for healing and to acquire *Arutum*. Yet contrary to popular thought, indigenous people do not need to imbibe plants to do this. They can simply open to nature's energy. The same is true for us.

In July of 2009, John and I hiked through Panamanian jungle with members of a partner organization, *Earth Train*. We headed for the Northeast edge of *Earth Train's* 10,000 acre preserve. One more ridge would have us at the Continental Divide and the boundary of indigenous Kuna territory which *Earth Train* borders now protect. As we made our way through thick jungle under-growth to the Mamoni River, we saw an area in the distance that was lighted by open sky. Much of the land *Earth Train* has earmarked for reforestation was slashed and burned for cattle but this parcel was felled for lumber. Illegally stripped, the most commercially valuable trees were targeted by helium balloons and plucked by helicopter. What remained was clear cut. We had only been in Panama a handful of days, yet, time enough to see widespread ecological damage. Hillsides were muddied and eroded. Once-pristine rivers stank of cattle urine. Sun drenched lands yawned vacant where lush forests had housed multitudes of animals, insects and birds. My heart hung heavy.

In reaching the river bed, we took off our outer clothes and relaxed near clear pools formed by cascading water. The journey had been long, hot and now, emotional. Yet the sights, the cacophony of birds and insects, and streams tumbling through this verdant pocket eased my grief. I watched several iridescent Blue Morpho butterflies pirouette through the air and recalled impressions from our hike. Leaf cutter ants by the hundreds carried tiny leaf bits. A huge Conga ant tended her nest and countless mud laden armadillo burrows bordered the trail. Delicate spider webs and infinite varieties of trees, vines and plant life stretched out before us. The forest pulsed with beauty. Yet the rape of adjacent lands was hard to put aside. We sat at the water's edge and John urged us to take in power. Indigenous people of these lands would know *Arutum*, though by a different name. I closed my eyes and listened to the melody of the falls. My body vibrated to the rhythm of cool rushing waters. When *Arutum* began to surge in me I breathed its life giving strength from the top of my head to the tips of my toes. I sucked in another deep breath and realized that my sadness had evaporated. In its place was fortitude. We and our world can change. I envisioned this force, *Arutum*, infusing the tens of thousands of seedlings being planted by *Earth Train* to restore degraded lands

We each can gain *Arutum* from the water and skies, from the land and trees. Its force that feeds us, and the life all around us, arises from the elements. These natural powers can be used unconsciously or malevolently, yet, ignorant or selfish gain never lasts; just as we see amazing advances in our times, humans are on the brink of extinction. So, we teach people to seek *Arutum* to heal and to gain higher direction in support of all life. The Quechua call this life force the Fifth Element, *Ushai*. Through it, and together, we can rouse confidence to transform ourselves and our world.

Arutum derives from nature, yet we can also discover it in dreams or shamanic journeys. In the process of discovery, we might encounter something ominous. For example our journey may pose us face to face with a huge spider, a jaguar, or anaconda. Snakes, ancient symbols of *Shapeshifting*, are associated with *Arutum*. Just as a snake transfigures by shedding its skin, *Arutum* can help us to transform. Perhaps snakes frighten civilized folks, in part, because they signify raw power. Think of the entwined Caduceus snakes of allopathic medicine, representing the power to heal. Consider the Minoan Snake Goddess, an omen of fertility, and the yogic serpentine energy, *Kundalini,* which awakens spiritual power. Juxtaposing is the snake of the Garden of Eden and the legend of St. Patrick banishing the snakes from Ireland. That St. Patrick banished snakes is debatable, but he did drive the earth-honoring ways from Ireland. Shamans, as did the Druids, cultivate power *with*, not *over*, nature. Snakes symbolize this raw alliance with primal forces which the Christians, for many reasons, feared. Whether ancient or esoteric, interpreted as good or bad, snake means power.

For this reason Shuar medicine people encourage people to approach the snake (or spider or jaguar) of their journey or dream and touch it, feel its energy. They even encourage their children to touch the life force, or *Arutum*, of dangerous snakes in the wild. Anacondas are voracious hunters. In fact, on one expedition we heard that a five year old had been eaten by an anaconda. But in mating season they pose less threat. At this time up to twelve males wrap around a female until she is no longer observable and all writhe trance-like for up to four weeks. The snakes are completely absorbed at this time; so much so that the Shuar have told us they urge their children to touch, even walk upon, these anaconda mating balls to take in power.

I was inspired by this story of Shuar children touching the *Arutum* of wild animals. For years I walked an isolated dirt road flanked by hundreds of acres of protected lands in Western

Massachusetts. In the spring when the black bears abundantly roamed the forests, my walks were stimulating as I never knew when I would encounter a bear. I was afraid, yet also excited, to meet one. I did not go looking for them, but did see four bears through my years of walking that road. I felt awe, terror and power. The emotions mixed into one as being so close to the bears and their cubs flooded me with *Arutum*. I was wide awake. The last one I saw ran out of the woods and crossed right in front of me on the road. I felt little fear this time. The animal was beautiful. I was exhilarated. This reminded me of when my son, Eben, had driven John and me on this road at dusk one night. We spotted a bear at the road's edge and Eben stopped the car. John jumped out and scampered over to the startled animal. Both bear and John then disappeared into the woods. Eben's mouth dropped open, "What's he doing?!" I said "John wants to touch the bear's power".

I do not advise that you look for, or run after, bears or any other wild animal. Yet, such stories demonstrate that *Arutum* can demand bravery and a willingness to step into the unknown. Those partaking in Amazon plant ceremonies sometimes encounter terrifying visions. Yet in rousing courage and touching what they fear, they gain vitality. This can be applied to everyday life. Think of a time when something terrified you, but you faced it. What did you feel, what was your experience? Recall rallying courage to make a public stand on something you felt strongly about. Remember admitting to a lover that your feelings have changed. Summon the memory of what it felt like to step into a daunting, yet important, task. In overcoming obstacles or following your heart, did you grow strong? Did approaching what you normally shy away from ultimately energize you? When the time is right, open to something you know you must greet, yet, would rather avoid. Like the Shuar, be mindful, as power must be respected. Again, I do not recommend running after a bear or touching a Brown Recluse spider, for instance. Seeking the exotic is also not necessary as each day offers ample opportunities for gaining power. Mindfully face life's everyday challenges and you will feel vital.

A Shuar hunter will seek to *Shapeshift* into *Arutum* to enhance stealth and stamina. Amazonians may do so for persistence in battling oil companies destroying their lands. A Shuar mother may rouse it to endure a trying birth, or even to redirect an errant husband. Elaborate customs surround the Shuar staple drink, *Chicha*, made by crushing, chewing and spitting manioc root into a large gourd bowl. The fermented brew is their primary fluid. Water is not consumed since rivers are full of organic matter. Yet, only Shuar women make or serve *Chicha*. If a husband causes discord his wife may withhold *Chicha*. Only when things are set right will she offer it to him to drink. With the help of *Arutum*, mothers *Shapeshift* into maternal warriors. They gain pluck to keep harmony in the family.

The Shuar of the Amazon seek *Arutum* for perseverance and to transform everyday circumstance. Its life giving force clarifies life direction. Gaining *Arutum* is becoming one with the power of life.

Windhorse / Lung Ta and Khiimori

Similar to the concept of *Arutum* is the Asian *Lung-ta*, (Loong-tah) translated as *Windhorse* (these words are used here interchangeably). *Windhorse* prayer flags flutter in the wind across Bhutanese and Nepalese mountains and waters, as well as from Buddhist homes and sanctuaries. The banners are adorned with mythical creatures invoking spiritual deities who remove obstacles. The flags depict a Horse in the center and icons in each of four corners. The Lion, Tiger, Garuda and Dragon represent the elements and four cardinal directions. These support the Horse in bringing prayers of good fortune to the heavens. One physically raises a *Lung Ta* prayer flag to diffuse prayerful energy. Likewise, personally raising *Windhorse* lifts the spirit and lightens the heart. It enlivens the Fifth Element.

Contemporary Western practitioners raise *Windhorse* when starting something new, whether a career or a cross country move. They may also raise *Windhorse* to tackle a social cause. *Lung Ta* rouses confidence so we can face important issues and make difficult decisions. Buoyed by the force of life, and aligned with clear intentions, we can empower ourselves beyond conditioning or pride. We have all known someone devoted to great causes but with too much ego at play for their own or the greater good. Even the best of us get caught up in the fight, succumb to abstract ideals that have little to do with the real world or get snagged by ego. Buddhists raise *Lung Ta* to consciously direct life force and to be wakeful.

Lung Ta is indestructible energy. Have you ever seen a horse gallop in the wind through an open meadow? In watching the horse's unbridled play did you feel a raw surge in your own heart and body? Likewise, recall hiking or walking when the wind picked up. Did you feel vigor as the breezes brushed your skin?

The Horse *Ta*, of *Lung Ta* represents innate goodness, likened in this example to the unselfconscious gallop of a spirited horse. Yet humans are often out of touch with fundamental goodness. *Lung* is exuberant like the character of wind. Just as wind is forceful, cleansing and liberating, *Lung* is our own pure energy. Raising *Lung Ta* is a way to lift our spirits. It is like sitting upon the horse to ride the wind; or taking our seat in our own good nature and riding, or consciously navigating, spiritual energy. The Mongolian word for *Windhorse*, *Khiimori*, is similar as it denotes spiritual strength or soul vitality.

Just as an Amazonian may spend days in the forest seeking *Arutum* we, too, can seek nature's life giving forces. As ancient Quechua infuse with *Ushai* by circumambulating revered volcanoes and bathing in sacred springs, we also can rouse the Fifth Element's power. Similar to a Mongolian shaman, who vitalizes the soul through prayer and ceremony, we, too, can fortify our spirit. As Tibetans do, we can summon our indestructible nature.

Although *Arutum* and *Windhorse* are evoked in practice and ritual, they are always available. We can rouse life giving energy anytime and anywhere. The last chapter, *Shapeshifting with Nature*, introduces ways we each can awaken to nature's power. Another way is to invoke *Lung Ta/Windhorse* or *Arutum Empowerment Huacas*.

Retrieve Empowerment Huacas

One way to connect with an *Empowerment Huaca* is to retrieve it in a shamanic journey. Use the same methods as those outlined in Chapter Three for retrieving *Spirit Huacas*. If you are stymied about which to retrieve, a *Windhorse/Lung-ta Huaca* or an *Arutum Huaca*, sense what calls to you. Or intend for the right *Huaca* to reveal itself in your journey.

Remember that *Spirit Huacas* can take any shape; as a ball of light, a person, plant, some other tangible object, a symbol, animal, or as feeling or intuition. *Windhorse Huacas* do often appear as horses and *Arutum Huacas* as snakes, but they also don unexpected forms. Whatever you encounter, stay present. Summon curiosity to reach out if something repels you. Fear is energy and in becoming one with it, we gain power. For example, as John suggests, "If a huge anaconda shows up with jaws agape and invites you in, consider climbing into its open mouth!"

I have experienced startling images in personal journeys and in those for clients. Early on, I sometimes questioned what I saw. Yet over time my trust grew as I discovered every form was perfectly fit to each person's needs, and the journey's intention. Power can display in unexpected forms. This is certainly true of Tibetan Buddhism's most awe inspiring icons which are grotesque. In meeting these multi-headed images, each with a grimacing face, your knees will knock in fear. They drink from skull cups filled with blood and pus, wear necklaces of human skulls, brandish daggers and are encircled by flames. They look demonic. Yet these wrathful deities are benevolent protectors with a high mission. Their fierce iconography cuts through ignorance and transforms the obstacles of ego.

Your experience with *Empowerment Huacas* may vary from journey to journey. As with dreams, shamanic icons compact many layers of meaning into a single image. Hidden or deeper significance is common. Yet unraveling this may take time and persistence. As these are *Shapeshifting Huacas* their external form may also change, similar to John Perkins's spirit guide, Manco, who transfigured into a ball of light.

Once you retrieve or attain an *Empowerment Huaca* do a separate journey to get to know it. Ask your *Huaca* how you can engage with it. Explore it from all angles. Experience its subtle aspects by *Shapeshifting* into your *Huaca* according to the suggestions in Chapter Three. Get to know it beyond form or image. How does this power feel? What are the qualities of its life giving force? Feel this in your body and open your heart to it. What is your *Huaca's* energy signature? Importantly, ask it to help you to clarify your *Higher Purpose*.

After you have obtained a *Lung Ta/Windhorse* or *Arutum Huaca*, and have journeyed with it, you may want to try the following approaches.

Awaken to Higher Purpose

Tending to a child's special gifts comes naturally for indigenous cultures. A Maya community reads the spiritual signs surrounding a baby's arrival according to the energy of the day, among other things. Some Quechua claim a baby destined to be a shaman will cry out from the mother's womb. Even modern midwives make note of babies born "veiled" or with a "caul", the Gaelic word for veil. The amniotic membrane is still intact, shrouding the baby's face as if veiled or hooded like on a monk's garment called a cowl. Folklore identifies such children as mystics. The veil symbolizes spiritual sight and that the child is protected by supernatural forces. Contemporary classics link children of power to a veil of a different nature, though with similar meaning. In *Harry Potter and the Deathly Hallows*, the teen-aged warlock, Harry, is able to observe from, as well as hide behind, a magical veil. Spiritual shielding also protects young Frodo Baggins, gifted with an enchanted Elven cloak by Lady Galadriel in *The Lord of the Rings*.

Whether we are born veiled with angels trumpeting our arrival, or under outwardly banal circumstance, a lot can be learned from a child's entry to the world. As with the Quechua, signals can even precede birth. This is one way a family or community can prepare to nurture a child's uniqueness. Most of us in contemporary cultures do not have Elders around to portend our special aptitudes, or parents waiting for us to signal them from the womb about why we are here. But despite that no one was listening, the signs were still there. Each child is auspicious. Tibetan Buddhism says human birth is as rare as a turtle that swims up to the surface of a vast ocean only once in a hundred years and pokes its head through a single hole in a golden yoke that has been tossed by winds and water.

We all have a reason for being. Perhaps the unsuspecting powers of young mythical characters like Frodo Baggins and Harry Potter intrigue us so because they tug at our own hidden gifts. Waking up and reclaiming power is especially important during these times. I once heard a visiting Tibetan teacher say the opportunity to become enlightened is so great now that thousands of beings are trying to rebirth on this planet.

No one may have been paying attention to why we came. Yet we each can embrace our *Higher Purpose*.

Explore Higher Purpose

The first suggestion for exploring *Higher Purpose* is to set the intention then take leisurely time in nature, whether at a park or rural setting. Try a practice from the last chapter such as *Aimless Wandering* or *Walking Like a Shuar*. If you are unable to get outside, engage this experience as a shamanic journey. Go to your *Sacred Place* then invite your imagination to take you through the experience below.

Begin by calling upon your spirit guides and consider taking along a *Physical Huaca*. Most importantly, *Shapeshift* into, or connect in whatever way feels right, with your *Windhorse/Lung Ta* or *Arutum Huaca*. Embody its energy. Intend this as a time to deepen your connection to your *Empowerment Huaca* and to discover your purpose, your unique offering to the world. As intention directs the journey be clear about yours, then relax. Trust that what you seek will come in just the right manner and timing.

As you wander, walk and commune with the earth, stay present and open. Take in the beauty and life all around you. Hear the sounds and smell the scents. Be alert to the sights and feel the textures. Taste the nuances. Tune into rustling leaves, chirping birds and insects, even if you also hear traffic or other noise. Smell the grasses. Study the details of leaves, flowers and plants. Feel your body as you move and each step upon the earth. Stepping gently and with bare feet is ideal. Breathe in nature's goodness. Ripple with her vigor. Pause at times to notice what is in the gap of your experience; magic surrounds us all the time, we are just usually oblivious. Slow down to meet nature as her rhythms are different than our habituated pace. Open your heart. Open your body. Call out to the *Arutum* of the trees, birds and skies. Connect with the waters, stones and insects, asking for *Lung Ta* to rise in you. Feel its life-giving surge wake you up. Ask your *Huacas* and spirit guides for help.

As you walk, feelings, ideas, or images may float to awareness. Whatever rises to the surface is fine, but do not involve with it at this point. Have a light touch. Observe what comes as if a by-stander to your experience. Let things come and go. Imagine sitting on a train and noticing the scenery of thoughts, feelings and images pass you by. Watch the images, notice the thoughts, allow memories or feelings. But, keep returning to the immediate moment. Some images, thoughts or feelings will arise and fall gently, like your breath, almost without notice. Others will be vivid, emotionally gripping, like a lightening cracking downpour that gradually lightens. No matter, make space for deeper attunement. Despite how enthralling a thought, image, or emotion may be, release it with the next breath out. Commit to a deeper way of being. This is how to channel *Arutum* and *Windhorse*. Feel at one with nature. Keep coming back. See, feel and sense. Deeply root in the here and now.

After practicing this way for awhile, you will feel grounded and present. You will be in cadence with cosmos and nature. When the time feels right, find a place to sit or lie down. Let everything go, immerse in the earth. Take a deep, refreshing breath. Take another deep, cleansing breath. Close your eyes if you are drawn. Take all the time you like. When you feel settled, ask the questions, "What do I have to uniquely offer the world? Why am I here?"

Do not try too hard for the answer, it will come. Again, have a light touch. Sense what arises or lingers. This can be a thought, vision or sensation. For instance, you may see children, a city, a book, or forest. You may smell or sense something familiar. You may think of your deceased grandfather or a quality that you and he shared. You may see that the disparate skills you have honed over the years form a cohesive theme.

When you think about these things or they pop up in your imagining, tune in. How does each feel? Where in your body do you feel this? How does your gut respond to each image or thought? What is your heart's sense?

Tune into body and emotion, notice nuances. What resonates and what does this feel like? What are the sensations? What does not connect for you, even if it is beyond what you understand? How does this feel? What feels right in your body and heart? What does not feel right in body and heart? Notice whatever you feel, even if it is un-nameable.

As you focus, let nature envelope and fill you. Connect with *Huacas* and guides. Ask them to wash away interference. Ask to connect with your *Higher Purpose*. If, and when, something feels right in your body and heart and from all angles, you can trust it. You may have found your purpose. We often have ideas about what we want, who we are, or what we have to give to the world. Yet, in perceiving more deeply we open the portal of the soul; our true path is revealed.

One time a nineteen year old at a *Shapeshifting* workshop shared that in journeying to his *Higher Purpose* he saw himself as a horse carrying a young boy he knew on his back. This boy was, in reality, the brother of a good friend. The young man felt a tremendous bond with this child and embraced the possibility that his life's purpose was to support the lad. He admitted to being surprised and more than a little disappointed not to receive what from his view was a loftier, or more global, mission. Yet, the vision of carrying the child rang true in his heart.

A week after arriving home from the workshop this young adult met the boy of his journey, who was on his way to swim at a neighbor's pool. Deciding to go along, our workshop participant playfully scooped the thirteen year old up and onto his shoulders. Carrying him on his back like the horse of his vision they arrived at the pool behind the house next door. In putting the boy down he looked up and said, "Thanks for carrying me. You know it's your life mission to carry me." The young man had not discussed his purpose outside the workshop. Any remaining doubts softened in that moment.

When the heart rings true it dissolves false ideas or those fabricated by ego. The humblest aspiration may have impact beyond measure. It may also ripple silently, which is just as valid. Most important is what rings true.

When you have found your life purpose, feel free to explore this more deeply. Go into those images and feelings within a shamanic journey. You can do this while still out in nature, or save it for another setting and time. Begin by relaxing into your *Sacred Place*, or in the current natural locale. Intend to probe in greater depth then see what comes.

Alternately, you can focus by consciously visualizing this reality. Ask yourself the following questions as it feels right to do so, or design your own exploration:

"What would this life look and feel like? What would I be doing?" Imagine this clearly. "What is the daily rhythm and how does it feel as I move through each day?" Look at it from every angle. "What concrete steps do I take to realize my vocation? How do I feel in taking these steps?" Notice the first actions you take and how you solicit support. "How does following my purpose integrate with my family's needs?" Also notice how it affects other relationships, responsibilities and community ties. Finally, "Does my calling honor nature and all life?"

Imagine vividly and see what comes. Sense and intuit. Feel the details of this life in body and heart. Try it on for size as if it were true now, as if this life were happening for you as you dream it. Pay attention to your instincts and what heart and body say. What do they say? Trust them. Whatever our calling, we have to translate it into everyday life. Imagination is a powerful tool. Doing so while attending to the impulses of heart and body helps to bring *heavenly* aspirations into *earthly* and practical life. This way, our highest wishes become possible. If we can imagine it, we can create it.

If after this exercise you feel clearer about how to direct your life, great. Consider asking your *Arutum* or *Windhorse/Lung Ta Huaca* for the power to *Shapeshift* into this life dream.

At the close of the visualization or journey, you can return to your *Sacred Place*. Release your *Empowerment Huaca*. Thank it, your spirit guides and nature for helping you. Whenever you close a session in a natural setting, it is good to leave a small offering. This can be some loose tobacco, flower petals or bread. It can also be a prayer, song or whatever inspires. Open your heart to the earth, feel gratitude.

You may wish to take notes while the journey is fresh, to reflect on later.

Live and Journey Fluidly

If you have found your vocation or calling through this process, that is wonderful. Hopefully you have taken time to connect with your aspiration. If you do not have a clear sense of purpose yet, do not worry. Chances are you have glimpsed something meaningful and feel closer to nature. Another method may work better, you may already be living your *Higher Purpose*, or this may not be the time. There is an old expression, "Don't push the river, it flows by itself." Once we set an intention the answer arrives in a timing and manner reflecting the highest good. It may be that nothing came during the exercise, but something is clear later. We may have an insightful dream. While out walking or sitting at our desk the next day we may have an "Aha!" moment. A prospect that feels just right may be suggested two months later by a colleague. Don't push the river.

Throughout these pages we have experienced that journey and dream imagery carries meaning beyond appearance. The Uncle Arthur of your dream may not be your Uncle Arthur. Your dream uncle may signify any number of things. Dreams and journeys weave multi-layered, malleable worlds. Characters and scenes may even morph before our eyes. Yet, mundane life is just as rich. Its greatest gifts often unfold serendipitously. Engaging life fluidly makes the mystery of the world come alive. This talent comes naturally for artists, musicians, writers and anyone partnering with creative forces. Eliciting this magic is innate; we just have to open to it.

You may explore or develop more approaches on your own, yet the exercise below is another way to clarify higher calling.

As with all the exercises in this book, feel free to modify this visualization as drawn. When guiding others on journeys, it is helpful to suggest they regard your words as a template. If their experience is different than you describe they can relax with, and trust, their own journey. For instance, you may portray a river, yet they are standing face to face with a jaguar. In such a case the person should engage the jaguar and not worry about the river.

It is also common for people to journey more slowly or quickly than the guide's verbal pace. Acknowledging this frees people to engage the journey they are meant to have, according to their own tempo. If you are still prompting people to connect with their *Sacred Places*, yet they have left and are flying on an eagle's back, they should not try to get away from the eagle. It is helpful to suggest for people to use the cadence of your words, and the sound of your voice, to support whatever is right for them.

Gentle drumming or soft background music is a great accompaniment to this next journey. Remember, though, that drumming or playing background music is not necessary. We can journey to the beat of our heart, the soft pelt of rain, to traffic sounds or silence.

Journey to the Reflecting Pool

Rest in your *Sacred Place*. Relax and take in everything around you. Look, see and feel. Smell, taste and intuit. Breathe in healing, comfort and safety. Feel the sanctity of your *Sacred Place*. Take all the time you like.

When it feels right, invoke the presence of or *Shapeshift* into, your spirit guides and *Empowerment Huacas*. How does this feel? Tune into the qualities.

When spirit guides and *Huacas* are present, look or sense beyond the region of your *Sacred Place*. Notice the larger environment. What do you see? What do you sense? There may be land and trees. There may be an ocean, lake, or a river. The sun may be shining or clouds may hang in the sky. You may sense mountains or a desert in the distance. You may see a village or city. Tune into the scenery surrounding your *Sacred Place*. What are its details, what is the topography?

Now, become aware because something may be calling to you. What is this? Tune in and you will know that it is your destiny that is calling. Where do you feel this in your body? Is it in your heart? Do you feel this tug of your destiny in your diaphragm or abdomen? Pay attention, allow its influence. You may experience a yearning, or urgency. What is the emotion, how would you describe it? That, which is calling to you, may be long forgotten. Yet, it will feel intimately familiar as you reconnect.

At some point imagine sitting, then standing up in your *Sacred Place*. As the call of your destiny strengthens, imagine walking from your *Sacred Place* and out to this land, by the waters, on the edge of the village, desert or city. Take your time. Feel each step as you walk, note the sensations. You may walk on beds of pine needle through the forest. You may walk on hot sand by the ocean. You may stride through tall meadow grasses or on a black topped road. Feel the texture and temperature. Notice the breezes against your skin. As you walk, deep inside you know what to look for. Your destiny calls to you from the depths of a clear pool of water. Your body, which is comprised mostly of water, intuits this pool's location. Open your heart and follow your instincts - trust. Observe and take in everything along the way. Take as much time as you like, enjoying and immersing in the sensations. Feel each step and movement. Longing may intensify as you near the water.

When you come to the reflecting pool, walk to and kneel by the water's edge. Gaze out across the pool. What do you see? What do you feel? Do you sense something beyond what you visually see? What is it? Still kneeling, intuit when you are ready to peer into the pool. When the time is right, bend over. Fix your eyes upon the water. Take your time.

What do you perceive about your *Higher Purpose*? How do you feel about this? Stay in your heart and body not moving too quickly into ideas and strategies. There is plenty of time for all of that. For now, simply look and feel. Take all the time you like.

When ready, bring your time by the reflecting pool to a close. Express gratitude for what you received. Feel your *Sacred Place* calling you back and retrace each step. Or find an alternate return route. Feel each movement of your body. Feel each step as you walk through grasses, marsh, streets or wherever you travel. Alternately, you may be back at your *Sacred Place* instantaneously. Or you may decide instead to remain by the pool of water. Wherever you close the journey get comfortable and take a deep, cleansing breath. Feel good, nurtured. Know you are safe. Feel sacredness all around and within you.

Take all the time desired to connect again with your *Sacred Place*, or with the sacredness of where you are. Then slowly come back into the room. When ready, gently stretch and open your eyes. You have just done an ancient scrying practice by peering into the water.

About Scrying

Gazing into a reflective surface to open spiritual vision is called scrying, from the English "descry", meaning to see dimly. Scrying comes from pagan and shamanic traditions, referenced throughout mythical literature. Scryers may gaze into water or a looking glass. They may look into a crystal ball, fire, or an open sky.

Tibetan, Mongolian and Siberian medicine people scry with mirrors. The mirrors are not always reflective, many are clouded. Tuvan shamans I have met employ them for healing, such as by scanning the body to detect illness. "Bad" spirits extracted from a client's energy field can also be trapped inside these discs. They are later released from the mirror and banished into natural settings where they cannot cause harm. Shamans attach the disc to a leather cord strung around their neck so the mirror hangs over the heart. This protects them from unwanted influence, reflecting invasive energy out. Alternately, shamans also use the disc to collect energy which is then beamed to a person to restore life force. Magic mirrors serve various other purposes.

Scrying is a powerful way to divine or influence energy, yet do reflective surfaces have power of their own? As with Tuvan Siberian shamans, these mystical tools respond to the user's directive. Whether we gaze into a mirror, a magic ball or doll, all are conduits for our intention. They sharpen our acumen as a seer or a healer. When you *Journey to the Reflective Pool*, what you view about your *Higher Purpose* arises from your own deep intelligence. Ultimately, nothing is outside you.

Reflective surfaces induce a mild trance state so the veils of ordinary reality grow thin. Expanded worlds, as well as submerged or unconscious material, are more easily accessed. Images may appear straightforward. Yet typical of these realms is to speak through metaphor. You may see clear forms or symbols, though meaning may be subtle. You perceive in direct measure to the clarity of your intention. Communication may come as feeling or intuition. Do not rely on thought alone to decipher what you sense or see about your destiny, take time to experience it. Open your heart, feel it in your body. You can also later do a separate journey to explore these images or feelings more deeply.

Once when scrying to understand more about my purpose, I was shocked to see a Catholic nun reflected back from the water pool. The vision was a reminder of the strong sense of vocation Catholicism instilled in me and which has carried through my life. Yet in attending to heart and body, my stomach felt anxious. The feelings were guilt and fear. Catholicism had clarified my destiny, yet it also blocked my power. Despite decades of transforming and distancing from parochial dogma, I carried an internalized nun of self-criticism. In a later journey I saw the beliefs that prevented my full expression. They were insidious, imbedded within my sense of self. As I had attended Catholic school for eight years since age five, this was not hard to understand. In the journey, these beliefs released and the nun transmuted into light. Continuing to liberate what suppresses my higher expression requires awareness, trust and love. I now access these qualities from an internal source of light that was once a critical nun.

The Wisdom of Heart and Body

Many of the exercises in this chapter, and throughout this book, invite us to fine tune our relationship to our heart and body. If we lived closer to nature, had low tech lifestyles and spent less time in cars and buildings, there might be less need to strategize how to stay embodied and heart centered. But modern life favors separateness and speed. These left brain traits deny the wisdom of body and intuition. They cut us off from nature and larger reality. Chapter Two encouraged a relationship to heart and body and here we go further to tap innate wisdom. There is a deeper way to know. This takes us beyond what the mind alone can conceive.

Cultivating body and heart knowing is effective. Even modern psychology says that mixing the mind's power with the acuity of instinct can make us good decision makers. In his best-selling book, *Blink: The Power of Thinking Without Thinking*, Malcomb Gladwell introduces breakthrough ideas about intuition developed by German social psychologist, Dr. Gerd Gigerenzer. Gigerenzer claims that those who follow gut instinct are adept at acting on simple signals they pick up on in the environment. They do so quickly, in part, because they focus on gut sense and ignore extraneous information. Likewise, shamans open to the instincts of body and heart which broaden perception; awareness is heightened.

The body can communicate through subtle sensations such as the goose bumps or prickling skin you can feel when something strikes you just right. Or your body can signal about something *not* being right through a queasy stomach or by the raised hair on the back of your neck. Dialogue from the body can also be indescribable such as the "feeling sense" or "gut knowing" healers get telling them where to focus energy. Some Quechua, Shuar and other healers even pass a client's disharmonious energy through their own body then regurgitate it. This is a conscious act directed by spirit allies and the shaman's body intelligence. It is different from unwillingly, or unskillfully, taking on another's energy. The latter can cause harm.

Symptoms, whether they manifest as a bad shoulder or a stomach ache, can indicate emotional or spiritual imbalances. They can also cue us to make good choices. A dramatic example is my own introduction to the body's intelligence. Many years ago I was torn between doing a plant spirit intensive and a rigorous course designed to awaken to the body's wisdom. I asked for a dream to clarify which program to commit to. That night I received a dream that seemed obvious. In the dream I sat in a classroom at a desk. On the desk rested a jar of water which held a bright sprig of forsythia. My dream self was happy sitting with the forsythia though nothing else occurred. Upon waking, I concluded the plant workshop was the right course to take. Being in a classroom, a place of study, with a plant on my desk, seemed clear. Nothing in the dream related to body centered studies and I was relieved to finally make a choice. Both were outstanding programs so, ultimately, what did it matter?

Later that day, I called the body program coordinator to say I had decided not to take the class. But although I felt fine before the call, in cancelling with this woman my stomach felt sick. Phone in hand, I leaned against the wall and slid down to sit on the floor. Illness seized me so suddenly that I suspected it had something to do with the phone call. I tuned in and on first guess thought I was picking up on bad vibes. But in focusing, going into my physical sensations, I intuited otherwise. I needed to do this body program. I told the woman I changed my mind, I would be there. No sooner had I uttered this, than I felt fine. The nausea disappeared as quickly as it came.

I arrived after dark in New York State at the body wisdom intensive. I found my room and within ten minutes had climbed into bed and fallen asleep. I awakened the next morning and upon opening my eyes, saw that the entire room was aglow. A huge forsythia plant was growing just outside my window; it consumed the entire picture window glass pane. Hundreds of delicate blossoms blazed in the sun, splashing my room yellow. What a perfect sign. The course proved of untold personal benefit and continues to be invaluable to my work.

Things are often more than they appear. My dream held meaning beyond what I could rationally interpret. But my body steered me loud and clear. Had I been more body aware in the first place, I may not have needed an exaggerated signal. Since these early experiences of awakening to the body's wisdom I consistently use my invisible senses. In fine tuning body-based instincts we can detect subtleties we may otherwise miss, including insights to help us navigate precarious health issues and changing times. Sharpening the body's acuity empowers personal response-ability. Everything has a vibration that our innate intelligence can detect.

The *Heart Math Institute* claims we are connected to energy fields that continuously unfold information via our body's sensory perceptions. The information our body picks up from this invisible field is what people call intuition. The institute also identifies the heart as a main intuitive vehicle, picking up on subtle signals quicker than the brain. This has certainly been my personal experience, what I have observed with shamanic peoples, and true of my work with others.

Shamans rely on body and heart wisdom for life direction and to *Shamanize*. One of the most powerful *Shamankas* I have met, a Tuvan woman, is a remarkable healer. Legend has it that she has even been known to raise people out of wheel chairs and from the death bed. Yet in the two weeks our small band traveled with her across the Tuvan and Mongolian steppe, she refused to teach us one specific shamanic or healing method. Instead, she instructed us to use our bodies and hearts to learn what we needed. She told us to develop our invisible ears to listen to the waters, stones and trees; to sway our bodies to feel the sacred circle of spirits and obtain information held in the earth; to revive our energy by "eating the wind"; to feel the pulse of stars in our hearts. For indigenous people, body wisdom and the heart's knowing are synonymous, as is oneness with nature. A snippet from an old Finnish shamanic verse expresses this beautifully:

I had the breeze to give me comfort, where the wind was there was comfort, where the breeze was there was solace. The sun when rising softly stroked me, the Lady Moon would braid my hair plaits. Trust in what your heart will tell you and trust in what your nature answers.

It is typical of higher calling to take us beyond what we feel capable; it can push our limits. It is also not uncommon for vocations to come up against societal mores and conditioning as in the example of my reflective pool journey to the Catholic nun. In such cases, following heart and body cultivates an internal system of guidance. This is essential to express what we uniquely have to give the world.

As you explore your *Higher Purpose*, open to the wisdom of heart and body. Not only do they offer feedback you can trust, they invite your higher aspects into everyday life.

Time, Space and Dreaming

Respecting intuition is second nature for indigenous cultures, which are dream based. Amazonian Achuar rise every morning, purge what is left in their stomachs from the night before then share their dreams. Dream content orients an Achuar to the day's events. Prophetic dreams are also taken seriously. Yet, "dream based" refers not only to tribes who honor night dreams; but to those who embrace life as reverie. Meaning lies beyond appearance whether a snake in the long house or a wilted plant by the edge of a trail. As is true of sleeping dreams, ordinary reality is pliable. In the trance of life, time and space are not solid. For instance, the luminous blue and white orbs that hover through the rainforest at dusk defy conventional logic. These are known by indigenous people to be beings from other times, locations, even other planets. Shamanic balls of light freshly caught my attention in Siberia.

While meeting with Tuvan and Siberian tribes I crossed paths with a compelling woman in Hakassia, Siberia. The cold overnight train rides had made me delirious with fever so I asked this large, cherub faced woman for a healing. She scraped me from shoulders to toes with a dull 24 inch knife, purged my energy field by placing the flames of a blow torch near my skin and kneaded my muscles with hands that resembled a cattle rustler's. It was excruciating. Yet, by the time Anga had finished with me I was healed. Grateful, I thanked the shamanka and gave her an Amazon seed necklace made by Ecuadorian Shuar women. In receiving it Anga beamed, "I travel through the rainforest all the time as a ball of light. I have never been there in this physical body, but I know that the rainforest is my true home."

Anga's words made it hard for me to reduce rainforest orbs to metaphor or myth. I pictured the Shuar of Ecuador or the Brazilian Uru-e-wau-wau watching Anga of Siberia, a radiant sphere, floating through their jungle. A few years later when a similar ball of light appeared in a photo taken of the birch tree grove my apprentices named the *Bridge of Light* (described in Chapter Four), we recognized that the orb was conscious.

According to indigenous view, past, future and even geographical distance are not as we think. All are here and now. Time/space travel is a given; expansive reality is in the mix of everyday. Extraterrestrial beings, dead ancestors, shamans from distant cultures, zip through the night sky as balls of light. Likewise, a shaman might see my dream forsythia inseparably from the forsythia at my workshop location. For most of us, reality stacks up neatly like a, b and c or one, two and three. Space is solid, each form separate from the other. Time passes in predictable, linear increments; the past has happened, the present is now, the future has not yet occurred. For shamanic peoples this is not true. Time and space are relational, part of a multi-faceted whole. Opening heart and body opens the gateway to the pliable and dream-like qualities of everyday life. We glimpse the greater whole and gain a better grasp of why we are here.

Trust your senses and follow your heart. Remember that life is fluid, illusory. Why are you here? What are your talents and skills? What do your heart and soul long for? Do not hold back. The legend of the flight of the Eagle and Condor portrays that heart and mind are destined to meld. There is within each of us, the ability to *Shapeshift*.

What is your purpose? What makes you feel alive? Regardless of what your society or culture thinks you should be; what role will you uniquely play to help all life on this planet?

Once you have defined your calling, or *Higher Purpose*, the following ceremony is a good way to empower it. This ritual can be performed individually, yet it is a commanding group exercise. The *Siberian Chalimar Ceremony* is presented here in circle format, but you can easily tailor it for solo use. It integrates very similar ceremonies performed by Hakass and Tuvan Siberian shamans.

Siberian Chalimar (Prayer Tie) Ceremony

To perform this ceremony, first enact the following:

Collect two strips of combustible, natural fiber colored cloth (for each person) that are 8 inches long and ¾ of an inch wide. Red, white, green, yellow and/or blue are good colors to choose from.Multi-colored fabrics are also fine. See what draws you. Strips cut from worn out clothes or cloth cotton napkins and sheets from thrift stores are good resources.

Collect one strip of combustible, natural fiber black cloth (for each person) that is 8 inches long and ¾ of an inch wide. Per above, strips cut from old black or darkly colored fabrics will suffice.

Collect fire wood and designate an outside fire pit or other means of having a campfire-sized (or smaller) blaze. You can also do this ceremony inside, using a fireplace or fire proofed container. Be mindful of safety measures when working with fire and construct it with reverence. The elements can destroy as well as empower, they demand respect. Be alert to fire bans, and if within city limits you may need a permit. Have a bucket of water nearby.

Identify a nearby tree on your property that lends itself to the ceremony; tune in and sense which tree calls to you. Then ask its permission to tie prayer ribbons, Chalimars, to it during ceremony. Or gather seven wooden poles, six that are seven feet long, the last pole can be about ten feet long. You will also need twine to tie the poles together. If you are opting to use the poles instead of fastening your prayer ties to a tree, erect an upright, tee-pee like structure (a Siberian Obaa as noted in the last chapter) within 35 paces from the fire pit, or in an area that calls to you. If your land area does not allow for a 35 pace distance, closer is fine. Ultimately, there are no rules.

Assemble drums, rattles and/or other percussion instruments. If you plan a group ceremony, yet live in a neighborhood, it is wise to alert your neighbors about the noise ahead of time.

If building a prayer teepee or *Obaa* consider doing so well before the ceremony, which people often perform at sunset because spiritual forces can be more easily perceived at sunrise and daybreak. Thank the forest for offering the fallen trees you use to construct the *Obaa*. As you assemble, hold the intention for it to empower the purpose of each individual in the group. Feel the life all around you and the spirits supporting this.

Several hours before performing the ceremony ask each person to choose two colored and one black strip of cloth. For workshop settings, a basket of prayers ties or, *Chalimars*, is set near the circle's center. Here facilitators, and group members, place sacred items. Pieces of paper can also be placed here, inscribed with the names of people outside our group who may need healing. Anyone can be included in the circle this way. Or people can inscribe on a piece of paper an environmental, social or global situation that needs support.

Each person will take at least one hour before the ceremony to venture out on the land to work with their *Chalimars*. If you live in a city, this is easily done at a park. If you cannot leave your 8th story apartment, connect with your *Chalimars* on a roof top garden, by a houseplant or window. Shamanism is flexible and it's what you intend that matters. This flexibility can be applied to anything. For example, fire is a powerful transformer, used by every shamanic culture to empower and heal. Yet at a Texas workshop our fire ceremony was called off at the last minute because a fire ban was instated. Our group graciously moved inside and we performed the ceremony by a small fireplace blaze. It was intimate and powerful. Similarly, clients who do the ceremony by themselves often do so inside their homes. In the absence of a fireplace they light a tiny fire in a large ceramic bowl. As with outside fires, a water source or bucket of sand to douse the flames should be close at hand.

The two colored *Chalimars* are used to empower *Higher Purpose*. Designate one color to support personal goals and the other colored *Chalimar* to empower global *Shapeshifts*. Sense the colors to which you are magnetized. The black *Chalimar* is for releasing and transmuting obstacles; anything that is in the way of manifesting your *Higher Purpose*.

To work with *Chalimars*, each person finds a place on the earth (or at home or wherever) that calls. Or, they may prefer to walk the entire time. This exercise should come from the heart. Its details can unfold as you go along, let your spirit guides and *Huacas*, especially *Empowerment Huacas*, direct you. The important thing is the intention, which is tri-fold in this case:

1) Infuse one colored Chalimar with wishes for manifesting your purpose. Blow your wishes into it, pray with it, or whatever inspires. Invoke your empowerment huacas; feel Arutum and Lung Ta raising the power in you to be who you are meant to be.

2) Infuse the other colored Chalimar with your wishes for global healing. Again, blow your wishes into the cloth strip, pray with it, or what inspires. Invoke the help of your Windhorse and Arutum Huacas.

3) Infuse the black Chalimar with any obstacles you perceive getting in the way of your ability to express your Higher Purpose. Call upon Arutum and Windhorse/Lung Ta for help.

Design how you would like to open your ceremony. Shamanic practitioners will typically open and close by honoring the four cardinal directions.

Half the group then forms a large circle around the fire. These people drum and rattle to support their community. The other half gathers in a circle closer to the fire, with prayer ties in hand, first taking out the black *Chalimar*. They circle the fire clockwise three times while tying a knot in the black cloth for each obstacle they identify. They put emotion into it, make it real. After circling the fire three times, this group offers the black tie to the blaze. As the cloth is devoured and the flames lick, each person reaches toward the fire to take back energy.

Fire is powerful in its ability to transmute one form to another. Ultimately, energy can never be destroyed, only change forms. Contrasting Western attitudes of "getting rid of" or "destroying" what gets in our way, we can recycle the energy. We offer our barriers and shortcomings as gifts to the fire and ask it to

Shapeshift them. Then we call this transfigured energy back to us to empower what is really in our hearts. The energy that surges in return is *Arutum, Windhorse, Lung Ta, Oushai,* the Fifth Element.

After the small circle around the fire has offered and taken back empowering energy from the black prayer tie, they take out the colored *Chalimars*. They dance around the fire three times again. This time, they ask the fire to empower personal and global wishes, yet these ties are not burned. Some dance and dangle the *Chalimars* over the flames. Some flail them over their heads and swish them around their body. Others sit next to, or walk slowly by, the fire and pray over their colored prayer ties. Each feels the power of the Fifth Element infusing their life calling via the *Chalimar*. The larger circle is still drumming and rattling, bolstering their community.

The inner group finishes empowering the colored *Chalimars* and completes three circles around the fire. Then they walk toward the *Obaa*, colored *Chalimars* in hand. The outer circle of people follows, still drumming, singing and rattling to support their community. All soon gather around the *Obaa*. The inner circle of people ties their *Chalimars* to it. Or they gather around a specified tree and tie the *Chalimars* onto a branch. The red, green, white, blue, yellow or multi-colored ribbons are tied anywhere on the tree or *Obaa* that inspires. When finished, each person from the inner circle takes an instrument from someone in the outer circle. The ceremony is then repeated and when finished, the directions are released and thanked.

Once the ceremony is complete, gather everyone by the fire. People can silently connect with, and thank, the fire. This is a good time to commit to concrete steps that will help to manifest their purpose after arriving home. Encourage people to ask the fire for help. Invite them to clearly see the steps to enact their vocation, feel them as possible. Purpose has been empowered and obstacles have been transmuted. Everyone has been infused with the Fifth Element and sees obstacles as illusory, energy. When redirected, this energy can be consciously applied to affect positive change.

Hearten participants to look into the fire and see their own, and global life, as they would like to see it. Ask them to feel this in their heart and body. In doing so, they may see images or sense a message from the flames. Whatever they perceive will be just right for them. Or they may simply take in fortitude from the fire. This reflective period is often followed by singing, drumming and dancing.

Whether on an *Obaa* or a tree, as long as the *Chalimars* hang they are empowered by the elements. The wishes they hold are carried far and wide by the winds. They are energized by sun and starlight. They are animated by rain and snow. They are vivified by the earth through the tree or poles. Tibetans hang prayer flags for one year then ceremonially burn them and hang freshly consecrated flags on the Tibetan New Year. Leave the *Chalimars* in place or burn them at the end of the year as the Tibetan's do, or when you feel is right. In doing so, create a simple ritual asking the fire to empower the wishes and goals the prayer ties hold.

Closing Note to Chapter Five

It does not take indigenous prophesies to tell us that life as we know it is in flux. Our understanding of reality and how we collectively envision life on Planet Earth is transforming. If the vibration many say the earth emanates now has intelligence, it is to instigate higher order. In the 1950's Dr. Hans Jenny, pioneer of Cymatics, applied sound waves to water and fine powders. The water and delicate particles responded to the vibrations by forming beautiful geometric designs. The results clearly showed the impact of auditory waves on matter. But the forms did not instantly appear. Each design was preceded by a stage of dissolution with no coherent pattern observable. During this interim period, the substances appeared chaotic.

Likening the impact of the earth's vibration on human beings to the effect of sound waves on fine particles, helps us reframe ideas about planetary chaos. Instead of fighting change or feeling victim to it, we can view disorder as an evolutionary stage. As in the designs that underlie the disarray in Dr. Jenny's experiments, we can look to the potential that planetary chaos conceals. Cultivating the knowing of heart and body helps us to intuit new patterns. We may perhaps even discover things that are now beyond the mind's reach. In doing so, we awaken higher global goals and invite fresh templates for living.

Shamans work with energy and ritual. Therapists work with words and insight. Both help their clients *Shapeshift* imbalanced dreams held in body and psyche to life affirming patterns. In the same way we, and our societies, can *Shapeshift* imbalanced dreams held in the collective human body and psyche. No matter how solid in appearance, reality is supple. Life is malleable. Whatever dream reality we slumber in we can wake up to and change. If there is intention to this *Shapeshift*, it is for life to evolve.

When we step into *Higher Purpose*, we invite *Higher Consciousness* into everyday life. This is the natural expression of our divine or Higher Self as it manifests here on earth. We will explore this next.

"Remember, the entrance door to the sanctuary is inside you."

- Rumi

CHAPTER SIX

HIGHER CONSCIOUSNESS AND THE LUMINOUS YOU

The previous two chapters noted the relationship between *Higher Purpose* and that part of us transcending personality and circumstance, often called the Higher Self. Our reason for being becomes clear when in reclaiming spiritual essence we remember that we are one with a limitless universe. This entire book is devoted to opening awareness of, and experiencing, this *Higher Consciousness*. Yet, here we explore straightforward ways to reclaim our essential qualities as well as how to enliven these connections for others. In this chapter I use the terms *Luminous Presence* and *Luminous You* interchangeably to describe the immortal, divine self, innate to being human.

The *Luminous Presence* has been portrayed in many ways throughout history and across dissimilar spiritual traditions. Egyptians believed one could merge with an immortal body of light to become a star in the heavens. The "Yoga of Light" was practiced for centuries by Hindus and Buddhists. According to the classic Yoga Sutra by Indian sage Pantajali as translated in *Yoga, Power, and Spirit* by Dr. Alberto Villoldo, it is the "True self, infinite with no boundaries...Pure essence, pure light engulfing the mind, the soul, the body, the invisible realm with its radiance." Tibetan Buddhist Dzogchen practitioners take two paths to manifest the luminous or "Rainbow Body": 1) practice to purify or exhaust karma and merge with the essence of the five elements, which is pure light, and/or 2) recognize, and merge with, the brilliance of each moment. Realized Dzogchen practitioners are said to, upon dying, transform the body into light leaving behind just the toe and finger nails, hair, and nasal septum. According to Eastern views, such beings can then fabricate another physical body from the radiant form and return to earth to en - light - en others.

Hebrew Kabbalistic traditions also point to the essence of everything, and each of us, as light. Similarly, Christianity depicts saints with shining halos around their heads or glowing cocoons which encase their entire bodies. The glow indicates divine light. Gnostic Christians maintain a comparable view, but with an important difference. Luminosity is not reserved for those recognized as holy or who have ascended corporeal reality into union with God, as exemplified by the resurrection of Christ. It is attainable for us all while we are still alive. Gnostics strive to unite with the internal Christ or Light-Presence. They wish to become one with the God within while engaging earthly human life.

Most of the spiritual paths mentioned here advocate years of dedication to expose higher nature. Many require concentrated practices. If everyone has an eternal self, if our light is intrinsic to our being human, we might ask "Why does it take so much to uncover it?"

Many religions infer that we each are crafted of the divine essence of Spirit, God, the Universe, or whatever expression. But most of us would agree that our natural brilliance is shrouded. Wounding, ego, fear, personal and collective habits cause us to forget who we really are. The human species has throughout recent eras viewed itself separately from divine essence, some looking to religious dogma, others to ancient and modern spiritual technologies, to find their way back. Yet, if predictions for the evolution possible during these times are accurate, coming back into the light may not prove the task it has been. This light may also present differently than we anticipate.

Embracing more whole values and sustainable life style changes are crucial at this juncture in global history. Simultaneously, this time forecasts that we can recover our true nature. As we do, caring for our planet will be held tantamount to caring for ourselves. Before going further with such discussions, let us gain a taste of this indestructible, boundless self.

The Luminous You Across Lifetimes

Explore Past Lives

One way to experience the *Luminous You* is to explore the part of us that continues beyond death and even across lifetimes. We begin by taking a journey to retrieve and view another incarnation.

There is mounting evidence for reincarnation, a concept that is integral to spiritual traditions all over the world. There are countless modern accounts of children who remember the details of previous lives including those who locate and are able to identify obscure minutiae about past loved ones still alive. Many of us in contemporary society are open to the idea that we have lived before and that who we are somehow continues after death. Tibetan teachers have even been known to be aware upon dying where they will be reborn. Well documented tales depict failing lamas who leave letters behind detailing where they can be found next. These include otherwise impossible to know facts about the family, location, and child they will return as. At the indicated time, monks seek this child who may be one to five years old. The youngster is given a series of tests to prove he or she is the reincarnated teacher. In one test, numerous ritual items are laid out in front of the child, among them, sacred objects belonging to the deceased Lama. The boy or girl must identify the items used for spiritual practice by the teacher when alive. If the young child is the departed teacher, he or she accomplishes this and delights in recovering the cherished objects. It is easy to imagine glee at rediscovering your own precious items which have been stowed away for years. The child will also show a high aptitude for Buddhist scripture, with knowledge beyond what is expected for one of such young age.

These stories are remarkable. Yet, striking as they are, believing in reincarnation is not necessary to use this approach to glimpse your limitless self. In the exercises that follow, simply tend to the journey story as it plays out. Experience it for what it is. Expanded reality speaks through symbol, metaphor and imagery. It may be that your life as a Nazi Germany survivor, for example, did happen. Or you may view it allegorically. Whatever scenarios unfold, and however you interpret them, they hold meaning. Remember that your intention guides the process. Be clear and trust the knowing of your heart and body.

Journey to a Past Life

In *Shapeshifting* workshops people are instructed to try this exercise with a partner. Partners find a comfortable place to sit or lie down. If reclining, as in any retrieval journey partners are to be touching at the ankle, hips and shoulders. They should not, however, be touching anyone else in the room. Some people prefer to sit back to back, or side to side. Each person then retrieves a past life for the partner as we beat our drums. This begins by both partners relaxing in their *Sacred Place*. The retriever may call upon guides and *Spirit Huacas* to help discover the partner's other lifetime.

When the past life is recovered, the person obtains all the information he or she can. The retriever may see the partner's past life clearly, or sense it. If you do not view another life in expanded reality, remember that sensing or intuiting the details is just as valid. There is no need to *Camay* (blow with the breath of spirit) this other life into your partner as we do in *Spirit Huaca* and spirit guide retrievals. Simply be curious about your partner's past lifetime and learn as much about it as you can.

Both partners journey to each other's past lives simultaneously, the retrievals are done at the same time. When each person is finished, they tap the arm of the partner. After the first person has tapped to indicate the journey is finished, she or he waits until the partner taps back to signify the partner's journey is also completed. Then both sit up and wait until everyone in the group has finished, after which partners share with one another the experience.

After each person has shared in depth about the past life of the partner, a new journey is taken. This is a solo voyage to view the past life, so people should embark in their own space, with no one touching another. Each now journeys to her or his own past lifetime, the scenario which was retrieved and described by their partner. It is important to view or intuit this life from a removed perspective and not experience it as if it were actually happening now. Be a detached observer, as you were when uncovering your partner's lifetime. Yet, now study the details of a past life of your own. Whether intuiting yourself as a woman in a distant land beating clothes on a rock or seeing a sheep herder in white garb and sandals from Biblical times, watch or sense these scenes as if it is a movie playing out before you.

The initial journey to discover a past life can also be done alone. Take time to stretch, relax and lie or sit down comfortably. Play a drumming CD or some soothing music if that helps you to relax. Begin in your *Sacred Place*, call upon your spirit guides, *Shapeshift* into one if that feels right. Sense what most supports your intention to visit and view a past life. Or ask what spirit influences are here to guide this objective for you. In solo journeys you are, of course, retrieving as well as viewing a past life at the same time. Again, experience this life from a detached vantage point. Observe or intuit its details unemotionally, as if you are an uninvolved bystander.

More On Past Lives

Keep in mind that no matter whether we are male or female, we may connect with, or have retrieved for us, the life of a woman or a man. Our past lives might also not always be as people, as we might guess. It can be shocking following a retrieval to be told we were a tree, or in retrieving a past life for ourselves to sense we are our favorite breed of cat sitting on someone's lap. Tibetan Buddhists, the Amazonian Shuar and other indigenous groups believe we have experienced many forms. We may rebirth as a person, a plant or an ant. Shuar do not view death as tragic but as an opportunity to return as something fortuitous. Because human life is challenging, the Shuar welcome the possibility of coming back as a hummingbird or waterfall. Workshop participants are often surprised at what they feel in viewing lifetimes as plants, animals, or even microorganisms. They are often moved to unexpected emotion. Such intimate exchanges with forms we might not consider sentient encourage respect for all life.

Our purpose for these journeys is not to immerse in, heal, or change this past life, only to view it. Yet, in the process healing and insights can occur. Influences and events from times we have lived before imprint subsequent lives. Until resolved, the effect of these incidents may penetrate future embodiments, meaning that other lives will display similar patterns. For instance, a woman with a bleeding fibroid tumor in the present may have been medically victimized in concentration camp experimentation on her uterus. Though, the same condition could arise for a woman who, in a past life as an American Revolutionary soldier, bled to death on the battle field. Likewise, in healing work it is not uncommon to view with spiritual vision, items such as a spear or bullet lodged in the body. These are not physical, but energetic phenomena. They represent the influence of wounds incurred, yet unhealed, from previous times. Commonly, people will exhibit current physical symptoms in the location of past life trauma. There are many resources and trainings offered for those interested in healing past lives including fascinating material by Brian Weiss. My own book, *Shamanic Reiki* (Roberts and Levy), offers energetic and shamanic approaches for healing past life scenarios.

While past life tragedy carries through lifetimes, the reverse is also true. Our gifts, talents and purpose can survive our death. Viewing a previous incarnation may deepen our understanding of why we are here. It can instill confidence to resurrect traits we have a passion for, yet, may suppress. This is true whether the lifetime is viewed as real or not. In his book *Adventures in Reincarnation*, based on the insights of 25,000 past life regressions performed over a thirty year period, Bryan Jameison explores this topic of reclaiming past life talents.

Whether viewed as symbolic or actual, past life snapshots are perfectly suited to the person you are retrieving for, or to you. Additionally, past, present and future are not as we think so you may recover a parallel or future lifetime instead of one from the past. Whatever your experience, it is just right, so open to what it has to teach you.

Access the Limitless You

Once you have discovered and viewed another lifetime, the next step is to look at this past life at the moment just after death. From a detached perspective, sense that this life you have studied, has come to an end. Do not experience this death or get entangled in how you died in this other time. If in the immediate moments following the release from this physical body you feel relief, sadness or joy, let that happen. Then observe what follows. Our goal is not to experience the demise of this life but to track the core, or essence, which transcends and survives it. Reliving the car accident or the pain this person incurred at death is not necessary or recommended; fast speed ahead to what happens after the actual moment of death. Connect with the instant that consciousness departs from the physical body. Your intention is to discover your boundless, authentic self. In doing so, you might gain understanding of this lifetime's purpose. Dying is not the end, your immortal spirit endures.

Tibetan Buddhism teaches that at the moment of death, essence leaves the physical body through the top of the head, or crown. Buddhist practices increase spiritual awareness to facilitate this exit when death occurs. Sensitivity to what happens when we die is not reserved for the monastic. My high school boyfriend's dad was a general medical practitioner and our family doctor. This was when physicians made house calls. I remember this man describing being in the room when a patient took their last breath. The M.D. felt a tangible presence, as if the spirit of the person left the shell of the body, hovered in the room for a time then departed.

What do you notice in your journey at the moment after your death as a person, plant or other life form? Let the experience unfold.

Of those experiencing past lives as a person, many describe the moment after death similarly to people who have had a brush with death or who have actually died, then were resuscitated. There is a plethora of books in New Age stores portraying such stories, instigated by the groundbreaking work of Raymond Moody in his 1988 book, *Life After Life*. What is it like on the other side? What do people have to say after they are brought back, or return to life? Descriptions of how some people have experienced the "other side" include: freedom from the body, floating as pure consciousness or as an energy body, viewing the physical body as well as those with the person at the time of death as if "from above", immersing in white light, hearing celestial music, feeling bliss, being in a tunnel of light, meeting angels or luminous beings or deceased friends and family, choosing to come back or understanding it is not time to die, among other things.

Such examples classically sketch the now popularized phenomenon, Near Death Experience, or NDE. Although scientists pose that the deteriorating brain creates the phenomena associated with NDE's, those who die and come back argue otherwise. Some return with healing and psychic talents, despite no prior inclination. This is true of my friend, Joel Kaplan, pronounced dead following a car accident due to a heart attack suffered while driving. Joel was revived after seven shocks by a defibrillator machine, standard procedure at the time being only to emit three shocks. Joel returned with amazing capacities, his story is told in the book, *Soul Companions*, by Karen Sawyer.

Although some, like Joel Kaplan, experience radical lifestyle changes after an interlude in the afterlife, not everyone does. Some take their NDE in stride. Over a decade ago my now seventy nine year old father had surgery for a benign growth. Medical intervention is precarious for my dad's side of the family, a delicate brood. After the operation he was recovering fine. Yet the evening of his surgery when I walked into his hospital room five nurses and a doctor were at my father's bedside. My dad was dying. The medical staff did not know why, yet I surmised the drugs overloaded his sensitive system. I stood at my father's feet amidst the panicked staff. I urged my dad to return to his body if this was not his time to die. After twenty four hours in the Intensive Care Unit my father recovered and life moved on.

Years later I sat with my son, Eben, and my father at my parent's kitchen table. There was a quiet moment. I had the inkling to ask, "Dad, did you experience anything when you almost died that time?" He said, "Sure. I heard the nurses yelling. At first I felt trapped, I couldn't breathe. You know those antique glass jewelry or candy cases? I felt like I was inside one of those. I couldn't move. Then suddenly I was free. I was surrounded by white light and floated above my body. I saw you there with the nurses and doctor but I didn't want to come back. I felt great, better than ever. That's all I remember." I was shocked. My dad had a quintessential NDE and it took me years to find out about it. He concluded, "I'm still afraid of how I'll die. But after almost dying I have no fear of death itself. What comes next is nothing to be afraid of." I suggested that my father need not dread how he dies, either. He had left his body, avoiding the pain of death, and could likely do so again. My dad liked this idea.

Donning an energetic body, as in the examples above, can be liberating. Yet, we may still feel separate from source. Wounds and personality traits from this and other lifetimes can linger into the afterlife. In viewing what happens after the past life your partner retrieved, look through such overlays to your primary nature. What shines through personality, karma or circumstance after the body dies? Take all the time you desire. Intend to witness the limitless you, your *Luminous Presence,* which permeates all lifetimes. Whether you see or sense this, allow your feelings. Open your heart. Each of us has a true self that is everlasting, indestructible. Here heart and mind are balanced, Eagle and Condor soar together. Our radiant selves are one with the essence of all things and the universe. We are divine.

However you experience the *Luminous You* after your past life death, engage it fully. Whatever happens in the moments following this death remember your intention to access your immortal essence. The core self does not fear death because it knows it is eternal. Be curious. If engrossed in a body of light explore that, feel its radiance. What are the sensations? What do you hear or see? What do you sense? Be aware. You may desire to merge with, *Shapeshift,* into the light that you are. If you encounter other beings in your journey open to what they share verbally or otherwise.

At the journey's close come fully back into your body and into the room. Take time to stretch, move and connect with someone if in a group. Share the experience in a way that feels right for you both. This can be by speaking, sitting together silently or sharing a hug. If you have done the journey alone, consider taking a gentle walk or spending time in nature. Ensure that you are grounded after this experience as your energy field is expanded. With this, sense of self and world can shift. Deliberate integration is essential when experiencing the *Luminous You*.

The first step of integration is to record your experiences and any shifts. Most people return from their journey to the *Luminous Presence* deeply moved. Some portray it as ecstatic, a remembrance of the eternally abiding spirit of all things. Like my dad who came back from the land of the dead with no fear of death, and those who clinically die then return with spiritual gifts, outlook on life can change in glimpsing what lies beyond the physical. What is your experience? Note any shifts. How does viewing your immortal core affect how you feel about life? How does remembering that you are limitless impact your feelings of death?

Upon returning from your journey, invite your essence to everyday life. The sections below offer concrete ways to do this. No matter how solid, life as we know it can dissolve in an instant, like elaborate sand mandalas brushed to the wind by Buddhist monks. Life's details are vivid. Yet, no matter how captivating, they are impermanent. Physical death is our biggest reminder of this. Yet coexistent to all that is transitory in this life and beyond is an undying core, light.

Revive the Core Self

All indigenous peoples I have worked with say this era will purge false concepts and instigate a higher relationship with life. Despite cataclysmic circumstance, it is most empowering to interpret this epoch as heralding a new cycle. Tibetan and Mayan Elders alike tell us we are moving from a Dark Age to an Age of Light. Many say this Light Age is already here; we humans just have to wake up to it. If this is true, how do we do this? How do we live from *Higher Consciousness* to shine our light?

The previous section outlines a way to experience your

Luminous Presence which is always who you are. A way to bring essence into everyday life is to retrieve and integrate its qualities. It is not enough to have isolated, exalted experiences. Our expanded self must suffuse the mundane. Our earthly personality is the vehicle for our heavenly light to shine through. Jungian psychology popularized the concept of shadow, the dark side of humanness often denied and projected onto others. From Jungian perspective, we are not whole until we accept our totality, including our shadow. Equally denied is our basic nature of goodness.

Two methods to retrieve our glowing essence are outlined below. The final section of this segment, *Remold the Self*, suggests how to confront modern day challenges from an expanded perspective.

Retrieve Vital Essence from Trees

Set time aside to spend in nature and consider doing practices from Chapter Four, *Shapeshifting into Nature*, such as *Aimlessly Wander*, or *Walk Like a Shuar*. Immerse in these experiences. Make nature come alive. Doing the *Siberian Mark Exercise* with a tree that calls to you, and that you have permission to exchange with, is appropriate to follow. This exercise will support our purpose here.

When the time feels right and you are resonant with the life all around you identify a tree that evokes a good feeling (if you have not already done so). Approach this healthy tree and ask if it will agree to help you to release outdated patterns and retrieve energy. Trust what answer comes, whether a feeling or tangible expression. When you sense the tree's consent, be sure to thank it and make an offering. Then elicit help from spirit guides and *Huacas* and follow your intuition. Tune into heart and body, as well as the tree. Intuit how to proceed. How can this tree revitalize and make you whole? How can it help you balance male, female, love, hate and other polarities? What does the tree suggest? Relax your body. Release cares and worries. Really listen to the tree.

A Quechua shaman once taught John to approach a tree and with each hand grab hold of a separate branch. Your intention in this exercise is to release into the tree through your right hand with each exhalation what prevents authentic expression. As tree and earth will recycle this energy nothing you release into the tree will harm it. When inhaling, as the shaman taught John, breathe in replenishing life force energy from the branch you hold with your left hand. Breathe in balance, luminosity. Breathe in *Windhorse, Arutum*. Breathe these fully into your body all the way from the fingertips and palm of your left hand, up through the left arm and into your heart. From there, let it flood your body. Only pure and radiant forces are breathed in, only that which restores and harmonizes. Feel this. Then again, breathe obstacles out through your right arm and hand to be absorbed and recycled by the tree.

Repeat this practice, breathing this way as long as you are drawn. You will energize and purge what habitually blocks the free flow of life within you. Trust when you feel complete. Thank the tree and any guiding energies for their assistance. Leave an offering such as loose tobacco, flower petals, singing a song or indulging a moment of reverence. Feel gratitude in body and heart. Radiate this out to the tree, really feeling your love and appreciation. Be touched by the tree's beauty, honor its presence.

Weather need not be an obstacle to practicing this way in nature, but if impossible to get outside, you can do this exercise as a shamanic journey. Or use a healthy indoor plant that offers to help you rebalance.

Breathe in Life Force

A retrieval method used by Tibetan shamanic peoples is similar to the one above and can be done anywhere and anytime.

Take time to center in whatever way appeals to you in a space where you will not be disturbed. Or sit or lie comfortably for awhile, resting in your *Sacred Place*. Call upon spirit guides and *Spirit Huaca*s. In particular, ask your *Empowerment Huaca* for help. Intend to release what impedes your highest expression, the *Luminous You*. Assert your desire to reconnect with, and bring into everyday life, your boundless spiritual core.

When the time feels right, place your left hand index finger over your left nostril and breathe out fully through your open, right nostril. In doing so, feel and know that you breathe out anything in the way of your core expression. Let it go. You may see obstacles release in your mind's eye as a gray smoke or clouds of gray pellets or grit. If you do not see what releases, do not worry. In this case simply sense what is leaving as you breathe out, trust it is happening. Engage your body, feel the release in whatever way it occurs. Also, do not worry about what you release. Trust that it is immediately regenerated into life affirming energy and will do no harm. Clairvoyants may see the gray clouds, grit or whatever, spontaneously transmute into sparkles of light. Feel distortions of masculine, feminine, love, hate and other polarities come into balance.

When your breath out has peaked, release your left hand from blocking your left nostril and place the index finger of your right hand to your right nostril. In doing so, take a full breath in with your newly exposed left nostril. Know that your spiritual guides, *Huacas* and compassionate energies have collected luminous forces for you. Sense them guiding these back through the pull of your breath. Feel these sparkling energies enter you as you breathe in. As they enter into your left nostril, feel them travel throughout your body. They will settle in your heart. Only pure, luminous forces enter, those connected with your highest good. Note the glow that permeates body, heart and mind. Feel awake.

Continue this alternate nostril breathing until you are vibrant and balanced. Feel life pulse through you unimpeded. When finished, release your hand and take a few deep, refreshing breaths. Offer a tangible item, a song, a prayer, a beautiful thought or vision to all who have helped to restore your core qualities. Let gratitude pervade body and heart. Do not be afraid to really feel this. Stop, and allow the world's beauty to penetrate you. Shamans teach that nature is responsive and we draw positive energy to us by showing respect and appreciation for all life. As our hearts open, we encourage the natural magic of our world to come alive.

These practices hold similarity to shamanic soul retrieval approaches. Given this, some might conclude that the *Luminous Presence* is indeed the soul. There are as many definitions for the soul, and how it interfaces spirit with form, as there are shamanic methods to heal its fragmentation. Indigenous shamans and trained Western practitioners can restore a client's soul pieces, yet we each can revivify our own vital essence. What is important to remember is that even when we do not experience it, we are always whole. We are radiant and eternal.

Tibetan Sending Exercise

Tibetan shamanism also teaches how to send vitality to, and retrieve the essence of, others.

Prior to this exercise, do several cycles of the practice, *Shapeshift into Earth and Cosmos*, from Chapter Two. When complete, stand with palms over your heart. Feel your connection. You are one with the earth, simultaneously infused by the cosmos. When ready, reach up again with your hands and arms to immerse them in the luminosity of the heavens. Feel light. Let your body sway, hands and arms becoming saturated again by the vibration of starry realms. Take all the time you like. Enjoy the sensations.

To complete the sending practice, perform the steps below.

1) *Stand facing a partner, with a little more than one arms length between you. Alternately, imagine a loved one or consenting person in front of you.*

Geographical distance is no obstacle; you can send energy to someone half a world away. If unsure of consent intend the energy to be received according to the person's highest good. If they are not open to receiving what you direct, know this beneficial energy will be directed to another person or situation open to receiving it.

2) *When the time is right breathe and pull with your hands, luminous sparkling energy down from the stars. Pass it with your hands through the top of your head, into your throat and heart.*

3) *When your hands reach your heart level, allow your dominant hand to face palm out to your partner (imagined or real). Your extended palm will be at your heart's level. Your non-dominant palm rests over your solar plexus. Imagine the starlight you have collected resting here in your diaphragm area. Let this light form a pool, or reserve, of energy.*

Note that #2 and #3 are completed on the same breath in.

4) *On the next breath out, send half these luminous forces out from your solar plexus to your partner. Propel them through your dominant and outstretched hand. In doing, simply extend the dominant arm toward your partner with a smooth thrust, palm out. Make a SHOO! sound as you extend your palm and arm.*

Sense, feel or imagine half the light from your solar plexus propelling out. Intuitively gauge where to direct this light, for instance to the head, heart or stomach. Make a forceful SHOO! sound to help move the energy.

5) *On the next breath in, retract your outstretched hand back to its original position close to your body at the heart level. Your palm will still be facing outward toward your partner.*

Your non-dominant hand remains over your solar plexus throughout the exercise.

6) *With a final breath out, send the rest of the light forces you have collected to your partner. Do so again by thrusting your dominant hand palm out toward the person. Make a forceful SHOO! sound.*

Sense where to direct this energy with your outstretched palm. For instance, your palm may focus on the person's throat, abdomen, or elsewhere.

On this final sending, exert an extra thrust to propel the last of the energy out to your partner as your arm completes its extension. Remember that what you send out to your partner is universal light. It is not personal energy.

Receivers stand with arms resting by their side or lifted slightly out from the body in an open gesture. Face the sender with eyes open or closed. Feel the star glow energizing and coaxing your essence to surface. Feel it balance feminine, masculine, love, hate and other polarities.

When finished, partners switch roles. The receiver then sends energy and the previous sender receives it. Then each person thanks the other in whatever way feels right, perhaps with a bow or a hug. Feel gratitude for the forces now awake within you. Note the sensations.

People gain rapport with their intrinsic self through the approaches above and throughout this book. We can also reshape our lives to essence, as introduced below.

Remold the Everyday Self

It is easy to set the intention to remold everyday personality to embody your *Higher Purpose* and integrate with your *Luminous You*. Yet, intentions are supported by action. Ask spirit guides and *Huacas* for guidance, especially your *Empowerment Huaca*. You do not have to do a shamanic journey to *Shapeshift* into them as spirit influences can be part of everyday experience. When your intention is clear and you feel supported by non-physical partners, notice daily circumstances as they may take on a new light. Aspects not aligned with your Higher Self may come up for revision so look carefully at what appears, as it does so for a reason. A past lover may show up, a bizarre situation may push your buttons, an indulgence or habit may be seen for the addiction it is. When we commit to express authentically, the ways we undermine ourselves can appear pronounced. Without judgment ask: "How do I block my light, when do I hide who I am?" "How do I react to past issues and, so, sabotage what I value most?" Alternately ask: "What feels right at my core, what brings a deep sense of goodness?" "Beyond what religion or society say - what reflects my true self and what does not?" Be honest.

You may choose to shift your life to reflect higher goals. Or you may simply decide that you need to relax more with who you are. People carry varying degrees of dissociation and there are myriad reasons as to why they have lost connection to the Higher Self. Our core can be hidden as if behind layers like those encasing an onion or artichoke heart. Many of us discover that these layers which wrap around us derive from low self esteem and values that are not our own; some come from childhood or other wounding. Of what are your layers made? What keeps you from being you? Only you know these answers. Be gentle and allow what feelings may come up as you review your life. Look at yourself at work and at home. Scrutinize how you are with your family and in relationships. Observe your role in the local as well as global arena. The only objective is to discover who you really are. What is important to you? What resonates with your core? What does not? Take a hard look at your onion layers. In workshops people are encouraged to journey to these layers then share what they witnessed with partners.

It is helpful to consider that within the layers that snuff our light are also lessons and opportunities. You may ask: "What areas of personality do these circumstances not aligned with my Higher Self prod me to develop? What do these reflect for me to see more clearly? How do I deceive myself? What needs healing, how can I feel more whole?" It is helpful to contemplate what you can concretely do as well as what areas in life you need to accept or stop fighting about. How can you be more genuine? Look at the messages, they are always there. Shamanism teaches that nothing is happenstance. Believe or imagine that every circumstance and encounter can return you to wholeness.

Emotions: Unleash the Real You

When the layers that shroud our essence are exposed, emotions may come to the surface. As these arise, feel them. Release layers of conditioning, illusion and pain behind which you hide. You may imagine yourself from infancy peeling layers off that you unconsciously accepted. You might imagine offering them back to those who deliberately, or inadvertently, imposed them. John and I invite people to writhe and release these overlays as a snake sheds its skin. We also bid people to pair up and go into nature, each helping the other to identify and bury aspects not aligned with essence. As you loosen these facades, you may feel anger or fear. There may be sadness and hurt. What do you feel? We all sometimes need to cry about what was lost and to laugh at life's folly. Or we may need to shake with fear or erupt with anger. Be gentle, but honestly scrutinize what has held you back. Touch the fabric of your onion layers to let them go. You will reclaim energy. Release what binds you and breathe in life force, *Lung Ta*.

I grew up as an extremely quiet child in an environment where being quiet equated to being good. Many of my relatives still reminisce, "You were such a good child; you were so quiet." This carried into my twenties when graduate school faculty suggested my character was ideally suited for work with autistic children. Was this quiet me the real me? It took me years to reframe these projections in order to appreciate the deeper gifts of my quietude. The process ironically demanded that I integrate a co-existent wild nature, typically expressed as rebellion. Yet, this fierce spirit fueled my creativity; I could not fulfill my *Higher Purpose* without it. In reclaiming these aspects, I felt sad and angry at having denied so much of myself. I was also sometimes afraid to fully own this part of myself. Would others accept my less tame aspects? Would I still be "good"? Could I effectively and safely express intensity? Though challenging, the journey makes me more genuine and whole.

In expressing some of what holds you back, remember that emotions are not right or wrong. What we feel is simply what we feel. This does not mean we desire to act on everything that stirs, but we do deserve to feel it. We may be ashamed or fearful, and so suppress emotion. Or we may cut off from our experience for other reasons. In contrast, healthy children liberally express what they feel and can quickly move from one feeling to the next. I remember my daughter, Sayre, at three falling down, whimpering, then jumping back to her feet laughing as though nothing had happened. Another time during dinner, food which she flicked from her fork landed onto her dad's cheek. He said "That's not nice." My daughter squealed with laughter, "But it's funny!" Uncensored children express freely. Keeping a lid on what we feel denies the authentic self.

Yet we should express safely and seek assistance if we cannot do this. Support from friends and professionals can help. It is vital to take responsibility for our well being and, likewise, not to push others to emotional edges we cannot identify or handle. It takes finesse to help people uncover wounds and deceptions. Recovering past traumas or unraveling aspects about ourselves we are in denial about can be challenging, even require specialized support. I participated in a cathartic emotional release program in 1990. On the last day a man entered the room with a finger painted face. He sat in circle with us, yet with his back to everyone. The chill that ran up my spine told me that this man was not enacting psychodrama as our facilitator suggested, but was at a dangerous edge. I voiced my concerns but the trainer ignored them. Two weeks later the estranged participant ended up in a psychiatric unit.

Contrasting this unfortunate story, years ago I joined Tuvans for a fire ceremony in a rural village. In the midst a girl of about nine appeared possessed. The girl shook then collapsed onto the ground. Had this been North America instead of the Asian steppe, such behavior would be labeled psychotic or a seizure. A shaman woman rushed over to the youngster, blew water onto the girl's face then yanked forcefully on her hair. She then pulled the youth up onto her feet. To us Westerners this was harsh, yet the intervention was skillful. It anchored the child's spirit back into her body after which she appeared fine. The girl was recognized as a shaman.

Unleash the real you and get all the support you need to do so. In uncovering your authentic self you will be freed to express your higher gifts. There is no better time to do this than now.

Consider, also, that liberating ourselves benefits those beyond the physical. We are not alone. In reclaiming our authentic selves we light pathways in other realms. I had a striking reminder of this when facilitating a workshop to transmute fear into *Higher Consciousness*. Lost spirits visited me throughout the final night of this program. Fifteen apparitions found their way to me through the walls of my room. At first, I was afraid, but I quickly understood the ghosts came only for help. As each approached my bedside I sent energy, light. The disincarnate person would then *Shapeshift* into this light, after which the next apparition would appear. The following day a dozen or so workshop participants expressed also having visitors from the grave. These spirits seemingly recognized that if we could liberate ourselves, we could also free them. Each was caught in fear or confusion. When we transmute our own fear we become a beacon for others, whether we are aware of this or not.

Shapeshift into Light in Daily Life

Releasing emotional layers frees up a lot of energy. In the process you may see areas of life, or habitual ways of responding, that you would like to reshape. Maybe you cannot find your way through hot debates with a neighbor about pesticide use. Perhaps you feel paralyzed about civil liberty issues and the global slave trade. Fear may grip about how to keep your child safe during a pandemic. Or you may feel stuck in relating to a family member or spouse. Recall the luminous body after a past life death or remember retrieving vital forces from the tree or with spirit guides. Feel goodness, energy. No matter life's circumstance, we are boundless. We may be afraid, grief stricken or ecstatic. We may be homeless or sitting in a penthouse tweeting our fans. Regardless, fundamentally we are vast, whole. This is independent to external conditions or even to our recognizing it. Yet for our world to change we must reclaim our core, which joins us with the essence of all life.

How does this translate into everyday reality? Ask your spirit guides and *Huacas* to help you *Shapeshift* into luminosity. Feel your light in each moment. As this happens new directions may appear. Strength and clarity will surge. Essence, which is beyond ego, reestablishes our relationship to the greater good. This fills us spiritually and eases material grasping so we can engage life more wholesomely. In seeing that we are light, we relax. Among modern cultures such higher relationship is often replaced by dogma, mores, and structure imposed by dominant groups. Contrasting this tendency to compartmentalize, our essence knows only connection. At our core we perceive relationally. This is why actions from our deepest knowing often appear unorthodox. Our essential self is attuned to the intelligence of each moment. As a result, we may intuitively coax the best outcome in a complex situation. We may say the most bizarre, yet perfect, thing. We may act at the most awkward, yet right, moment. As we do, grace can unfold, sometimes beyond our wildest imaginings. Beyond convention or story line, our essence detects deeper patterns and relationships.

As you *Shapeshift* into light you may observe spontaneous changes in life. Or with the help of spirit partners, effect changes aligned with your core. To remold traits and be more authentic, keep practicing. What feels right in your body and heart? What feels right on a soul level? You may not even know what this means, but you will discover it over time. You may need to slow down and reflect more instead of acting or speaking out of habit. You may feel compelled to shift how you respond to situations or people. For instance, using the scenarios above, you may get to know and appreciate your neighbor before broaching his pesticide use. Or you may stop arguing and, instead, engage your community to create a "pesticide free" zone. You may become an activist and/or join a meditation group to confront painful injustice issues. You may cultivate inner peace and think positively instead of getting lost in fear. You may use natural means to boost your toddler's immune system and choose intervention consciously. Along the way, you may see that fear, global economics, and personal health are related. You may break through emotional paralysis by helping someone: the widower next door or a political prisoner thousands of miles away. You may follow the message of an insightful dream or seek therapy to confront what is blocking your relationship. These are only examples; yours will be your own.

Such re-patterning can light a path through uncertainty. It can empower us to positively impact our world. We can meet the demands of contemporary life by being more flexible and following our heart in everyday matters.

Following deeper wisdom is not about being correct, good, or perfect. It is about being present. In tapping authenticity we empower deeper expression. I once dreamed I was attempting to do yoga with a room full of adepts. I failed miserably. But suddenly I levitated and flew around the room surprising us all. I needed no special training, the ability was inborn. Similarly, have we forgotten enlightened ways are natural? Living from higher nature takes us beyond what we think and what we deem spiritual. As in the discipline of yoga, and the practices in this book, methods can help us remember who we are. Yet, our core is self-existing. It does not depend on dogma or discipline. Accessing it can be simpler than we imagine.

Breathe genuine presence in and breathe it out. Shine your light in every moment, understanding there is no pat formula for doing so. Be present to who you are. As we *Shapeshift*, we remember we are whole.

Awaken to Luminosity with Others

Another way to recall our *Luminous Presence* is to enlist the help of community members as outlined in the approaches below.

View a Partner's Essence

Have you ever walked through a train station, airport, or on a busy street and unexpectedly been mesmerized by a stranger? Perhaps it was a lady with twinkling eyes, or a hunched adolescent that touched you in some way. Similarly, have you ever known someone for years, then one day for no explainable reason, saw them as if for the first time? It would not be what these people looked like, what they did, or what they said that grabbed you. It would be something deeper and beyond the personality level; their essence. Recall this presence. What did you feel in such cases? What was your experience? Remember the moments.

Chapter Four noted how most of us travel through life with superficial awareness of the natural world. The same is true of our encounters with people. We can work with, even live next door to, someone for decades but never glimpse who they really are. This is, in part, because we look at others through lenses that blur deeper perception. These lenses are comprised of our ideas, hopes, and fears. They are crafted by ego and social condi- tioning. Most of the time we do not see people, we see our projec- tions of them or superficial layers of personality. Because the most useful practices are those we can translate into daily life, this exercise opens us to look beyond concept and habit. It hones us to perceive the core qualities of others. We have already explored how to tune into nature's essence. Here, we flex our perceptual muscles to appreciate who people really are - beyond what they do, look like, or are associated with.

To begin this practice, find a comfortable place to sit facing a partner either on the earth, on a floor with cushions, or on chairs. Consider playing soothing music in the background if you are not outside listening to the sounds of nature.

Remember that even if you live in a city you can connect with nature. As well, you can integrate any sound or distraction into your experience.

The instructions are simple. First, you will each take time to open your heart to who you really are. *Shapeshift* into light, feel your essence. Then, look at each other for at least five minutes. If you can do ten minutes, that is great. As you look, allow a soft gaze. There is no need to study every line and detail of this person's face. Just open your heart to feel a connection with them. Go beyond convention to see this person fundamentally. In other words, do not gather factual information, in fact, do not talk at all. If you have a proclivity to detect subtle realities this is not the time to read auras or scan energy fields. Forget about doing psychic evaluations or looking at past lives. Simply see, and appreciate, this person beyond concept or strategy.

As you look at this person, you will obviously perceive physical details; the shape of the face and color of his or her eyes, the line of the jaw, or the wrinkle of a brow. Yet, relax this focus. Remember, we are acculturated to see a fraction of reality. Open to seeing more fully and deeply. To attain this, simply intend it and be mindful. Be open and present. If you are thinking too much, relax. Soften your gaze. Let go of each thought with each next breath out. Feel your body against the earth, floor or chair. Open your heart and let it inform you.

If you are anxious about looking so intently at this person, who may or may not be someone you already know, do not be concerned as this is common. Allow nervousness, feel the qualities of discomfort and breathe. As this energy ripples through your body, focus attention on your next out breath. Come back to the person sitting across from you. They are unique. Softly gaze into the person's eyes. What does that feel like? What do you see beyond the physical? What do the eyes say? Feel it in your heart. There is a texture to deep looking. You will feel it and sense it. You will know it in your body and heart.

You may begin to sense things beyond the person you are looking at, or have unexpected emotion. It is not uncommon for either or both partners to tear up during this process. Keep looking and keep feeling. Touch the essence of this person. In doing so, the experience of your own luminosity will grow. You may see yourself through the eyes you gaze within, recognizing the goodness that radiates through us all.

When the practice is complete, partners can close the session in whatever way feels appropriate. People often hug, though some simply bow or nod. Some like to share the experience verbally and others prefer to take a walk, write in a journal, or have time alone after the experience. See what feels right. Reflect upon how you can bring this experience of viewing people's essence into everyday life.

The above practice of viewing the essence of another person is ideal preparation for the following two exercises. These demonstrate powerful tools that families, communities and other groups can use to encourage the essence qualities of members. Engaging with people in deep, authentic ways, such as demonstrated through the practices below is fulfilling. It slows us down, awakens us to what is important in life and to the richness of every moment. This can only benefit us and our world.

Read Essence in Groups

Gather a small circle of people. If you are working with a larger group, break them into circles of about six. Participants can be sitting in chairs or on cushions on the floor and one drum, rattle or bell should be provided for each group. Yet, any percussion instrument will do.

One person is designated as the beginning point in the circle exercise. This person is the first to receive an *Essence Reading*. The person directly across from this participant holds the drum, rattle or bell.

To begin, the person to receive the reading will close her or his eyes. The person is instructed to sit comfortably and open to what is received. Taking a few deep breaths will help the recipient relax to feel the love, energy and insights directed to him or her. The participant holding the percussion instrument softly begins beating the drum, shaking the rattle or striking the bell. The other group members have their eyes open and focused on the person receiving the reading. As the sound carries, each becomes heart centered and *Shapeshifts* into their *Luminous Presence*. The group opens to looking through the eyes of the heart to see this person's essence. The intention is to perceive beyond personality or circumstance. They look with love and respect to fundamental qualities, which may be masked by day to day persona.

The percussion is sounded for about a minute as the group focuses and the person receiving the reading relaxes. Then the sound ends and as each person in the circle is moved, they express in a word or a few words the essence of the other person. Sometimes words overlap as one person speaks and another is also prompted to speak. Sometimes there are small gaps of silence when no-one speaks. Each person shares only when moved, when the heart propels expression.

Essence Reading is deeply bonding. We begin by connecting with our own essential nature. This allows us to look at another beyond story line and beyond judgment. We drop ideas about what we do or do not like about this person to perceive inherent goodness. We may see as never before. We look to wholeness, yet this is not abstract but tangible. We feel it. We know it. We mirror it back.

Examples of essence expressions are: Warrior. Loving Mother. Strong. Goddess. Protector of Animals. Fearless Nature. Relentless Journeyer. Word Crafter. Beautiful Presence. Gifted Voice. Tender Heart. Poet. Son of Hope. Steward of the Earth. Wounded Child of Light. Shapeshifter. Knower of the Ancient Ones. Wisdom Keeper. Manifestor. Visionary. Wounded Healer. Fierce Planet Lover. Hard Worker. Children's Advocate.

Our true essence exists beyond the spoken word or tangible human quality. Yet, each word or phrase emits energy affecting a glow upon the person receiving it. Hearing beautiful, positive things about ourselves strengthens us. It awakens our unconditional presence. Reflecting a person's essential qualities stirs her or his inner potential and the desire to integrate these into the earthly journey. Qualities that have been forgotten or denied are confirmed and encouraged to come to the surface. People describe this experience as "Healing", "Profound", "Being held in love". It is not uncommon for people to be so moved that they cry during or after their reading. It is rare for a group of people to focus on us so unconditionally and to express with such love. We feel seen, and nurtured, on a fundamental level.

Each group member may express five or six times per reading, yet there are no set parameters. The reading is complete when each person has spoken what has arisen and nothing more comes. The silence signals to the person receiving to open his or her eyes. Or a circle member can gently tap the receiver on the shoulder. To close, this person may look at each member of the circle, feeling gratitude. Or they make a simple bow to each participant.

Following this, the person who drummed, rattled or chimed passes the instrument to the person on her or his left. This person now softly beats the drum, shakes the rattle or strikes the bell for several minutes. As this occurs each member of the group *Shapeshifts* into her or his *Luminous Presence*. Then the group focuses with open eyes and heart on the person to the left of the member who just received a reading. The whole process is repeated until each member of the circle has received an *Essence Reading*.

Perceiving from the eyes of the heart, such as in this exercise, can help when confronting those we consider beyond reform. From a distance we can journey to the essence of anyone we imagine, whether a prison inmate, or a political leader half a world away. The belief that all humans are radiant at their core, and that everything is universal light, is hard to sustain in the face of tragedy. It is vital to acknowledge conflicting feelings, yet important to consider that the most terrible acts conceal the deepest wounds. In such cases, heart-centered visioning can spark empathy that is otherwise hard to rouse.

Dr. Gabor Maté is the author of four bestselling books including, *In the Realm of Hungry Ghosts: Close Encounters with Addiction*. Dr. Maté treats hard core addicts at safe injection sites to reduce addiction related financial and health burdens to society. Research shows, without exception, that addicts have endured acute adversity from childhood in the form of neglect, abandonment or abuse. The unconditional positive regard that harm reduction site caregivers offer may be a person's first compassionate encounter. A moving side effect is how such benevolence motivates people to enroll in detoxification programs.

The process of reading a person's essence prompts us to act skillfully as it is grounded in clear seeing. We are not naïve and neither do we hold unrealistic expectations. Yet our heart is open to appreciate the fundamental goodness of a person regardless of their circumstance. Productive ways of relating to difficult people and situations can result.

Retrieve Essence in Groups

The above exercise of reading essence in groups is ideal preparation for the next step of retrieving essence. The following practice designed to encourage a deeper experience of the core self, supported by a circle of caring individuals.

To facilitate the experience of retrieving essence, gather up to eight people together in a circle. Participants are ideally sitting on cushions on the floor. One member of the group lies fully clothed, comfortably in the center of the circle, on a mat and covered with a blanket. A pillow can be placed under the head if desired. Another mat, pillow and blanket should be placed outside, yet nearby the circle, in a comfortable setting. A drum, rattle or bell is also provided for each member of the group. Yet, any percussion instrument will do.

To begin, the person to receive the retrieval will close her or his eyes. Instruct that the person to lie comfortably and open to receiving. Taking some deep breaths will help the recipient don a receptive mode, to open to essence. As this person does this, the circle members who are holding percussion instruments begin softly beating their drums, shaking their rattles or striking their bells. These group members have their eyes open and focus on the person they will retrieve for. As they sound their instruments, each person in the circle connects with her or his core essence. Then each opens to perceiving another through the eyes of the heart. The group is to look beyond personality or circumstance; beyond good or bad or what they do not like about this person. *Shapeshifting* into their own essence to begin helps them look beyond health or illness, to see this person in perfection. There is nothing to heal. There is nothing to fix. There is nothing to change.

After a minute or more of making sound with the percussion instruments and when this person's essence is tangible, each member stops sounding drum, rattle or chime. This often occurs spontaneously. Group members then place the instruments down and retrieve essence. To do this the group focuses on the person lying in the center of their circle. They relax their minds, and follow their hearts and bodies. Some sing to the person, coaxing essence to surface. Some lay their hands on the person, awed by their beauty and light. Each retriever maintains loving admiration.

It is important to see this person as whole, perfect. Feel this in your heart and body. Be touched by this individual's radiant core. Feel essence, light. Again, there is nothing to heal. There is nothing to fix. There is nothing to change about this person. You see only perfection, wholeness. You sound, touch and move to encourage these qualities to surface. You feel only gratitude.

After several to five minutes, the retrieval ends. With such loving focus and clear intention little time is needed. Each member sits back and remains present, feeling replenished as if by a deep well of love. The person who was retrieved for knows to slowly open her or his eyes. If the receiver does not appear to know this, a group member can gently touch the person on the shoulder or whisper into an ear "Take your time and when ready you can open your eyes and slowly sit up." When the person's eyes open and he or she attempts to sit up, group members can offer to help. Then, they close in a way that feels appropriate. Some circles do this by inviting everyone in the group to wrap their arms around the person for a few moments. Others simply allow the space for the person to transition on their own.

Following this, the person who received the retrieval is led by a member to the mat, blanket and pillow located outside the circle. The person lies down here to transition from the retrieval experience. When the recipient is led to the transitional mat, the next person moves to the center of the circle and the whole process begins again until everyone has experienced an *Essence Retrieval*.

The person on the transitional mat rests for the duration of the next retrieval. The person returns to the circle when the next freshly retrieved person moves to the transitional mat.

Points to keep in mind as you perform and receive *Essence Retrievals*:

1) *One person can be designated as a time keeper. Or groups can use a timer set to four minutes to indicate when to close retrievals. Ending spontaneously is also fine, if that is desired, yet keeping time parameters works well. After the timer sounds, or a person indicates four minutes have passed, the retrieval is brought to an end over the next minute.*

2) *Essence retrieving is not about doing a healing. We firstly feel our own wholeness then perceive the goodness and wholeness intrinsic to another. We affirm this and coax it to surface. If you are a healer who does energy or shamanic work, this is not the intention here. Connect on a level deeper than wounding, to the core of this person that is whole and perfect. Perceiving and affirming wholeness is profound beyond expression. Hold back the tendency to read energy fields, balance chakras, or employ other healer's habits. Redirect the orientation to detect imbalance and disease. For this exercise, you must perceive more fundamentally. Otherwise, you will miss its power. The heart needs no strategy.*

3) *The percussion (drumming, rattling, chiming) raises the circle's energy vibration. It helps each person to feel their Luminous Presence. This includes the person receiving the retrieval. Energy is amplified when a group gathers with a clear intention. As individual immune systems are known to be boosted by massage and other body work, our energy systems and consciousness are boosted by the above ingredients. This gains the group, as well as individuals, resilience and power. It also helps everyone in the circle to access, and perceive from, his or her own core self.*

It is important to recognize that group members may be sensitive to touch. Some people are "thin-skinned" or neurologically delicate. Others have abuse issues or there may be further reasons that people shy away from being touched. Be explicit about asking permission, as well as touching sensitively and always appropriately – this is crucial. Ensure that participants feel safe and have the opportunity to verbalize when they do not feel safe or to express other needs. Encourage personal responsibility. For instance, a person may not want to be hugged at the end of the session, but is fine with having group member's hands rest on his or her back. Or someone may choose to lie down in the circle face down instead of lying on his or her back, face up. Another may request not to be touched on the face. It is important for the circle to know about, and honor, such needs. Whatever occurs for a person, or is expressed, within the circle is confidential and not shared beyond the group. This should be the parameter for any group engaged in authentic sharing and it is important that everyone in the group expressly agree to uphold each member's privacy.

Doing *Essence Retrievals* is optimally performed with groups which are already bonded. When people are aware of each member's journey it is easier to create a safe container. When a circle is held sacredly tremendous healing can occur. People relax and open to broader dimensions of self. Such intimacy can be nurtured for groups by following the practices throughout this book. Alternately, employ methods of your own or work with already formed groups or communities.

As is the case with *Essence Reading*, *Essence Retrievals* are deeply moving. We look through veneers of personality and our own judgments to a person's indestructible radiance. We perceive wholeness and encourage it to come to the surface.

Closing Note to Chapter Six

In looking at the Mayan Prophecies people typically focus on the Long Count calendar, ending December 21, 2012. This closes the last of five 5,126-year cycles. The fact is that many Mayan calendars end at the same time and what this all means is hotly debated. The decades surrounding these "end times" are often viewed as ominous and linked to Christian ideas of apocalypse. It is true that this era of closure, which extends far beyond the year 2012, coincides with environmental and social crisis. Yet for original peoples, reality is cyclic or spiraling. It does not plow a steady trough, nor does it truly begin or end. Each part of reality, time included, is dynamic and relational. Mayan calendars are likewise inextricable from human consciousness. This end period of the Mayan Calendar resounds with myriad prophecies and is said to correspond with the arrival of the sun at the center of our Milky Way Galaxy. This and other factors drive many to conclude that the true apocalypse is the destruction of constricting ways of being. The change that can birth from these times, they surmise, is the recognition of our true form as light.

Spiritualists and scientists alike tell us that matter is vibrating energy, a perspective that transforms who we think we are. Given this, now think of the many things that seemed fantasy when Jules Verne wrote about them in the 1800's. Verne's visions included horseless carriages, computers, subway systems, calculators, electricity and other, now commonplace, technologies. John Perkins often asks, "Why did Christ heal and raise people from the dead?" John poses that Christ did this not to set Himself apart, but to show what we are all capable of. If we each are fabricated of divine light, we embody the universe's potential. The supra-natural attributes of yogis, saints, even Christ and the Buddha, then, are our own. Such expanded human qualities could help us navigate challenging times. It is probable, as with the musings of Jules Verne, that many things we now only imagine will someday feel natural. All the more reason to dream what is really in our hearts and souls, and what we know will benefit the world.

Humans are material and physical, yet we exist well beyond the corporeal. We are luminous, limitless. This force, which is who we are, is more fundamental than notions of subtle energy bodies or chakras. We each are an undying flame of love that is one with a sentient universe. In remembering our *Luminous Presence*, we reclaim this love and connection. In recovering who we are we remember why we are here. New understandings emerge as the Light in us awakens.

In the next chapter of this book, we apply *Deep Feminine* perspectives to help us transform the perils, and embrace the promise, of these prophesied modern times.

"Another world is not only possible, she is on her way! On a quiet day, if you listen carefully, you can hear her breathing."

- Arundhati Roy

CHAPTER SEVEN

SHAPESHIFTING WITH THE DEEP FEMININE

John Perkins and I presented to Central and North Americans at a Panama City gathering in 2009 to promote rainforest preservation, sponsored by the non-profit organization, *Earth Train*. In attendance were several members of the Panamanian Kuna and Embera tribes and their families, beautiful people with distinct traditions. Fiercely independent, the Kuna are known the world over for their colorful *Mola* tapestries. A memorable moment of that evening came when a Kuna chief dressed in jeans and a blue striped cotton shirt stood before us. All eyes focused on the small, yet sturdy man as he delivered the following words:

"Here in Panama the Great Creator made a bridge across the oceans three million years ago. It transformed one ocean into two: Atlantic and Pacific. That single act brought together the North and South. It also changed climates – changed the world. Then the Yankees came and tore a hole in that bridge with a huge canal. It changed everything once again. Since then we have all been divided - people from nature, people from each other, North from South, East from West. Everything went crazy. Now, it is up to us to build a new type of bridge."

According to *Earth Train* founder, Nathan Gray, the Kuna command international attention as the "poster children" of global warming. Much of the tribe lives on densely settled islands on the Atlantic coast of a semi-autonomous territory in Panama. Yet, with the rising ocean levels, storm surges now flood their tiny island villages. Of the many indigenous groups whose lands are threatened by swelling waters, two of the Kuna's islands are uninhabitable two months of each year (as of this writing) due to flooding. Just as glacial melting causes Arctic wildlife to migrate, rising shorelines are forcing the island-living Kuna to abandon their homes.

Some still argue that planetary warming is not due to human activity. Even if this were so, there are countless indicators that more than a century of heavy industrialization has resulted in severe global impacts. Sometimes it appears as though this has happened overnight. Yet it has not. Long term accumulated results of rampant materialism are simply at a tipping point.

Given this, we can take heart that the leap of consciousness predicted for this era is equally slow to appear. If human evolution reaches its own tipping point positive global change could then outweigh the rapid deterioration of life we see now on this planet, also as if overnight. There is a rising wave of social activism that makes this wish viable. Fine examples are found in *YES!* Magazine's true to life stories of ordinary people transforming the world. Models for sustainable living are featured at *Green Festivals* and *Bioneers* events and paradigm shifting *Awakening the Dreamer* programs, presented all over the planet, also give hope. Those involved in such movements - women and men, young as well as old - show us that change is possible.

Indigenous prophecies, and common sense, tell us that we must harmonize with nature in order for our species to continue. Some native teachers say that "cosmic vibrations," light frequencies never before experienced on the earth, stimulate in us new levels of unity with nature, each other, and life beyond our own planet. Just as we teeter at the threshold of doom, forced out of denial about the trajectory of materialism on Planet Earth, the flood gates of human potential appear to be opening. Many, who now take advantage of this portal, dare to imagine and act on their dreams. The wise adage, "Crisis prods brilliance," applies to thousands who are forging new ways to live, *building new types of bridges*, as the Kuna Chief so aptly expressed.

Of the thousands of examples of inspired change, one that stands out is the "living building" concept, such as demonstrated by the *Omega Center for Sustainable Living* (OCSL) in Rhinebeck, NY. Biological wastewater schemes at the OCSL clean water using earth, plants and sunlight. Purified water is then returned to the local aquafir which recycles it into the systems of the world's largest holistic educational institute. The processes use on-site produced renewable energies. Solar power fuels passive heating and lighting providing net-zero thermal comfort. The living building is successful because it mimics the intelligence of nature.

The template for higher living is here. We just have to *Shapeshift* our mindsets and habits to manifest it. Now is the time to act from our deep love for life, bridging mind with heart, science with nature, materialism with spirituality, to implement a new reality.

Many say the necessary, albeit, missing, ingredients to do this - to *unite* people with nature and people with each other - are feminine values. Among others, of primary importance are *Deep Feminine* orientations which nurture the earth and all life upon her. It is not hard to see how repressing such impulses have resulted in human and environmental degradation. This contrasts with indigenous, matriarchal cultures which knew their place in the cosmic circle and held women and the earth as sacred.

The approaches throughout this book are based on *Deep Feminine* principles. Here we explore further ways to activate the creative power of the feminine.

Wild and Womanly Ways

In investigating the *Deep Feminine*, it is interesting to note the design of commercial honeybee hives, refined just as the

Industrial Revolution reached full swing. I began exploring honeybees quite unexpectedly when on a Vision Quest I heard one sing. Not a buzzing, but a melody. I had been singing my own songs on this canyon quest to appease the springtime population of rattlesnakes. My guides, Anne Hayden and Sheila Belanger, explained that although snakes do not hear as we do, in using a soothing voice we become calm and secrete pheromones that the snakes can taste with their tongues. Anne said that in doing this the rattlesnakes can "read" how we are feeling towards them. Our singing can strongly affect the snakes because of how it "changes our own inner climate of fear and possible aggression to curiosity and calmness, even allurement through love".

I sang to three snakes the first day. The last stretched its tightly coiled body into a luxurious wave and relaxed its "poised to strike" head. It then sat there as if entranced. The snake and I stared eye to eye for some time.

I chanted prayerful songs thereafter, though not expecting to be sung back to. It was when I was scaling up a big horn sheep trail on a high rock field one afternoon that I heard the soulful tune of a bee, humming as it gathered nectar from tiny yellow flowers on an outcropping of rocks. Later, on my three day solo an hour's hike from base camp, one honeybee visited me each day. Its greatest interest was my necklace of carved stone bears, a gift from a Native American medicine man when I was gravely ill. This was lying on my altar amidst other stones and sacred items. The golden insect traipsed its tiny feet over my bear necklace for extended periods each day. I had thought bees were "busy", but this one seemed to be on vacation. That it was alone intrigued me. On my final solo day, the honeybee walked gingerly over my bare feet and hands. Lastly, it crawled into my curled left hand and settled into my palm for a half hour as if taking a nap.

Following my quest, I happily observed, *Shapeshifted* into, and read about honeybees. I ate local pollen and raw honey, embarked on shamanic journeys into alternate reality to glimpse hive structures, morphed into the psyche and body of bees, and had delightful exchanges with log-nesting feral bees in forests and at beaches accessible only at low tide. My obsession magnetized honeybee energy so keenly that for several days my home buzzed with bees that had found their way to me.

Although I began knowing little about honeybees, once I started studying them I soon learned that people have domesticated these charming creatures for centuries. In the late 1800's the man-made hive model produced honey with such efficiency that it changed bee lives and culture forever; that model has not been tampered with since.

It is tempting to romanticize about honeybees and there are certainly valid mystical associations (for example, shamans who apply bee stings during healings and ancient orders of honeybee initiates). In his book, *The Shamanic Way of the Bee*, Simon Buxton even mentions that beekeepers rarely get cancer or arthritis. Yet, these are human benefits. We may ponder whether the high, unnatural honey and pollen production of Industrial Era hives has made honeybees into workaholics. Everyone is aware that in recent years unprecedented numbers of worker bees have left their hives causing the hives to die. Beekeepers I spoke with said that hive evacuation may be due to viruses affecting immune-deficient bees. Of the culprits blamed for weakening the immune systems of honeybees are chemical and electromagnetic stressors. It appears that honeybees have reached their own tipping point. Beyond targeted causes, unnatural exodus from one's nest indicates that the feminine principle has been compromised.

What of the elusive feral honeybee, such as the one with time on its hands during my Vision Quest? Those I spoke with knew little about such honeybees beyond that they lived more leisurely and in smaller clusters, some perhaps even solitary. None gave much credence to wild honeybees beyond their function in wilderness ecology and their help in pollinating food for human consumption. Why is the wild all but invisible, apart from its benefit to humans? First ask "When did we step out of our own natural state?" As people project what they want, as well as what they fear, onto the untamed world, the true powers and magic inherent in the wildness of nature, as well as our own true character, elude us.

Modern society's resonance with nature and *Deep Feminine* ways can seem all but snuffed out in industrial-techno cultures. But, there are hopeful signs. These include the holistic "new science" paradigms; cooperative leadership strategies; technologies that apply feminine principles; wilderness and nature-based therapies; the growing number of businesses committing to socially and environmentally just standards, co-creative agriculture, bio-mimicry and sustainable design, to name a few. Contemporary individuals reclaim wild and womanly values quietly in their homes and gardens, publicly through social and environmental activism, spiritually such as through popular "Gaia" and "Goddess" movements. People are waking up to spirit, nature, and acting to preserve local and planetary biology. For support, many look to traditional and shamanic worldviews which revere the untamed world and the feminine.

Although there are exceptions, ancient peoples' reverence for the feminine ensures that the home, children, and the natural world are nourished. For instance, a Shuar Amazonian woman maintains a private section of the long house that men do not enter without her permission. The children gather here and the mother prepares the food. The woman, also, honors the plants that sustain her family and sings to the goddesses of the earth and waters to help her plants grow. Women throughout history and across diverse cultures wielded the power of home, food, and the earth, thus holding the well-being of family and community. In support of this, I once heard a North American Medicine Man say that if a husband threatened the harmony of his home, he would likely return to his teepee after the hunt to find his bowl and blanket waiting for him outside. Mick Dodge, raised in an extended Welsh family in the Hoh Rainforest in Washington State in the United States, tells a similar story. Mick (the *Barefoot Sensei*), observed that while growing up, his grand-fathers obliged all their wives' demands. Confused as to why these burly Celts were subservient, Mick asked "Grand-Pas, why do you do everything Grand-Ma tells you to?" They both replied "Grand-Ma knows how to nest."

It is true that modern women may not desire traditional roles. Yet, regardless of who plays the part, communities flourish and people live in harmony with nature when the feminine principle is intact.

How strong is the feminine in current times? To respond, we can look at our own nests. Do our homes help our children thrive? Do our institutions enrich our communities? Is our larger nest, the earth, healthy and cared for? Everyone these days agrees that environmental pollution is like dumping garbage and excrement in our collective living room. From a "nesting" perspective such activities are absurd. The same is true of allowing industries to destroy waters and lands. In plain view now is that fact that first world lifestyles kill plant and animal life, enslave third world sisters and brothers in sweat shops, and are unsustainable.

How can we meet the overwhelming challenges humans face today? We can *Shapeshift* our attitudes and ways of life. A wise place to begin is to revive *Deep Feminine* perspectives that inspire us to greater harmony with each other and our planet.

The guided journey below will help you awaken the deep woman within and reclaim the possibilities for life that are the birthright of man and woman alike.

Reclaim the Deep Feminine: Journey to Catherine

Prepare to Journey

Journey note: The ancient art of story-telling can help us connect to the *Deep Feminine*. The tale below is shared for this sole purpose. Despite that it may entail similarities to historical people and events that occurred in New England in the United States at the close of the 17th Century, and in Europe from 1300 through the 1700's, the details presented here are only loosely based on fact. The characters are fictional. If in reading this journey you or participants do not want to enact it, skip over this exercise and/or do it at another time. Trust your resonance and readiness.

This journey is ideally performed in a group. Before you or group members begin, gather any *Physical Huaca(s)* desired for the experience. The facilitator should decide if soft drumming or music is preferred. We employ a combination in our workshops, using gentle drumming during the guided journey and applying music as indicated below.

When positioned, each individual places her or his *Physical Huaca(s)* on the body, floor or ground, or holds them in hand. Journeying without sacred items is also fine. We remind people to summon the energy, power and wisdom unique to each *Huaca* or to imagine *Shapeshifting* into these qualities. Participants can also *Shapeshift* into guides as the experience begins.

Spiritualists as well as scientists tell us that our conventional notions of time and space are more mutable than we are conditioned to believe. Shamanic journeys bypass habitual thinking patterns that compartmentalize reality, opening us to a larger view of ourselves and our world. Imagine that your body can pass through the bounds of time and space. Affirm that you can propel into the past and future, or into any era or location. Time, physical barriers, even vast distances present no obstacles. You can travel anywhere through your imagination. This renders the wisdom of all times and spaces available. You will see, hear, sense these realities, or there may be another way you perceive them. There are no rules.

Establish the Journey Environment and Set the Intention

To begin, invite a few deep breaths. Let go and allow the body to soften with each breath out. Imagine sinking deeply into the earth. Feel the earth's support and her loving embrace. Continue to relax and sink more deeply into the earth. Take some time.

Take another deep, refreshing breath. When ready, go to your *Sacred Place*. Immerse in your *Sacred Place* with no agenda other than to notice its details and feel its nuances. Again, relax physically, deepening and softening your breath. Absorb the feelings of safety and comfort. Bask in this sacred and healing environment, feeling the sensations and allowing them to expand with each breath in and out. Take ample time to experience your *Sacred Place* and as you do, allow the *Shapeshift* into your *Luminous Presence*. Feel your essence become tangible, open your heart to who you really are. Feel yourself as light.

Now, you, as a light form resting within your *Sacred Place*, will set the intention to journey geographically to Salem, Massachusetts in the United States. Intend that you will travel back in time to the Salem of the late 1600's.

Remember that energy and experience follow intention; commit to witness the life of an evolved woman of this period named Catherine. Your interest in Catherine is the link she offers to *Deep Feminine* wisdom which transcends time, culture, and even gender. Please note that, as engrossing as Catherine's life may be, you will view its details as a distant observer. You may experience this as if watching a film play out on a screen before you. As with a movie, you may have feelings about what you see and what occurs for Catherine, yet, you will do so as if from a distance. You are witnessing, yet not experiencing the lifetime you see. Recall how shamans *Shapeshift* into animals and other forms as if trying on a well-fitting set of clothes. These shamans do not lose sense of self, or their clear intention, in the process. Neither will you.

Keep in mind that regardless of setting identical intentions and embarking on the same journey, each person will experience uniquely. If one's journey pace or content differs from the facilitator's description, the sound of the facilitator's voice and his or her words can be used as a backdrop. In this case, participants are encouraged to simply allow the cadence and tone of the guiding voice to support the journey they are meant to have.

Once your intention is set, linger for awhile longer within your *Sacred Place*. Again, relax your body and open to being safe and comfortable. Feel sacredness and healing infuse you with each breath in and out. Feel your indestructible luminous qualities; let your whole being soak these in.

At this time, summon the help of *Spirit Huacas* and guides, if desired. You may ask "What guides are here to join me on this journey?", or simply invoke what energy feels right. You can alternately *Shapeshift* into the energy of your guides now, or later. Or simply stay with the experience of being a luminous presence, a radiant form of light.

When ready, allow your luminous body to grow lighter and lighter until you feel yourself lift off the ground and float high into the sky.

Imagine rising high into the air and passing through the ceiling of the room. You may sense that time ceases to exist. Space may feel permeable. You, with the aid of your imagination, will float through the ceiling and roof of the building. Imagine yourself feather-light, drifting into the sky, above the tree tops. When you feel ready, look down from this high vantage and notice what you see. (If none of these suggestions work for you that is fine. In this case, simply embark on the journey experience in a way that works for you.)

Imagine now that you float higher, through atmospheric layers and into fathomless space. Your body is energy, light. This light is indestructible. You travel rapidly, beyond time and space. Feel the sensations, listen to the sounds and note what you see. Track what you sense. Remember that as you are guided by your clear intentions and spirit allies, nothing more is needed; simply open.

Travel in your imagination back in time and to the Northeastern United States. In coming closer to the land, note its topography. You may also sense the qualities of the time periods you pass through; history may unfold before your eyes. When you arrive, hover in the skies just above Salem, Massachusetts. Linger close enough to watch the inhabitants and details of life in this village during the late 1600's, yet know that you are not seen. Look down now as there is a woman at the ocean's edge…

Journey to Catherine

Rest unseen as if you float in a time/spacecraft made of pure light. Watch from above as a woman named Catherine stands by the water's edge. In looking down you see her aged woolen dress, a muted color, is wet where it touches her ankles. Catherine wears the Puritan fashion of these times, yet her long hair freed from its confining cap falls wildly to her waist.

Take a few moments within the journey space now to look carefully at, or to sense, this woman named Catherine. What do you notice? In studying, or sensing, Catherine's face, what are her features? What color are her eyes? Does her hair hang in thick tresses, or is it thin and straight? What shade is it?

How old does Catherine appear? Note the texture and pattern of her dress and whether her body underneath is full or slight. What else do you sense about this woman?

As Catherine stands at the water's edge, you see that she is not alone. Another woman, ripe with child, stands a short distance from her. Catherine suggests that this young mother synchronize her breathing with the waters. The two breathe deeply as they gently rock their bodies back and forth with the rhythm of the incoming and outgoing waves. The wind brushes their faces and the water washes over their bare feet, soaking their dress hems. Luminous flowing strands of seaweed encircle their feet like green, writhing snakes.

Catherine is a midwife and herbalist. She is often seen with pregnant women like this one at the water's edge, or with her herb basket walking in the deep forests or in the open meadows collecting medicinal roots and flowers. Catherine *wildcrafts* the feminine and healing plants: Motherwort, Echinacea, Belladonna, Blue and Black Cohosh, Yarrow, Witch Hazel, Skull Cap, Shepherd's Purse and others. Her grandmother began tutoring her in the healing ways when Catherine was just a young child, as long back as she can remember. Her grandmother's own grandmother had instructed her before that, fulfilling an unbroken line of woman healers and those who facilitated the birthing into this life as well as beyond it. Catherine, as did her grandmothers before her, sits by her neighbors' bedsides offering sea vegetable broths, applying pungent poultices of freshly crushed plants, massaging their babies and guiding the dying.

Awake to her *Higher Purpose* since she was a young girl, Catherine is able to vividly recall other lifetimes: sitting in ancient circles in Africa, reading the alignment of stars in Egypt and Atlantis, lighting ceremonial fires in Mongolia and South America, meditating in dark caves and monasteries in old Tibet, gathering at the *God Stone* in early Jerusalem. Catherine, a seer through many cycles, chose to be here. She is conscious of her purpose to transmit a deep knowing that is beyond time, location, and gender. This wisdom, she knows, belongs to a future time that will be ripe to heed it. Catherine immersed in these understandings through each incarnation, whether she lived as a man or a woman. Within those lifetimes, she saw this time, now, the dark era of the late 1600's, when she would impart energy, power and wisdom for future generations.

The period of this present life is dangerous for women who

know the wisdom of the earth, and cosmos, as their own and draw from these forces. Countless European women have already been killed at the hands of witch hunters. As the tension in New-England grows, Catherine is careful to veil her power. Visible to her community as a healer and midwife, she cloaks her deeper knowing. A wisdom carrier, Catherine transmits compassion and wakefulness to other times and places, holding deep communion with invisible helpers and the sentient earth. Concealing these ways is necessary. Catherine knows that the abuse of women and suppression of feminine power seeds imbalance and disease for generations. Hence, she desires to impart her gifts when they will have the most impact. For now, she follows her impulse to wait and to camouflage her deeper purpose. She serves her community, and the earth, and remains aware.

As the unrest in New-England and in her own village of Salem grows, Catherine sees fear in her neighbor's eyes. She smells hatred as if an acrid odor is hanging in the air. Her own husband looks at her as though she is a stranger. Catherine's healing abilities have gained her a reputation causing the suspicion that she is aligned with unnatural forces. Her facility with native plants and their good effect appears greater than human and some consider it black magic. Several women, "witches," from other New-England territories have recently been hung. Their lifeless bodies were afterwards burned.

Watch from your indestructible body of light, the time and space craft of your *Luminous Presence*, as one day Catherine wakes to the angry sounds of a mob. Her husband allows them entry into their humble home on the outskirts of the village and the men who seize the stunned woman cut her hair. They grasp her wrists and ankles and tie them with ropes. Catherine is carried, ankles bleeding and wrists bruised, to the central commons. To the mob's surprise, the woman they grip does not move or protest. The loathing in their eyes tells her they are poised to kill. Fear burns in her chest like a hot coal, yet Catherine knows nothing can change these circumstances. Grief weighs upon her as if a granite slab. Frantic, she screams to her ancestors, "What of imparting this wisdom?!"

In hearing her own voice bellow through the crowd the vice that grips her heart suddenly releases. A deep love now envelops Catherine as she imagines herself resting in the grandmothers' arms.

View the following scenes safely from within your light orb. Nothing can penetrate or impact you beyond your conscious choice. Watch as if a movie plays out on a screen before you. Open your heart to what occurs, but do not go into the experience of this life or become a part of it. Feel your body and securely anchor into who you are; your essence. Remember that Catherine, the woman you watch before you, is the link to Deep Feminine wisdom transcending time, gender, and culture. Nothing can harm her spirit or weaken her intention, not even her death in this lifetime. Her death, in fact, conceals her purpose. Upon the demise of one body, her essence will reincarnate, and as a man or a woman, she will continue her mission.

As you look down from within your body, your luminous vehicle, you see that piles of wood are placed in the center of the commons. You watch as a crowd gathers.

Catherine is dragged, along with another woman, to the woodpiles. She glances toward the other woman, communicating love and fortitude with her eyes. Both are tied against poles high on separate stacks of wood. Catherine's long, worn nightdress is torn, her bare feet caked in mud that is red with her blood. Her hair is cropped close to her head, her eyes are wide open. She looks to the crowd seeing mostly men, but women and children also gather. Some appear sad and some are visibly afraid. Are they afraid of the devil that they think inhabits her or are they afraid to watch her burn? Most have fire in their eyes, their hearts choked by terror and ignorance that clouds their radiant core. Catherine's heart aches for those who will start these fires and also for those who will watch her die. These dark times are fraught with pain, uncertainty and hatred. Yet she envisions a future time when light, mystery and goodness will prevail.

A man sets the pyre ablaze and the audience roars. Hands wave in the air and the people scream "Vanquish evil! Burn the witch!" Catherine smells the burning wood. The smoke stings her eyes and chokes her lungs. As her nightdress is scorched, then afire, panic grips and she tries to catch her breath. Catherine braces for the agony of being burned alive yet even as her body is consumed by flame, the pain does not come. Catherine has left her body. Her spirit, a ball of light, has departed her through the top of her head. The light orb lifts into the skies above the lifeless body known as "Catherine" which now expels its final breath.

Catherine is free, luminous. She remembers this lucidity from countless times between other lives. The essence of Catherine looks about in this space and sees that other lights encircle her.

You are invited to look toward Catherine, this conscious radiance, from your own glowing presence.

What do you see? Sense the consciousness, Catherine, and her *Higher Purpose*. These orbs of light that surround her – you - are the wisdom carriers of the future that she is destined to transmit to.

Watch the brilliant form before you, the ball of light. This essence known as Catherine in the late 1600's has donned many names and bodies as men and women in diverse lifetimes. Take some time. Search your heart. Will you open to her?

If this does not resonate for you, or if it is not the right time, simply observe and be moved by whatever experience unfolds in the next few moments.

If it is right for you to receive the transmission of this evolved form you have come to know as "Catherine," consent to her. Open to her gifts whether seen, heard, felt, sensed, or experienced in other ways. Take your time. Catherine may open you to: ancient dreaming arts, nurturance, the interior life, nature's power, transforming strategies for institutions and communities, forgotten healing ways, or any variety of things. Relax with what occurs and however this unfolds, safely from your indestructible body of light. At any time during this experience you may be drawn to merge, become one, with this light-filled consciousness representing the creative force of the feminine. Catherine's gifts awaken us to compassion and higher knowing.

Journey note suggestion for facilitators: Play gentle, inspiring music now for ten or more minutes. We use Dakshina by Deva Premal, in this instance.

Give ample time.
When resuming the guided journey, begin soft drumming again and slowly lower, then stop the music.

Allow your time with the conscious sphere of light known as "Catherine," to gently come to a close. Feel yourself as a vehicle of pure light. Look out from this luminous vantage to Catherine. Take the next few moments to close this experience in whatever way feels right to you. There may be final things to say, feel, or insights to share.

Take a short pause for this experience.
When you feel complete, take the next moment to express your gratitude and to feel the power, energy and wisdom you carry for future generations.

Again, take a moment to pause.
When the time is right gently lift high into the atmosphere. The scenes of the village life of Salem, Massachusetts in the late 1600's grow dim as you float away. The balls of light which hovered near you embark on their own journey. Floating higher and higher into fathomless space, your luminous space vehicle as your own body of light, travels back. Feel the sensations. Listen

to the sounds. Note what you see. You are being called back, guided by your clear intentions and spirit allies to the present time to your *Sacred Place*. Open to your experience.

You may propel through cosmic wormholes or simply sense the wheel of time spin quickly forward. You may sense land masses or qualities of times you pass through. When you arrive, float above the building or place on the earth where you began your journey. Now, slowly drift to the earth, back into this body, time and space.

Anchor into your *Sacred Place*. Take some deep, refreshing breaths. Breathe in sacredness, and healing. Then, breathe these qualities out. Fully return to your body and to this time and space. Wiggle your toes and fingers and do some gentle stretching. Take all the time you need and when ready, you can open your eyes. Slowly come to a seated position.

When performing this journey in a group, invite members to connect with another person following the experience. Ideal is for people to crawl from where they sit over to someone else. This childlike gesture is grounding and synchronizing after an involved journey. Sharing non-verbally is preferred for the first transitional moments; people can simply sit together, hold hands, or hug. Partners can converse if they desire, however, heart-centered and embodied sharing is essential. Invite people to stay with their experience and not move to a "heady" place.

If doing the above journey alone, do also take time to crawl around on the floor and drink some water. Take gentle time in nature or go for a walk to integrate what you saw and felt. Come fully back into this reality.

Remember your feelings as the journey unfolded. What was this like? What came up for you?

Feel the gifts Catherine has opened for you. How do these affect you? What is their intent and how is this related to your *Higher Purpose* in life?

When you have taken some time and space to fully assimilate back into physical reality, it can help to write down, or concretely express, this journey's insights. Create your own questions for reflection; ponder and integrate this journey in what way you choose.

To assimilate your experience of connecting with the conscious ball of light, note how you feel. How *do* you feel? What do your heart and body say?

When the time is right, after reflecting, consider how you might bring these insights into day-to-day life. How can they benefit everyday circumstance personally and on a societal level? What actions can you take to honor your experience? Consider how you might integrate these. Whether man or woman, how will you access, and express, your own *Deep Feminine* creative power?

Take a walk, engage invigorating movement, or spend time in nature before moving on to the next experience.

Balance Male with Female

It is important to consider that although the above journey depicts the life of a woman, Catherine has also lived as men; she has expressed her essence through both male and female bodies. Chapter Six introduced this essence self; our luminous aspect beyond time and space which is immortal and indestructible. Essence is beyond concept, including gender. Whether we are a woman or a man and, regardless of our sexual persuasions, our core is undifferentiated and whole. We each are boundless, eternal. At the same time, the dance of polarity such as: light and dark, material and spiritual, male and female, weaves the fabric of relative life. This is expressed by the Chinese *Yin Yang*, the East Indian and Tibetan *Figure Eight* and other universal symbols for infinity.

Across history and cultures female and male archetypes are the main props for this life play. This synergy is found in the internal anatomy of the hemispheres of our brain. Tibetan Buddhism and Hindu yogic traditions likewise teach that our energy anatomy includes subtle conduits that channel both female and male forces. In addition to inner, spiritual realities, original peoples have, for centuries, also charted the gender characteristics of the outer, physical world. A good example is a ring of volcanoes encircling a vortex valley high in the Andean mountains. The "male" volcano is revered as a transformative force. Shamans *Shapeshift* into his power through fire-blowing practices invoked during curative rituals. Quechua people I have worked with believe this volcanic male is wedded to a snow-faced summit, a "woman" peak, whose restorative qualities are feminine. Other crest, spring, lake, waterfall and cave personas form a sacred web-work with the volcanoes of this valley, topped by a mystical apex to the North. Quechua lore says this silent, Northern ridge is lover to the others; the husband as well as his wife. We can imagine this mistress of the North to symbolize the primal feminine ground through which male and female come together.

Given the obvious and inherent interplay of female and male, it is fair to presume that "Manly Ways" are not for men alone and that "Womanly Ways" are not for women alone. This is especially visible in original cultures. As a case in point, North American and European women and men are struck by the sculpted bodies of Shuar men. Strenuous navigation of hand dug canoes on rain swollen rivers, animal hunts using spears, and the abundant rigorous activity rainforest living requires, makes strong physiques. Westerners see Shuar men as "quintessential male", yet, their feminine side is also apparent. Attuned to plants, children, animals, the spiritual and living world around them, these men who can kill with their bare hands are tender guides on excursions. I have experienced a similar mix of qualities in the indigenous men in Panama, India, Siberia, Guatemala, North America, Tibet, and in the Andes.

Equally, as it is common for both sexes in indigenous groups to comfortably display what is viewed as feminine as well as masculine traits, the women I know in shamanic-based cultures are as fierce and forceful as they are nurturing. My shaman woman healer, Anga, in Siberia, was soft-spoken and compassionate yet her "massage" was as brutal as it was effective. What I describe as "torturous, yet expedient" body work is common in Siberia and Tuva and Shamankas (female shamans) employ it with great success. As another instance, gentle as they appear, Shuar women are fearless protectors should a wayward poisonous snake or a wild boar find its way into the longhouse. They are also known to growl like panthers at husbands who inadvertently kill more animals than the family requires, or cut more trees than their longhouses demand.

The woman knows her family nest is interdependent to the larger nest of nature, so she subdues the over-industrious provider. This regulating voice, all but lost in modern women and men, is necessary for human survival and reflects clarity about the place of humans in life's circle.

Step into the Sacred Circle

Awareness of place in the larger circle of life is expressed through basic aspects of aboriginal life, such as in how women, men, and children walk. Whether living in Mongolia, the Amazon Basin, high in the Andean peaks, in the Australian Outback, or on the plains of the United States, native people "walk softly" on their Earth Mother in relationship with everything around them. In this way, they express reverence, connection and receive the energy of the earth which is nourishing. John and I teach this walk in seminars (ie: *Aimlessly Wander* and *Walk Like a Shuar*) and Mick Dodge gives in-depth instruction in his *Earth Gym* trainings. The ball of the, preferably bare, foot touches the ground first as opposed to the dominating heal-pounding approach. Through this gentler walk we are receptive and any good reflexology practitioner will attest to the benefit of stimulating the thousands of nerve receptors in the feet through "bare-footing". Natural materials protect the feet in colder climates; Tuvans and Siberian shamans even design yak fur boots with upturned toes to remind them to walk softly upon their mother, the earth. Try bare-footing, the soft walk, and not only will you feel great and gain a better outlook on life, you will sense your rightful place on this living planet.

Since ancient times, indigenous people have espoused intimacy with the earth for individual and communal well being. Antiquated wisdom and modern science meet in revolutionary books such as, *Earthing*, which poses that reconnecting with the power and energy of the earth offers significant health benefits for humans.

In addition to making us healthy, gaining energy from the earth can also shift us out of an overly material and self serving focus. As a simplistic illustration, for several months I was finding feathers everywhere. Whether walking in the forest or stepping out of my car in a parking lot, feathers routinely appeared. These delightful gifts renewed my respect and curiosity for the world's winged creatures. Some of the feathers came home with me and I prayed over those left behind. I took this bit of magic in stride, appreciating the message while not investing in always having to find a feather. Despite this seemingly enlightened attitude feathers finally beguiled me. One day while hiking, I *wanted* feathers. Recognizing the folly of this did not deter me. I did find a small, battered owl feather an hour into my hike. Then, mile after mile, I found nothing. My distress was shameful. In coming upon a grove of evergreens on a ridge I gave up on finding feathers and took off my shoes and socks, fluffed up my coat for a pillow, and lay down on the sun-warmed pine needles for a nap.

I awoke refreshed and ready to continue hiking. My bare feet felt so good that despite the now chilling weather, I walked barefoot. My soles soaked in the coolness of the mud. Each step was so sensual that I slowed to a crawl in order to savor every moment. I entered a relaxed, hypnotic state. After about forty-five minutes I sensed an invitation to step off the path, yet held back for fear of hurting the fragile alpine terrain. But the urge was so pure it seemed to come from the land itself. I gingerly stepped onto the alpine grasses. The softness of the natural landscape against my bare soles was ecstatic. How could so simple an act bring such bliss? Recalling my feather desperation, I laughed out loud. I did not need to keep finding feathers; I merely needed to be fully present. Mystery evades us when we try to grasp it. In that moment, I could not want for more. Oneness with the earth is humbling, and it fills us.

Inseparable from our gain or benefit from the earth is that we must respect this mother. All original people I know ask permission, show gratitude and offer back to the natural world. Circles initiated by humans were traditionally enacted with integrity. Relationship to the living world is direct and honoring whether done by a Siberian Shor wild-crafting mushrooms and pine nuts, or a Tuvan skillfully incising a ram's chest, reaching in with a hand, and stopping its beating heart. In the traditional Tuvan sacrifices that I have seen animals suffer minimally and are prayed over. Every part of plant or animal is used and appreciated. Offerings are made to the being and to the earth. Compare this with picking up fast food and eating it mindlessly in the car, or buying plastic-wrapped slabs of meat labeled "chicken", whose feet never touched the earth.

Do we honor our circles? Do we complete our relationships? Are we awake to our impact on life? Let us renew our relationship to our physical body, the food that sustains us, the children we bring into this world and to our communities which include the larger circle of plants and animals we share each breath with. Animals suffer because of all sorts of human addictions including vanity, food, sport, and human pollution. Prisons overflow and developed countries consume most of the world's natural resources. Life is begging us to move into higher relationship.

To take our proper place in the scheme of sentient life, we bring the masculine and feminine into balance. When we step into the sacred circle, its mystery unfolds.

Balance Male with Female in Society

If you are confused about your place in the circular flow of life, explore what feels lost or forgotten. What is missing? What do your heart and body say? You may want to investigate what makes you feel whole and fundamentally good, versus what makes you feel fragmented or incomplete. It can help to identify how the masculine and feminine archetypes, however you view these, play out each day.

Look at your home and other physical environments, at mealtimes and social interactions, at business transactions and your decision making methods and any other daily activity. Ask yourself some fundamental questions: Amidst the busyness, is there space to dream and feel? Is there room to play? Is "being" of equal value to "doing"? Are friendships and relationships fulfilling? Is my heart and creativity in my work? Am I connected to, and do I protect, nature? Is my breath deep and full, how do I regard my home and my body? Do I move in fluid, or rigid, ways? Do I cultivate and trust intuition? What care do I bring to others? Do the institutions I support and the activities I engage embody feminine principles? Do they nurture people and honor the earth? Are the feminine aspects of life alive?

Given the above insights, and the examples offered throughout this book, consider what you desire to shift about yourself and the flow and feel of each day. Identify actions as well as attitudes. Consider, also, what you would like to shift about the institutions and communities you engage. Further, what actions can you take to support these changes in yourself, in the environment and in your community?

It is a mistake to sacrifice any moment to frantic modern pace, consumerism, or even global tragedy. Fear and pessimism mount whenever we obsess over the news on television or in the newspapers. Yet, fear dulls our instincts about what is true and suppresses the creative powers of imagination. Thus, fear can be used as a strategic tool to manipulate the masses. The answer is not to deny the world's pain, but to channel our emotions to generate more goodness. Despite the day's turmoil and busyness, we all need to breathe, eat, rest, and manage the energy of each moment. Grounding in the basic rhythms of the day is a feminine wisdom that keeps us caring and connected as we sail the turbulent seas of change. Then we can dream, act effectively, and inspire others. The well being of the earth's and our own future depends on our ability to do this.

In compromising the feminine we have stepped out of the *Sacred Circle of Life.* Yet, many ask "Why, given the success of the Women's Movement is the feminine of modern culture ailing?" Although the Women's Movement has empowered women beyond typecast roles many women still feel measured by male yardsticks. Our men express feeling equally stressed and we still raise boys to conquer. The poignant line, "The girls go to school and the boys go to jail" from the Clint Eastwood movie, *Gran Torino,* speaks to just one example of such societal gaps: that of low-income, urban boys. It is tragic for a woman to sacrifice who she is in order to climb the corporate ladder. Equally awful is a · boy who is destined to be a gang member or a workaholic. These losses devastate individuals and they ruin our communities.

The time is ripe to embrace the feminine and we must revere nature if we are to survive. As one solution, modern initiation rites and Vision Quests offer healthier models for young adults. Those designed for boys channel inborn warrior instincts to benefit the family, community and natural environment. A wonderful case in study for bringing this into the mainstream is a colleague who transformed an East Coast boxing gym into an ethnically diverse center for youth at risk. Vincent Santo Ferrau helped distressed young men divert potentially violent tendencies through rigorous boxing training. Beyond this, Vincent brought into his curricula counseling services, poetry events, job searches, and cultural outings. Later, in adding shamanism and martial arts, the youth melded physical prowess with mental and spiritual powers which also honored nature. By blending masculine and feminine strengths, the highly respected program transformed troubled, urban boys into integrated young men. Vincent went on to instate similar projects in New Mexico, achieving a 100% success rate *Shapeshifting* directionless youth into viable members of society.

Two well-known social change movements that likewise integrate the feminine with masculine are Majora Carter's *Green the Ghettos* and Jane Goodall's *Roots and Shoots* programs. *Roots and Shoots*, in one hundred and sixteen countries around the globe, mimics nature's ability to network and create foundations through its root systems, at the same time sending up life shoots against all odds. With a solid foundation in the earth, fragile plant shoots can even make their way through brick walls if they have to, in order to reach light. *Roots and Shoots* youth create positive change through diverse projects and bring people together over a common cause. Similarly, Majora Carter renews the hope of inhabitants of New York City's South Bronx, Carter's childhood home. *Green the Ghettos* addresses environmental and economic inequity, setting examples for other urban centers through on-the-ground activism.

The feminine is a force that must rouse in men as well as women. This will ensure that all of the earth's children are nurtured. *Higher Consciousness* is about marrying heart with intellect and balancing the woman and man within. In doing so, the eagle and condor will fly together and we humans will step rightfully into life's sacred circle.

The above examples demonstrate concrete measures for mainstreaming more whole expressions of humanity. There are also subtle applications for the *Deep Feminine* principles which can help us heal and become more aware. We explore these next.

Cultivate Awareness

Of many ways to perceive that are resonant with what we term the *Deep Feminine*, John and I learned the following strategy from a Maya teacher when leading a group with the Prophet's Conference. The slender man who was our guide exuded a gentle air and when he spoke his eyes smiled. In his characteristically affable manner Mario asked us to walk for fifteen minutes amidst the ancient ruins focusing on the "modern" aspects of our surroundings: the people, the directional signs, the gates and reconstructed pathways, the sounds of airplanes and other noises such as humans talking, the clothing and watches visitors wore, etc. Then, for the next fifteen minutes we were to stroll while concentrating on the antiquated and natural aspects of the site: the pyramids, the sight and sound of the howler monkeys, the eyes of people, the trees and sky, the mounds of land indicating hidden structures, and so on. The effect was powerful. The concealed world came alive. A dual perception was achieved which firmly rooted us in the present yet, which, sharpened our acuity of the normally undetectable.

The practice our insightful friend, Mario, employed to open seekers to subtle energies at ancient Maya sites can be applied anywhere, even in cities. As challenging as it may seem, anyone can develop simultaneous perception and urban areas offer an ideal environment for this practice. On your own walk, begin by noting what is contemporary: the people and their clothing, the objects such as cars and street lights and buildings, the mechanical sounds, etc. Then, on the next fifteen minutes of your stroll shift your attention to the timeless, the antiquated and the natural. Note the plants and sky, the eyes and emotional quality you sense of those who pass you by, watch the birds and the squirrels in the trees and listen to their sounds, observe the old buildings amidst the modern cityscape, etc. Focus on what propels you back through time and connects you with richer details of the human and natural world while, for a time, ignoring contemporary or surface traits. Even when with a group or inside a building, you can note the obvious then shift attention to the subtle. In doing so, you will pick up on feelings, energies and nuances routinely filtered from awareness.

This orientation sharpens intuition and grounds us to consciously interact with the world. We open to the spaces in between objects, things, thoughts and habit to the many worlds that coexist with our own. In touching the expanded field of energy that comprises our reality, shamans can detect the "energy history" of locations, the emotional tone of persons or animals passed on, or of the lands and waters, as well as engage the spirits of locations, non-visible helpers and the elements. Each place, item, person and environment has an energy we can tap into. Imperceptible from common view, these are readily discerned through shamanic tracking, as in the exercise above.

Attuning to the subtleties makes us receptive so we can participate more fully with life and also understand how the invisible impacts us and our societies. Many life forms exist beyond our own and every action, emotion, and thought leaves an energetic imprint that we can pick up on and may also be affected by. For these reasons, shamanic peoples enact rituals to impact the energy of those passed on, of land, objects, and turbulent or otherwise significant events. Through spiritual means they may be guided to draw upon for guidance, enhance the well being of, or even exorcise, unseen influences.

Highlighting the relevance of the non-visible is the story of a group who visited a shrine containing their teacher's relics. The small group of followers walked directly to the sanctified building soon after arriving at the isolated retreat center, at which time one person with no history of epilepsy had a seizure. Though stunned, the person recovered with no recurrence and the seizure was considered a fluke. In later visiting this retreat center myself, I was struck by the shrine's spiritual interaction with the surrounding mountain peaks which created a commanding vortex of energy. That the small entourage walked straight to the relic building indicated that the group was obviously unaware of this. Otherwise, they would have connected first with the land and honored the larger circle of relationships. This would also have helped them acclimate to its energy. I cannot say whether or not this person's seizure was induced by these intensified energies. But it is always wise to enter sacred sites respectfully and with awareness of the larger circle of beings who reside there.

Holding deeper attention is all it takes to illumine what is invisible. Then we must properly greet these presences and ask their permission in order to understand how to relate to them. The exercise above and those in Chapter Four offer great ways to do this. Second nature to indigenous people, even those who are spiritually oriented can miss the subtleties. Yet, in doing so, we tap only a fraction of what is happening, not only at sites of power, but in daily life.

Heal with the Deep Feminine

The journey of Catherine's life, death, and the transmission of her *Higher Purpose* is riveting for workshop participants. The wounds and profound wisdom of women across the planet, as well as throughout history, reverberate within each of us - man and woman alike - and the feminine is persecuted to this day. In the *Journey to Catherine*, Catherine cloaked her deeper knowing to avoid peril. There are many methods and reasons to engage the subtle yet these wisdom ways remain dormant as long as mystery and magic are denied. In retrieving the *Deep Feminine*, we arouse innate healing forces that positively impact the visible and unseen worlds.

Demonstrating this are the countless miracles I encounter when applying feminine principles such as those practices that are found throughout this book. Not uncommon are physical, psychological and/or spiritual *Shapeshifts*, or for people to arrive at workshops with injuries who later return home to their doctors healed. A recent example is the story of a man who attended a week-long *Shapeshifting* workshop. He practiced techniques he had learned at the workshop and he had a miraculous experience. His doctor, who had no explanation for the man's rapid recovery from debilitating pain, postponed the surgery scheduled for his condition. Months later, the pain still had not returned. This is just one of many stories.

Being physically present at workshops is not required. Of those whose names placed on the altar in the center of the circle of participants, many benefit just as routinely. Infections and sprains have eased, Intensive Care Unit patients have stabilized, addictions and chronic pain has disappeared, and malignant tumors have *Shapeshifted* into benign masses. Some people claim to know the exact moments these *Shapeshifts* occur. They describe with certainty that positive change has occurred, which is later medically confirmed.

No one can predict or explain such occurrences and no one is credited for them as "miracles" are part of the natural mystery of our human legacy. We only know that in applying feminine strategies amazing things can, and often do, happen.

I hear similarly from friends and colleagues. Driven by her love for a sibling, one woman spontaneously produced twice as many stem cells as considered normal for her brother's transplant. Increasing numbers of physicians report abiding by feminine principles, some strategically employ the body's inborn ability to heal. One such pioneer, an acquaintance now deceased, did so primarily by supporting the body's natural defense through fever. This man lost no patients to a deadly flu that swept through North America in the early 1900's.

The deep woman instinct, of men and women, knows that reality is mutable and that love can *Shapeshift* energy and form. The Tibetan Buddhist practice below is resonant with such perspectives. It helps us become less self absorbed so we can hold genuine empathy for others and the environment. By embracing each moment unconditionally we can open to the world's suffering, and even to our own pain, without resistance. Then, in accessing our deep reserve of goodness we can extend well being, compassion, love, and healing to any being or circumstance.

Transmute Suffering ~ Sending and Taking

Tong Len Tibetan Buddhist Meditation
In traditional Buddhist teachings this practice is grounded in a mindfulness-awareness discipline. As workshop participants often do not have formal training in meditation, we prepare them with the *Breathe Presence and Light* and other exercises in Chapter Two that help us to be present with a relaxed mind. It is important to establish a foundation of awareness before attempting the practice

Transmute Suffering.
After reading the description below, if it for any reason does not resonate, trust your impulse not to do it and move on to the next section.

It is always good to stretch and shake out tension in your body before settling into any practice. After this, you can sit comfortably in a room or outside space where you will not be disturbed. Take a few deep, refreshing breaths allowing your body to completely relax. Invite peace and calmness to pervade your mind. If this does not occur, or if you feel agitated, simply breathe with that. Then devote ten to fifteen minutes to the light breathing approach from Chapter Two, which should by now be familiar to you. When you feel complete with the practice, bring it to a close as instructed. Then you are ready to begin the Tong Len practice, yet read through each step thoroughly before enacting the practice.

Feel the Universal Life Force, radiant primordial light, completely fill and surround you. Sense the indestructible quality of this light and its loving intention. Take time to open your heart and immerse in these sensations. This light is you. Make this real.

Now, remember a time in your childhood, or in the recent past, when you experienced great love and happiness. See this time as clearly as you can. In your mind's eye, look carefully and closely at its details. Where were you? Who were you with? What were the circumstances? Look with curiosity to this time when you experienced great joy and a deep sense of well being.

As you look at the details of this happy and loving time, allow the sensations of love, happiness, and goodness to flood your body. Feel these as if this time were happening for you right now, make it real. In particular, allow the feelings of love, peace and connection to permeate your heart.

As this peaceful and radiantly happy time generates loving feelings in your heart now, allow these feelings to build. Intend for them to grow stronger. As you do this, focus on the feelings exclusively; allow the details of the situation to fade from view, yet stay with how you feel. Take some time until you feel the love, joy, and well-being as a force that radiates from your heart.

These are good feelings that you have generated and strengthened. Feel the peace, love, joy and connection that pervade your heart. At the same time now, imagine (or see in your mind's eye or, sense), someone sitting six feet in front of you who is suffering.

Alternately, instead of one other person who is suffering, you can imagine yourself in this place. We all experience pain, fear, and confusion. Or, you envision animals of an endangered species, natural disaster victims, an area on earth that is environmentally degraded, or a world location where life is filled with anguish. Another option is to imagine in front of you one whom you consider to be an "enemy" or that you have difficult relations with. Take time to see, or sense these people and situations clearly. At the same time keep feeling the sensations of your radiant and loving heart.

As you notice who is in front of you, imagine the energy of suffering gather around this person or situation in a thick mass. Suffering manifests on many levels: physical, emotional and psychological, and spiritual, and in energetic form you may sense that it is hot in temperature, it may appear heavy and weighted, or it may have a claustrophobic quality. You may even sense this energy as a tarry substance with a specific shape or see it hang about the person or situation like an ominous cloud or a dense smoke.

As you clearly sense or see this, keep coming back to your open and radiant heart. Stay rooted in goodness, healing and love. Feel compassion for the confusion and suffering of yourself, another, or situation. You may some sadness and the growing desire to extend kindness and care.

On the next inhalation, breathe toward you this thick, claustrophobic energy. Lighten suffering by breathing the heavy mass of energy toward you. Open and feel your radiant, loving core and your heart, as you do. Remember your loving intention and the indestructible quality of light, filling and enveloping you. When the mass touches this light and love that is you, it immediately transmutes into light with no trace or heaviness remaining.

(Traditional practice of *Tong Len*, under the guidance of a Buddhist teacher, instructs the practitioner to bring suffering into her or his body and heart and to transmute it from within the practitioner.)

On the very next exhalation, expel with your breath, goodness, healing and well-being. Propel the qualities of care, kindness and love with the out breath all the way back to whomever or whatever sits in front of you. Sense confusion and pain lifting. Imagine the suffering is lightening and easing.

Repeat numbers 7 and 8 for ten minutes or for a shorter period of time. To close the practice, simply relax the focus and let the visualization completely dissolve. Come back to a normal rhythm of breathing.

With regular practice, the steps to *Transmute Suffering* become second nature and can be done on the spot; breathe pain toward you, transmute it, then breathe out loving kindness, relief and healing. For example, you might apply this at the scene of an accident on a busy street corner, or to transmute your own difficult emotions.

The more we acknowledge, instead of back away from, what distresses and pains us, the greater is our ability to transform our own, and the suffering of another. The practice of *Tong Len* helps cultivate empathy and resilience by "holding suffering in a non-judgmental state of mind" as my daughter, Sayre Herrick, writes in her third year college essay entitled *Regenerative Breath and Soulful Healing*. Sayre continues, "The practice strengthens the meditator's capacity for acceptance, non-judgment, and transmutation of suffering. Tonglen practice breaks the ingrained habit of pain avoidance. It is a profound way of using breath and intention to transform suffering and encourage selflessness and compassion." It also positively impacts the object of our compassion: who or what we direct our love and energy to.

Closing Note to Chapter Seven

Through the last century and beyond, dominant cultural mindsets have suppressed feminine values. Earth-honoring ways were pushed aside and ancestral peoples, their lands, and their wisdom, were sacrificed to superficial and material goals. Yet, the *Deep Feminine* inspires us now to awaken. In acknowledging the feminine we can bring our lives, and the global climate, back into balance. In living in harmony with the earth, revering the mystery and creative forces of life, and of our feelings, we step back into the *Sacred Circle*.

To support a sustainable future in which people live in

greater harmony with each other, and for the earth to be healthy, we must arouse our deepest longings for life. Let us, firstly, dream good dreams for humans and for all sentient beings. Then, let us act on our heartfelt wishes to ignite the universe's intelligence within and make the world we dream of become real. The concluding chapter, *Shapeshifting into a New World*, encourages ways that we can do this.

"Our life is composed greatly from dreams, from the unconscious, and they must be brought into connection with action. They must be woven together." - Anais Nin

CHAPTER 8

SHAPESHIFTING INTO A NEW WORLD

The approaches presented throughout this book are based on the timeless wisdom of our ancestors. In essence, they include: being embodied and expansive, respecting every living thing, relating consciously with the earth and the cosmos, engaging transforming forces to remember and empower highest human potential, and expressing our essential nature for the good of all life. In being fully present, we can heed the signs of our times and walk the *Shapeshifter's* path through change. As we remember our world as sacred, new road maps for life on Planet Earth will be revealed. A vital step in this direction is to transform our individual and collective dreams.

Shift the Dream, Change Reality
Indigenous shamanic individuals, as well as their communities, interpret nocturnal dreams and take their meaning to heart. Shamans also regard the signs and omens of daily life because each action has impact and everything is in relationship. John tells the story of Shuar members calling a late night meeting to discuss the message of a wilted plant found by a trail. The tribe decided to close the forest path. Plants offer themselves as spiritual allies, medicine, food, and they also share the living bionetwork with humans. A sick plant may indicate that a path is overused, so keeping it open would serve neither the rainforest nor the people who live there. Unnoticed, more plants

could deteriorate and potentially hurt the animals, waters and humans living in that area. Consequence to the tribe is direct as people depend on the jungle's resources for food and shelter. Humble regard for one plant shows non-hierarchical respect and it also acknowledges the interdependence of humans with the living world.

As a hypothetical contrast, a modern community might not notice a feeble plant. If it does, or if many plants ail, pesticides might be applied which harms the animals, waters, and ultimately, the people living near the trail. The path might be widened into a road or gravel may be laid, without regard for the life and spirits inhabiting the area. There may be no thought to the displacement of wildlife or the systemic implication of unhealthy plants.

To listen, and respond, to nature is necessary for humans to survive; the warning signs are clear. Yet, we believe (dream) that we are separate from the living world. This supports a dominating stance which threatens our existence. An example is Tikal, Guatemala. Each year when John and I facilitate expeditions to Tikal we focus our work at complexes dating back to 800 BC. We also do ceremony at the Gran Plaza, built from a different mindset than the earlier structures. I am awed by the prominent temples of the Gran Plaza. The massive stone pyramids, "Mask" and "Jaguar", that face one another across a broad expanse of grass, are daunting and magnificent. Just as the three major pyramids of Egypt mirror the stars of Orion's Belt, these, and other pyramids in Tikal, align with the Pleiades. Mayan guides also tell us that these tombs (Mask and Jaguar), erected for royalty around 734 AD, were built on the backs of slaves. Although today teeming with plant and animal life as the now heavily forested region was in its original state, during the time of the Classic Maya the land was stripped of trees to fashion the grandiose scheme. The pyramids of the Gran Plaza are an amazing testament to what humans are capable of, yet, what if we channeled this brilliance in a different way? Despite its splendor, the complex harmed people and nature. Its ultimate abandonment is no surprise.

The same dreams of dominion which annihilated thriving nations of the past drive current humans into crisis. Just as we do not see the wind, but can see its designs as it flutters the leaves of a tree, destructive attitudes are invisible. Yet, their effect is as evident now as in eras gone by. Contemporary beliefs propelling nature's abuse may include: "The wild world is frightening and dangerous. Animals exist for humans to exploit.", and "As people are at the top of the evolutionary ladder, as well as the food chain, they should shape the planet according to whim and need." In apprenticeship programs John and I facilitate journeys for people to examine such personal, familial and collective beliefs. Participants scrutinize unconscious fears and separation then, exorcise these through ancient ceremonials (banish spirits and thought forms from the energy field that do not serve the higher good). This is one way to *Shapeshift* "negative" into "positive" energy that fuels life honoring outlooks and behaviors.

Which attitudes about nature were you brought up to believe? Or, what other perspectives shaped you? Imagine where these ideas came from; why do you think they came about? How do these dreams, perhaps largely unrecognized, affect you? How have they influenced the way you live? What is their societal impact? Similarly, what paradigms separate us from, and, promote suffering for, children and people around the world?

Such exploring makes conscious the insidious ideas we live by. Just as body type determines what we look like clothed, life takes on the appearance of our values. Attitude and observable reality are so closely linked that our health, wounding, outlooks and beliefs can be read in our bodies. We shuffle when sad, when excited we skip. These are crude examples of an articulate physiology that acts out every nuance of our psyche and - through eye movements, gestures, facial expressions, posture, gait, voice inflection, and so forth - tells the world what sentiments and ideals we live by.

In the same manner, we can read the interior mechanisms of families and societies by looking at familial and social structures. Bhutan, a small democratic country in South Asia, exemplifies a nation that understands the power of conscious values. Historically, Bhutan was strongly influenced by Tibetan Buddhism as evidenced by temples and monasteries built in the eighth and later centuries. Loosely joined by warring clans until the 1600's, it was unified and renewed by an enlightened Tibetan military leader. After he died, Bhutan fell under British, then Indian, influence. Buddhist ideology and traditions guide its existing leader and King, Jigme Khesar Namgyel Wangchuck, who fulfills his ancestors' dreams of promoting compassion, prosperity and peace for Bhutanese people. The nation of Bhutan is molding itself according to higher ethics. Other countries commit similarly. Two examples are Sweden, which vows to promote socially responsible business and sustainability, and Ecuador which has became the first country to include the inalienable rights of nature within its constitution. The latter transpired in 2008, the same year that Bhutan transitioned from being a monarchy to a parliamentary democracy.

Whether transforming person or nation, we can begin by shifting the agendas that shape them. To foster people living in harmony with the natural environment we may adopt dreams such as: "The natural world is welcoming and intelligent," "Wildlife deserves our respect," "Appreciation and curiosity open us to co-creative possibilities with plant, mineral and animal species," "Humans, as is true of all other life forms on earth, are designed to live in accord with the natural world."

Try on the above attitudes and behaviors as if they are true; act in ways that make them real. How does it feel to give these dreams substance? Is there also a tangible effect? What do you think could happen if you energized such outlooks over time? What might result if you inspired others to do the same?

We can dream consciously and transform the world. The following segments help us to dream, and act on, the world of our innermost longings.

Dream it Possible, Make it True

In introducing the journey below this section I invite people to imagine a world that reflects their highest dreams for life on earth. As adults, we often shy away from exploring our deeper desires. Participants sometimes say, "I can't dream of the life I'd love because isn't possible." Or, "I feel foolish and afraid I'll dream something absurd and unpractical." Many of us have, from a young age, been conditioned to suppress our longings or been told to keep them to ourselves. Sometimes people fear getting lost in illusions that will only make them feel good; what if they forget, or give up on, the real work that needs to be done in the world?

We must be realistic and keep our feet on the ground in order to help those we serve and love. Yet, as we face the challenge and uncertainty of these times, we, and those we care for, will only benefit as we open our hearts and let our imaginations soar. Just as the creative projects of children, artists, writers, musicians, and similarly inventive people are often spawned by dreams, our musings can inspire a new world.

The power of dreaming was emphasized for me many years ago by a brilliant teacher who had completed a six-year mediation retreat. I was happy to see this man on a brief visit back to the United States to put his worldly affairs in order before re-entering retreat; this time for life. My mentor looked radiant. His soft blue eyes sparkled like sunlight dappling the ocean's surface. During our moments together I asked how it felt to be leaving everything he knew behind. I will never forget what my teacher, now a Lama, said: "It was one day suggested to me that I would be better off living by myself in a cave. The person who told me this was extremely frustrated by my isolative tendencies." The white haired man cracked an impish smile, "I was struck by how much that idea appealed to me! This dream was within me, but I hadn't recognized it." My friend concluded, "Llyn, wishes are everything. The deep wishes of our childhood, those we may not even remember or identify as wishes, can unfold our destiny if we give them credence. Our heartfelt longings hold untold power."

As with my mentor, the realm of dreams and wishes may at first feel foreign, yet, we can reclaim them. With a little coaxing people relax and agree that embracing our heartfelt desires makes a better reality possible. Dreaming can restore morale and optimism. It helps us to be flexible thinkers not stuck in habit or fixed ideas of how things must or "will always" be. Because opening to our imagination ignites our passion and invites our inner genius to come out and play, we can uncover fresh solutions to problems and glimpse previously unconsidered possibilities for living. Once we uncover our deep longings for life, acting on them is like aiming an arrow in a bow and releasing it toward a desired target. A spiritual archer's feet are firmly planted on the earth. The spread bow is like an open heart. The breadth of bow and the archer's arms, as well as crown of the head, align heart and mind with the heavens. Relationship with body, earth and space is intuitive, precise. Aim and vision are guided by this alchemy which ripens in the heart. The arrow releases when heart and goal are one.

In the same way, in giving our wishes energy we open to a synergistic relationship with others, nature, and the universe. Made conscious, our wishes and longings are like magnets that attract resources, people and auspicious events to support them. In acting upon and experiencing tangible results from our actions, we can shift limiting belief and lifestyles. Spiritual manifestation technologies, such as those in books and movies like *The Secret*, work because they apply these same shamanistic and metaphysical principles. Many fashionable personal growth approaches are ego-driven, yet they understand that consciously directing energy encourages what we desire. To strengthen our intention we reflect with deep feeling; then relax and let the arrow fly. Feelings are like cosmic fuel. The more impassioned our wish, the more power is generated. Think back to when you accomplished something that did not at first seem doable. Was there a critical moment when you almost gave up but, instead, kept going and met your goal? What characterized this change, how did you feel in those moments? We have all heard of people saving loved ones by moving a fallen tree deemed impossible for a person to budge; of a mother exerting equally inhuman strength to rescue her child pinned under a two and a half ton car; or of those walking with bare feet over glass or on 1,000 degree coals in ancient fire walking rituals. These are dramatic examples of how we can transcend fear, and focus the human will, to make what is otherwise impossible within reach. They show us that the dream is pliable and we can change it.

Energy is ultimately neither good nor bad and we all strategically, as well as unconsciously, influence reality. Cultures or individuals largely ignorant of the power of thoughts, feelings, and dreams, propagate imbalance. The same is true of those who adopt goals that are short-sighted and self-serving. If we shine the light of consciousness on acquiring four million dollar mansions, or building opulent pyramids based on worship, these we will manifest. Similarly, if we focus on sacredness, these intentions are magnified and manifested. Instead of using our inborn talents to bolster our ego or to yield windfall profits at nature's or at another's expense, why not direct them to benefit all of life? The following journey helps us use our dreaming powers to do this.

Prepare to Dream

The journey experience below helps us retrieve our deepest longings and honor them through action. I have introduced it to shamanic practitioners as well as to social and environmental activists who know nothing about shamanism. Whether with ten or two hundred people of any background or age, or doing this exercise alone, there is no better time to revive our highest hopes for life on Planet Earth. After reclaiming our dreams we then must fearlessly act on our heartfelt wishes.

Choose an indoor or outdoor location where you will not be disturbed. If inside, lie down on a soft, carpeted floor or mat, or sit on a cushion or chair. Lie, or sit, where appropriate if out of doors. If working with a group, people should not be in physical contact with other journeyers. Have *Physical Huacas* or small sacred items on hand or nearby, if desired.

Go to your *Sacred Place* and invoke the presence of, or *Shapeshift* into, *Spirit Huacas* and/or your essence, as you are guided. Hold *Physical Huacas*, place them on your body, or rest them near you.

If introducing this experience to new journeyers, help them to relax. Using the suggestions offered throughout this text create a peaceful environment and induce a restful state.

The following guided visualization is helpful for those who have not established a *Sacred Place*. It is also a good preliminary step for anyone doing this journey. In connecting with the earth we invite dreams that support her, and are guided by her intelligence; we open to the earth's deep dreaming. (Consider exploring this further at another time by taking a journey to merge with the earth's consciousness. Look at this dream called life from her view.) In integrating our bodies with the earth we become present and energized so we can effectively manifest in the material world. Breathing with the cosmos takes us beyond personal and collective identity to essence, and what some term, *Universal Consciousness*. This way we merge with our expanded self so the creative forces of life can express through us. These are centered in our hearts.

As this exercise is adapted from *Shapeshifting into Earth and Cosmos* from Chapter Two, you can alternately do that practice.

When facilitating the experience below, speak the instructions slowly. Enact and feel them yourself as you guide people. Allow adequate time for each segment.

1) As you sit or lie, rest your hands upon your heart. Allow your body and mind to relax. Take three deep, cleansing breaths. (Facilitator takes three audible breaths.) As you breathe, feel the warmth of your hands against your chest and the soft beat of your heart against your hands. Allow each breath to deepen your sense of peace and rest.

2) Return to a normal rhythm of breathing. Place a light focus on each breath as it moves in, through, and, out, of your body. Feel the gentle movements that coincide with your breathing. How does this feel? Enjoy the sensations. If thoughts or concerns arise there is no need to push these away. Simply allow them to flow with the rhythm of breath and body. Thoughts may become spacious or change.

Keep returning to your breath and body. Feel your hands over your heart. Feel the movement of the breath within you. If you have cultivated a Sacred Place feel each breath return you to center.

3) When relaxed and present, feel the earth beneath you. If inside, envision, or sense, the earth beneath the floor and foundation of the building. Whether inside or out of doors, imagine the earth's many layers down to its core. Feel power and energy emanating from the earth. Sense her solidity and support. Feel her sustenance.

Feel also, now, the weight and solidity of your own body. It is good to be in a human body. You are the earth. Know this. Breathe the goodness of this in and out with each breath. Feel this particularly in your heart area. Sense the energy of the earth collect here.

4) Now, anchored in your body and the earth, become aware of the space around you. Sense the spaces in between people or objects if you are in a room. If you are outside, feel the space between trees, stones, or what surrounds you.

Expand into this space. Continue to feel your body, breath, and the warmth of your hands against your heart. Stay fully present while you simultaneously expand awareness out.

5) Fully present, expand out further with your awareness. Sense the space that comprises, and lies beyond, the walls of the room or the natural locale.

Imagine everything as energy; trees, stones, water, chairs, people, walls. Nothing is purely material. You can penetrate, as well as travel through, matter. You sense the space of atoms and cells, and can travel into these vast spaces.

6) Fully embodied and present, travel even further. Through your imagination, expand into the open skies.

Move beyond the blue of the skies. Expand awareness out with each breath. Sense the space around the earth and limitless expanses beyond. See or sense planetary bodies, quasars, and stars. You are also this space. You are one with a boundless universe. Breathe this in and out with each breath. Feel this cosmic energy collect in your heart and mix and integrate with the energy of the earth.

7) Take a nice, deep breath with all of this. Breathe oneness with the heavens. Breathe oneness with the earth. Anchor oneness into your heart and body. Make it real.

Once more feel your warm hands resting over your heart. Tune into the soft beat of your heart against your palms. Take a deep restorative breath. Relax and open.

After completing this experience, or practicing *Shapeshift into Earth and Cosmos*, you are ready to facilitate, or experience, the journey below.

Dream It Possible

Guide this journey with the soft beat of a drum, or play a musical CD that induces a deeply restful state so the rational or censoring aspect of the mind can relax. If you enact or assist this experience outside, do the same or invite people to journey to the sounds of nature.

In the journey space invite people to openly consider, or to leaf through the pages of an imaginary text entitled *The Book of the Future* to view, the following: "What would I like to see fifty years in the future? What world is possible? In what ways would I like humanity to evolve by this time, even if this appears impossible judging by normal standards or in looking at the current state of global affairs? What are my deepest longings for earthly life; how can we, as a species, optimally live? If humans could inhabit this planet in any form or manner, and attain this in fifty years, what is my highest vision?"

This is similar to the journey to *Dream Harmony on Earth*, in Chapter Three. In this instance, visualize, imagine, feel, or sense, the details of how humans can evolve and live. What could earthly life be like in fifty years if we expressed our highest creative potential? What does enlightened community look and feel like?

Invite specifics and trust that the journey will reveal them. Things that most provoke or move you will naturally appear. Yet, you may ponder or suggest: "What does my home, and what do cities, villages, families, neighborhoods look like?" Explore the character and role of corporations, schools, organizations, and institutions in your future visioning. Survey the economic, global and local social climates. Ask, "How do people appear; how do they subsist, interact and relate?"

Reflect upon, or look into *The Book of the Future* to see the routines of each day; how people subsist, eat, and dress. What is the predominant medical model? How do we view health? What are the social and political systems? How do people get around and travel? What world do you see? What is the outcome of our current and pressing problems? How do diverse populations, races and cultures relate? What is the fate of indigenous groups? Does your imagined reality include life beyond our planet? How do we view nature; what are our relations with the forests, waters, land, air and animals? What does stewardship of the environment mean for enlightened community? Is there co-creation with nature? What does this look like? How does it affect daily life?

Contemplate all life strata. What are your visions? What dreams open your heart and stir your soul? Follow the threads of your own deep mystery to the heart of your longings. What reality opens before you as you leaf through the pages of *The Book of the Future*?

Let your imagination fly. Dip deeply into the vast reservoir of human potential. Do not hold back. Your heart and body will know when you perceive the highest dream. Allow this reality to reverberate your whole being, try it on for size. Does it feel right in your gut? Is it true in your heart? If it does not, then what needs to adjust? Invite what makes your heart sing, and your breath relax and deepen, to unfold before you in the journey space.

When your dream world feels just right, allow its energy to suffuse you. Breathe it in and breathe it out. Take in and expel power. Feel the beauty of this world and allow every part of you to feel that it is possible.

After sharing the above suggestions, people can then journey and dream unguided. Allow ample time - fifteen or twenty minutes - for this exploration.

To honor the world of our dreams, to make it real, we apply love and attention. The following is a concrete way to do this. It helps us identify and act on those visions we want to give life to.

Make It True

In the final ten minutes of the journey ask people to identify three actions to make their highest vision of life on Planet Earth come true. What three things can they do to nurture this dream? What actions, projects, or attitudes can they adopt to foster personal and global harmony? (These will resound with *Higher Purpose*, explored in Chapter Five.)

You may ask participants to: "Look carefully at these tasks. Scrutinize what they require and how you will enact them. What materials or skills will you need? How will you acquire these? Who will you collaborate with and ask for support? How will you give energy to this heartfelt vision? Be specific. How can you help *The Book of the Future* come into being and encourage wholeness in the world?"

Then, as with the dream, invite people to feel these commitments in their entire being. "Tune into heart and body. What are the qualities? What is the feeling when you focus on higher values? In your mind's eye, see the attitudes, actions, and projects you have identified as if they are already true. How does this feel?"

Allow five or ten minutes for the above process. When complete, bring the journey experience to a close. Invite people to open their eyes when ready and do some gentle stretching.

Lastly, suggest that participants find a partner to share the journey. Also, one at a time, each can share the actions she or he identified to empower the world that is possible. What will each person do to make enlightened community span the globe in the next decades?

After the partner's exchange, invite five or six people to share with the larger group. It is powerful to hear what others are dreaming and the similarities are often striking. The attitudes and behaviors people choose to energize their visions inspire everyone. Examples include an animal communicator who is already giving energy to her dream. The vision urged her to educate the public about how we can learn from animals. So moved by the power of dreaming, a young man committed to facilitate "dream groups" in his home state to help communities dream and act together. A woman realized her dream of facilitating trips to the Himalayas. People give energy to the world of their heartfelt desires by creating wakeful schools and institutes, organizing community projects, shifting lifestyles and attitudes, writing books, composing music, enacting plays, creating art, instating non-profit organizations, communing with nature and preserving it, and other ways. Make your dream world come alive.

You, or those you guide, can revisit this journey to the future world of your dreams at anytime to reconnect with its details. It may be enough to rouse the tone and feeling of the visions. Or, revisit the pages of *The Book of the Future* to determine new actions or perceptual shifts to adopt when the initial ones are complete. Formally journey as above or go into the dream at will. For instance, recall images and insights, and enliven intentions, while on a break at work or sitting on a bus. When you have a few idle moments, daydream about, and breathe in the reality of, your ideal world. Feel it. Make it real. You can also write about these and track the progress of the projects and new ways of being you give energy to. Consider entitling your journal *The Book of the Future*. Or give it a name that feels just right.

Open your heart and embody your dreams. When you dare to step into the world of your deepest longings, life will become an inspired adventure. Giving substance to your highest dreams for humanity expresses the brilliance within. This light shines far and wide.

Obstacles as Gateways

As we create the world of our dreams, obstacles will naturally arise. Yet, obstacles are simply fuel or energy and they usually have something to teach. What obstructs us can empower us; to garner its gifts we open the gate and walk toward what gets in our way. Presented next are methods to do this.

When difficulty or resistance occurs the exercises, *Access and Apply Higher Consciousness* from Chapter One and *Shapeshift Views of Global Dilemmas* from Chapter Three, can help. Yet, instead of *Shapeshifting* into the sun or a spirit guide, you may alternately do so with a person you admire. This can be someone famous or a historical figure you have never met, a favorite high school teacher, or anyone whose character you respect. This strategy works well for people of all walks of life; we apply it in varying settings. Follow the steps outlined in the above-mentioned sections and imagine looking through the eyes of a person you esteem to survey your dilemma from his or her vantage.

If particularly resilient, you can do the opposite and *Shapeshift* into your adversary to understand what dreams drive the person or situation that denies your dream. Always come fully out of the experience to your own body and identity. (If merging with your adversary feels threatening, do not attempt it!) Whether the adversary is a political leader, a corporation that runs sweat shops, or a family member who sees change as threatening and thwarts our expression, standing in our antagonist's shoes can help us understand our reactions. We can apply this method to institutions, corporations, situations, or people who put up roadblocks to the world we dedicate ourselves to. Just as shamans survey dreams held in the energy field to determine what causes sickness, we can look at what propels businesses, groups and individuals.

Begin by visiting your *Sacred Place* and connecting with your guides and helpers. *Shapeshift* into light, merge with your essence self as described in Chapter Six. Take your time.

Next, open to another's experience, or the situation. Intend not to take on its energy or impose your own. Simply ask to see through clear lenses. Open to looking from a closer vantage for the benefit of all involved. Take your time and then given what you sense or see, explore how you might better relate. What does this situation call for, how can you act more effectively?

Later, you may want to go more deeply. What do you feel when exploring this person's outlook? Or, what is the character or tone of this organization or predicament? What do you sense or see beyond the obvious? Take your time and have a light touch as you connect. Open to the essence of this person or circumstance. (Review the essence approaches from Chapter Six.) Again, what do you sense, feel or see? Take your time.

Now, completely let the practice go. Upon letting go, feel spacious and resilient. Breathe in *Lung-Ta*, life force.

When complete, release your helpers and guides. Come fully back into your body and the room. Gently stretch and take some deep, refreshing breaths. Go outside if you can, and place your bare feet upon the earth. Or ground in other ways. Take time to write or reflect on how to follow through with what you detected. You may understand what underlies the problem and relate in a cleverer or more empathic way. Surprised at how much your own ego is at play, you may try a different tack. After confronting the fear of what happens when you express the truth, you may stop enabling the person or situation and push even harder for what you know is right. Or, do all of the above. These are just examples.

Wake Up, Lighten Up, Persevere

Wake Up

As we regard obstacles as gateways we should also not be discouraged when our goals for a new world are met slowly. The deep restructuring of reality has phases that are unpredictable and unstable. As a case in point, many of us now confront enormous shake-ups in our lives. Whether encountering the death of a loved one, loss of income and security, a major move, life threatening illness, or a shift in relationship dynamics, the familiar ways we know are dissolving. This is equally true for the world at large. As of the time of this writing, our systems look as if they are collapsing. Violence escalates in our streets, environmental and corporate atrocities mount, third world dilemmas multiply, and the economy is still spinning out of control. It is not hard to imagine why these decades surrounding the mystique of 2012 are called the *End Times* and why so many people fear the world is actually coming to an end.

When you feel lost in the gap between the old and the new, try to see the chaos as integral to change. Remember that intelligence underlies it. In workshops I invite participants to journey to look at, and communicate with, the deeper rhythms of personal and global reformation. We can tap the wisdom of shifting cycles and find our step in the beat of transformation. Consider a fragile sprout that disturbs the soil as it breaks through the earth in its unfurling and ask, "What new life unfolds simultaneous to (and perhaps depends upon) the interruption of familiar and known patterns? How can I nurture the seed of a new me?" Just as vital forces disrupt the soil in thrusting a fresh, green shoot through the earth toward the sun, envisage the spirit of life dismantling old paradigms and awakening *Higher Consciousness*. You might ask, "How can I evolve and encourage change? How can I inspire others?" Look to your *Higher Purpose* and your dream of humanity's highest potential for these answers.

Personally, and globally, the sloughing off of the old can feel treacherous and unruly. In walking through these times it is easy to become lost in anger, sadness, or fear, or to numb through addiction or distraction. No extreme is helpful. There is wisdom to our agitation as it can push us to where we need to go. Admitting to the anguish, terror, and rage we feel liberates energy that can be used constructively. We are bound to feel lost at times. Yet, we can swim to the next shore. This is a profound time of reorganizing. Each of us must find our way and care for ourselves and each other as we do. No matter what circumstances swirl around us we can talk with our spirit guides and ask nature to heal and give us strength. These good influences can guide us. It rarely helps to push feelings away. That energy needs to flow. We can breathe, and move, with what we feel following each moment back to center. As this is often easier said than done, the suggestions in this book will help.

As uncertainty escalates, each of us can guide ourselves by the living intelligence of these times, with which we are inseparable, to nourish the tender seedling of a new reality. Within the womb of dissolution quickens a world of untold beauty.

Lighten Up

As we navigate these times wakefully, it helps to move, laugh, to be light and joyful. There are untold health benefits to laughter and joy. We can access these by being like a child. In workshops we do so in a variety of ways, see what appeals to you. We sometimes crawl on the floor to get back to our seats after journeys; meander through the circle of people bumping hips as we return; drum and dance between sessions. Sometimes we even gallop together like horses to traditional Tuvan throat singing music (*Back Tuva Future* Ondar, songs #1 and #2) ask first for a "lewd," then a "crude," then lastly a "silly" story from three participants, and apply other light-hearted strategies. I am struck by the glee, intimacy and healing these antics elicit and how they nurture authentic sharing. They excel in helping people to integrate overwhelming feelings or heightened states that can accompany deep shamanic work (as well as global and personal change). Synchronizing body and mind in playful, childlike ways also makes it easier for people to translate their experiences and insights into ordinary life.

Likewise, we can invite our child-self to come out to play every day, even in serious circumstances. An outlandish example is a story told by a Celtic friend whose family held a wake for an elderly uncle who had died. The tone was at first subdued. Soon the mood lifted and the room filled with the small clan's celebratory sounds as they recalled their loved one's life. At one point, as relatives stood near the opened casket, one of the remaining uncles peered into the coffin as if investigating his brother's body. Without turning to face the others he said, "Hmmm. That's a really nice pair of shoes he has on." Everyone laughed, which just egged the old man on, "Yes, that's a *very* nice pair of shoes! He certainly doesn't need those shoes now, but I could use them." The uncle reached into the casket, then gently untied and removed the dead man's shoes. The family was at first shocked. Yet, as they were familiar with this one's antics, the cousins, siblings, uncles and aunts soon laughed until they lost their breath. Some moments later the elderly gentleman peeked into the casket again, "Hmmm. That's a really nice belt he has on."

This is not unlike the "silly" and perhaps, "crude," stories told at our workshops. We might not desire to do a comedy act at the next funeral, but few of us would argue the therapeutic value of laughing. Our spirits lift when we are happy, our physiology hums and we gain a more spacious angle on the world's, and our own, problems. Well-placed humor and joyous movement loosen us up. We become more flexible and able to integrate complexity.

Whether we are a spiritualist, activist, or whatever, when we take ourselves and our views too seriously we can lose vitality, as if we have sewn shut the entrances to life's magic and mystery. Contrastingly Einstein, proponents of the new physics, and others expand our view of reality. According to these vantages everything is space and potential. Likewise, the Maya Elders and guides we know remind us that their prophecies are not about destruction, but transformation. The Mayas and other cultures we have worked with tell us this is the portal into a new era that has the potential to create more compassionate and cooperative human societies. The promise of upcoming decades is that we will transition from fixed to more fluid ways, just as the new physics shifts us from a Newtonian world of parts to quantum fields of energy. We must nurture a personal relationship with the living intelligence of these prophecies, beyond trendy or intellectual interpretation, and do our part to make the changeover smooth. A little humor goes a long way to help us rouse the good energy needed to pursue positive change.

Persevere

As we lighten up, adopt a non-linear tack and open our hearts and bodies to epic shifts, it helps to put hopes and fears into perspective. The earth needs our attention as do other species. It is also ironic to obsess about our own enlightenment, or what catastrophes may befall us in the decades that trail 2012, when most people in undeveloped countries live under daily threat of disease, starvation, poverty, natural disaster and annihilation. Indigenous people the world over have endured crises for centuries. Remarkably, and despite severity of suffering or whether afflicting person or culture, Tuvan shamans I know never question what is possible and never give up hope. The shaman affirms: "I can overcome this disease and disaster." This is true whether it is a physical hardship, or the fierce affects of historical genocide and cultural oppression, such as is seen in the environmental degradation, suicide, and alcoholism in rural villages that dot the Asian Steppe. Aboriginal Eurasian cultures have been decimated, yet their shamans are dedicated to restoring their people, lands and traditions. *The Last of the Shor Shamans* by Alexander and Luba Arbachakov and *Spiritual Wisdom from the Altai Mountains* by Nikolai Shodoyev preserve such legacies.

Whether living on the Asian Steppe or in the Amazon Basin, a shaman follows heart, body and soul to heal each circumstance at its root. This burden is ecstatic as it is not taken on alone. The shaman asks the spirits and nature for help. The trees, the flowers, the stones, the earth, and the life force in everything that grows upon the earth, share their power. The healer roots deeply into these forces. When this power grows very strong, the shaman intuits how to direct it for higher good. She or he then transmits these healing forces out to community or patient.

Like shamans all over the world we can draw upon our own,

and nature's power, and rely on the spirits, to help us dream and act for higher good. As the shifting of personal and societal dreams forces us out of denial, we can guide ourselves into a future that nourishes not only the human, but also the plant, animal, and mineral species of our planet. No matter how comfortable, those patterns which do not serve the larger environmental and global family, or our own higher good, will not persist. Given this, the reality we know is indeed coming to a close. Yet, inspired groups that span the globe tell us the templates for healthier living are already here.

Motivated people from all walks of life are rising up to seize the opportunity of this era and build a new world. As in ancient death and rebirthing rites, we may feel as if we are dying as we let go of fantasies about life, and ourselves, to live genuinely. Yet, the richness of being real eases the release of outdated ways.

Now is the time to join with like-minded others to dream and act together. We must fix upon the higher paths that open now and walk steadfast in their direction. As we do so, it is vital that humanity remembers it is boundless; we are one with infinite potential. The following visualization helps us ignite the creative intelligence within.

Merge with Universal Light

This experience is wonderful to share with a group. If guiding, take your time. Immerse fully in each part of the journey, simultaneously staying aware of the group. Remind participants that their journey may proceed faster or slower than you speak. The content may take an entirely different route, yet, whatever is meant to happen, will. In this case, the cadence of your voice will support them.

We play soft background music and use no drumming. The music we use for this journey is *Shamans' Healing* by Shastro. Consider increasing the volume at those times when you invite people to go deeper into their experience, as suggested.

You may want to adjust the first two paragraphs below accordingly as the wording assumes an established relationship with a *Sacred Place*.

Merge with Universal Light

Find a comfortable place to lie or sit where you will not be disturbed. Gently stretch and take several refreshing breaths. As you relax, settle into and immerse within your *Sacred Place*. We each can create an inner sanctum. Although some locales and experiences may be similar to others, no *Sacred Place* is exactly like ours. Our sacred haven is our expression. It reflects our relationship with ourselves, the earth and universe, spirit guides, and our *Higher Purpose*. Breathe in the sacredness, healing and comfort of your protected place. Take all the time you like. Relax further with each breath.

Allow time.

As you lie in your *Sacred Place*, feel the presence of spirit guides and *Huacas*. See, sense, or simply know they are there. Take a deep, cleansing breath with the beauty and power that surrounds you. Breathe in safety, sacredness. You are protected, resting comfortably in your sacred haven. Rouse its presence with each breath in and out. Your *Sacred Place* lives within you, as well as in the journey space.

Allow several minutes.

Now, notice. Something or someone calls to you. Feel the presence tug at your awareness. What do you notice? Where in your body do you experience this? Allow this longing; it is the desire to connect with something intimately familiar, yet which you may not be able to name or even remember. Allow this sensation to grow. Give room for it. You do not need to name it. Trust and take your time.

Allow time.

This calling now prods you. Stand in your *Sacred Place*. Feel yourself slowly rise to your feet in the journey space. When ready, walk from your sacred haven.

Explore beyond this sanctuary to the surrounding scenery. Take your time. Sense what direction calls. Enjoy each movement and sensation as you walk. Feel each foot as you step upon grass, sand or whatever is the surface. Look down. What do you walk upon? As you move, what do you see and smell? What do you hear? For instance, do birds sing, are waves crashing, do breezes blow? Is the sun warm? Do plants brush your skin? What is happening for you?

Allow Time.

Look ahead now to where the landscape opens. A large vista and sky spread before you. Gaze upward. Are there clouds or is the sky blue and clear? As you gaze into space, sense the longing you feel grow. Something magical is about to happen. You can feel it.

Continue to look skyward. Something remarkable occurs. A faint light radiates high in the heavens. It is like nothing you have seen. Your heart aches. What is this feeling? It may be as if your very soul is being touched. Take a moment. Allow the deepest part of you to surface. It yearns for something. This is indescribable, yet, ultimately familiar.

Allow Time.

The light grows brilliant and a sparkling beam emerges. A luminous shaft slowly descends from the sky. Look at, sense, or feel, this heavenly beam of energy. What do you feel?

If drawn, walk slowly. Make your way to the glowing column which descends toward the earth. Feel each movement and each step. Listen. Open your senses. Move closer. The pure white shaft of light has a hint of color. Is it a golden or violet hue? Or what color is it? The tube of light vibrates. You hear a hum. Or you may just sense it in your heart and not hear it with your ears. What do you feel? Take all the time you like.

Allow time.

The transparent light ray moves closer to the ground. It gently touches the earth within feet of you. Its width spans seven feet or more. Feel this light before you. What is its quality? It is alive, conscious. Look carefully at it and listen. Open your heart. Move closer to the dazzling beam if you desire. Gently step into the glowing force field, if and when it feels right.

As you immerse in this field of energy, bathe in it. Feel divine light. Take on the shimmer of this light. It tenderly touches your face and heart. What do you feel? Allow sadness, love, joy or whatever feelings to bubble up and through. This light touched your soul. It heals and loves every cell, organ, muscle and bone. It nurtures those parts that feel whole equally to those parts that feel fragmented or wounded. All of you is welcomed and celebrated in this light. Sparkling energy embraces and fills you. Take a nice, deep breath with all of this.

Allow Time.

Now, go more deeply into the experience. Feel the loving power and wisdom of this light as it swirls through every part of your body, mind, heart and spirit to cleanse and release old patterns. Sense it spiral within and all around you lifting deep, subconscious layers that no longer serve you. Feel these sweeping up, out, and liberating from you. You may not even know what they are. Trust what occurs. This light, that is inseparable from you, can only act for your highest good. Take your time. Know that you can *Shapeshift*. This light merges with, and dissolves, false beliefs. It evaporates conditioned ideas about life and the ways we separate from ourselves, others, spirit, and nature. It ignites an inner flame of wisdom that lights up dormant spiritual centers in the mind and body, transforming every physical cell. Your DNA glows in this firelight. This flame restores internal and external balance; it burns from a deep desire to be one with *Mother Earth, Mother Time,* and *Mother Universe.* This is your authentic presence. You are home. You are vast. This light is conscious and it is you. Really go into this experience.

Allow ample time here with louder music.

When complete, and ready, gently step out and away from the luminous beam. As you separate physically from this light source its loving vibration remains with you. A palpable hum may fill you. Your mind is spacious, light. You may feel warmth or sense a glow. You may feel deeply peaceful, impassioned, or you may feel something else altogether. Fresh ways of being are on the horizon. Humanity is poised to uncover expansive, new ways to experience life that will feel totally natural. How does this feel?

Consider now taking a few steps back from the light beam. Gaze again toward the heavens. Something spectacular occurs. A radiant human-like form glides down the beam of light from on high. A being of pure, swirling light descends from the heavens. The form appears tall, weightless. It moves effortlessly through the tube of shimmering energy. What do you see? What do you sense?

The being comes closer. You see that it wears a simple robe with sleeves to the wrists. The garment is crafted of fabric that appears to be pure energy or light. It is like no material here on earth. The being arrives closer, floating down the light column directly in front of you now. Discern the robe's color. What do you sense? What do you see?

The gown may be embellished with patterns overlying a simple background color. If this is so, what are these patterns? Are they stars, swirls or leaves? Is it a design of birds or grasshoppers? Or is it geometrical? Is it something else altogether, or of varied, or changing, images and colors? What adorns the light being's robe? Look at it. What do you feel?

Allow time.

The translucent being's toes light upon the earth. It presses both feet firmly onto the ground. The human-like form of light then carefully steps from the glowing shaft. Upon the earth radiates a circle of light many inches beyond its toes and feet. This happens with every step the light form takes. Look at this light emanate from its feet as it walks upon the earth. What do you feel?

How tall does this form appear? What does the being look like? How do you feel standing there? Go into these feelings. If drawn, open your heart and gaze into this one's face and eyes. What do you see? Keep feeling.

Allow ample time.

If it is right for you, open to exchange with this cosmic friend. This is your essence, the embodiment of your unlimited potential. This being, crafted from the universe's own deep longing, mirrors your authentic presence.

Open to this enlightened one; feel it. This being links you to the vast reservoir of cosmic intelligence, the creative force of the universe; it holds the keys to personal, and global, transformation. What does this stir for you? What do you feel as you engage this being? Stay in your heart and body. Actual words or thoughts may not form; you may not want to talk or ask questions. In this case, simply be. Bathe in essence. Take a deep breath as if drinking in light from the air.

If you do ask questions, you may not hear this being with your ears or understand its responses with your mind. Instead, you may feel them in heart and body. This is intimate beyond what language could be. As mind and heart are inseparable, you may think and converse differently, through feeling and vibration. This happens instantaneously and with a depth of feeling that words could not convey. Connect with the light being in whatever way feels absolutely right in this moment. Surrender to infinite consciousness. Open heart and body to who you are.

Allow ample time here with louder music.

When your exchange comes to a close, take time to transition. Express your gratitude for this time you have shared. What feels right?

Now, look to this loving being's outstretched hands. There, a robe rests on its palms. What colors and patterns do you see? This robe is for you. If it is right for you to receive it, communicate this from your heart to the being's heart.

If you consent, allow the luminous presence to unfold the robe, lightly place it onto your shoulders, and wrap it loosely around your body. Feel the garment's texture and ambience as it gently enfolds you. The fabric is weightless and seamless. It may glow or you may sense its life force in other ways. It envelops and penetrates every part of you without judgment. What do you feel? What are the sensations in wearing it?

The celestial robe soon becomes a transparent mesh of light upon your body that absorbs completely into your skin and body through your clothes; the radiant webbing dissolves into you and disappears. You, and the being of light, are one. You, and the column of light, are indivisible. In merging with this robe feel its energy. What does this awaken? You are never separate from source. Immerse in, and breathe deeply with this.

Allow ample time.

The light being now holds a gift in its outstretched hand. Look at this gift. What does the being hold and what do you feel in looking at it? It may appear material, as real as anything in this world, yet it is also translucent. The object, like the robe, may have a soft radiance or glow. It is crafted of a spiritual fabric, much like the glowing garment. Open to its energy if this feels right for you. Take your time.

Allow time.

If resonant with the gift held out before you, allow the luminous form to place it into you. If you consent to the being placing the gift inside of you, note where this is. Is it placed into your heart? Is it guided to your forehead at the third eye area or where is this gift gently placed? Go into the feelings and sensations. You may see images or connect with beings or energies beyond time and space. The spiritual qualities of this gift permeate you. What is this like? Open your heart and body to the sensations.

Allow ample time.

Your exchange with this infinite one comes to a close. Gaze once more into the being's face and eyes. What do you feel? Does a question linger? Allow it to form in your heart. Forget the words now, feel your question. Really feel it, make it strong. Your own feelings reverberate within the being's heart. This enlightened one is moved by your heart's longing. A swirling light may emanate from its heart, and softly touch your own, in response. Feel its touch. Open to a deeper way of knowing.

Allow time.

Before departing, your heart grows full with a question to you from the light being: "Will you bring wakefulness and compassion to the world?"

Take your time. Feel this response in the deepest part of you. Beyond thought, what is the feeling? How will you respond? The answer must come from your innermost self.

Allow time.

The being now slowly turns from where you stand and makes its way back toward the luminous tunnel. The light beam vibrates and hums. What do you feel as this one steps into the light to leave? Open your heart, do not hold back.

Watch the being ascend. It rises into the heavens and the sparkling tunnel vanishes beneath its feet. The form soon glides high into the sky until the light grows faint. The vision then evaporates; a wisp of heavenly light remains.

How do you feel?

Allow time.

When ready, slowly make your way back to your *Sacred Place*. Feel each step and sensation as you walk. The being's presence pervades you. You are not separate; this being is you. Feel the gift deep inside of you and the robe of celestial fabric that is inseparable from you. You are one with vast potential that you can bring into daily life. The universe blazes within you.

Take all the time you like. Meander back to your *Sacred Place*.

Notice the sights, feel the sensations, take in the smells. Feel the fire and light that is you.

Allow time.

When you arrive at your *Sacred Place*, be aware of the position you began the journey in. Rest your body. Connect with your sacred haven. Look at, or feel, its details. Smell and touch. Sense and listen. Take a deep refreshing breath where you sit or lie. Feel present, alive. Thank, and release, your spirit guides and helpers.

Now, gently make the transition from your *Sacred Place*. Come fully back into this time and space. As you return to your everyday world, give room for this wisdom fire that transcends words, struggles and polarity. Co-create a *new* world from your flame's desire. Feel it burn deep inside of you, igniting a passion that incinerates resistance to infinite intelligence. Be authentic, convey compassion. Wake up to this planet.

Wiggle your toes and fingers and do some gentle stretching. Bring your awareness fully back into the room. Take your time. When ready, open your eyes.

If facilitating a group, draw from the many suggestions given elsewhere in this book for how to close and integrate shamanic journeys. Give plenty of time for participants to reflect upon their experience. Be sure to invite them to identify concrete ways to be, or act, to bring the power of this journey into the everyday world.

It is ideal to take a walk, move in invigorating and playful ways, or spend time in nature before moving on to read the final section of this book. Or, do something silly!

Open to Mystery, Invite Magic

As we merge with the fire and light that we are, we radiate benefit to everything, and everyone, around us. Mystics tell us this happens naturally and extends farther than we know. We can also channel the benefit of our higher nature through how we act, as well as consciously direct tranquil and spacious energy to people and situations of all time periods and locations.

Offering wakefulness is similar to the Buddhist practice of "Dedicating the Merit." Whatever calm and happy state of mind is gained through meditation is dedicated to the enlightenment of all beings. Buddhists do not offer merit only to people. Included is all life on earth, animate and inanimate, those beyond this planet, spirits, entities, thought forms, other invisibles, including those that inhabit other times and dimensions. These lie well outside the boxes of Western thought yet it is time that modern cultures recognize subtle influences. We must have compassion for the countless unseen beings we co-exist with and admit to our impact on each other. For instance, although we live in an epoch of untold advances we are habituated to the violence, the greed and the ignorance that passes from one century to the next. The waters and air, the lands where we dwell, and from which we eat, hang heavy with the nightmares, and spirits, of the past and the present, impacting how we feel, act, and live. It is no wonder that modern human societies are based on exploitation, war, and materialism rather than compassion, cooperation, and spirituality. Just as dreams and values shape us, and our societies, so do unresolved spirits and energy.

John Perkins devotes his life to bringing the global community into balance. He and I encourage workshop participants to act on social and environmental issues. We also teach shamanic methods that support these goals including ancient exorcism rites (in advanced programs and apprenticeships) to *Shapeshift* confused energies that negatively influence us and our children, grip our leaders, and which are encouraging institutional corruption.

Entities and spirits at unrest experience inner, as well as perpetuate outer, turmoil. Yet, we, in turn, also affect them. We feed their havoc as much as we do our own. Conversely, as stated in Chapter Six, when awake, our light shines like a beacon for confused and lost spirits to find their way. This occurs whether we are aware of it or not. In her work, *Medicine for the Earth*, Sandra Ingerman demonstrates how embodying the divine self can even transmute environmental toxins. Our light has a profound effect on the nonphysical, and the material, world. It is vital that we shine it.

Be authentic, shine the light that you are. Bring this to everything you do. Illumine the dark shadows of our collective journey and together we will *Shapeshift* this life dream.

As our higher nature transforms the visible and hidden worlds, it also links us to transcendent individuals. These may be saints, yogis, wisdom keepers or healers from other time periods, past, as well as, future. They may be light beings as in the journey above, ancestors, ascended masters, Bodhisattvas or angels. Although having a high vibration increases the chances of perceiving such presences, you can still connect with these beings by journeying to them. Enlightened ones are here for us, whether or not we believe they are real. In workshops we invite people to *Merge with Universal Light* or *Shapeshift* into essence then journey through time and space to sit in a sacred council of beings, such as those mentioned above. Participants bring personal and worldly concerns to these light ones and request their assistance. The light ones in the council usually ask something in return. They know that you, a person, are better suited than they to translate the wisdom from "higher" realms into actual earthly life. Raise your consciousness and open your heart to wise councils; take your place within their circles. Feel these circles with you as you walk through each day. Do your part to bring heaven to earth. You can make a difference in a world that seems to be on the brink of disaster.

When we look through habitual eyes it is easy to see everything wrong in the world today. Unrest appears to span the globe. The biosphere teeters. Our children seem to be walking into the future of a species gone amok. Yet when we awaken to the eyes of the heart, we see differently. The human family is capable of greatness; every moment breathes with this potential. We just need to wake up to it. As dire as life appears for our own and all the earth's children, the dream of harmony with each other and our planet has never been so strong. All we have to do is remember to look for the beauty, mystery and intelligence of life to see that it is everywhere. In doing so we glimpse what heaven on earth could be; and we make it possible.

Final Entry

That the earth, like the heavens, is filled with glory was affirmed for me on my Vision Quest last year in the canyon lands of Washington State. My goals were for *the wild world and me to know each other as one,* and that *the magic of the world show itself to me as I am.* I wanted a phenomenon. Contrary to many questing approaches, I would not fast, do overnight vigils, or ingest mind-altering plants. I was no stranger to enchantment. Now I invited nature and the universe to come alive as never before. I asked for a sign, an irrefutable example beyond the subjective, so I could share with fellow journeyers just how wondrous this earthly existence really is. This had to be without spiritual gymnastics on my part because, no matter how holy, these come from feeling separate and believing we need to strategize our way back to grace. The promise of these times is for the magic, intelligence, and beauty of the "transcendent" to be totally natural.

I imagined my intensity might make it hard for nature to produce anything that would really satisfy me. Yet, the very force and clarity of my intentions opened me wide. Splendor was everywhere, a feast for the senses. The towering ponderosa pine trees, the swift river cutting the ancient designs of the canyon, the birds and snakes and bees and butterflies, the black rock fields that comprised many of the canyon's walls, the occasional flower clusters jutting from stone crevices and the big horn sheep families that set these stone people crashing to the canyon floor at dusk, the constantly changing weather vacillating from hail to crystalline blue skies and everything else in between; the natural world was ecstatic. Who could ask for more? Yet, I did receive more:

It is my first morning alone in the canyon and upon waking I hear singing. I open my eyes and listen. This sound is different from the song of the honeybee (see last chapter). *Then I realize the canyon's own choir is seducing me. I hear these melodies as normal music with my ears. Yet, they begin as a warm feeling in my heart that then becomes audible. I am "hearing" with my heart. I get excited about this but, then, after twelve hours of listening I feel disoriented and panicked, "Maybe I'm mad!" I do everything I can to stop the songs now, but, to no avail. Then I realize I am getting what I asked for. So, I climb once more onto the back of the horse named Euphoria and gallop with her into the melodic sounds. I am again one with the canyon's harmony.*

I stick to my resolve to follow my own, and nature's rhythms, in each moment, with no strategy or involved rituals. Being sacred in a folksy way has already opened so much.

From that first day I listen to, and sing with, the canyon, watch the honeybee walk over my stone bear necklace, put my coat and gloves and hat on when the sky becomes dark, take my coat and gloves and hat off when the sun comes out, climb inside my makeshift shelter when it rains and hails, climb out again when it stops, eat when hungry, drink when thirsty, etc. I laugh in remembering how worried I was about getting bored with three days alone. I feel one with the rhythm of this place, I belong here. The animals and insects crawl under the leaves and blades of grass and move into their holes and then out again with the changing weather, just like me. Their rhythms are mine. My long hair becomes knotted, feral, and the scent of my own body odor almost overwhelms me. I love it.

On the second night I cannot sleep. My toes are freezing as the feathers in the old, down sleeping bag I borrowed have shifted, leaving the lower part of me un-insulated. Yet, it is not so much the cold that is keeping me awake. I am agitated. I try to push it away and jump onto Euphoria's back. Then I catch what I am doing and open to what I feel. Yes, I am agitated. As much as I try not to be, I am. I have to embrace this. Damn! I take a deep breath and resolve to greet what underlies my agitation freshly in the morning; open to its gift. I sleep.

The next morning the sky is clouded but I am not cold. I sit at my altar on the ground and the honeybee visits my bear necklace and me. When it leaves, I find a spot to sit on the earth and welcome my feelings. Anger catches me quickly in its grip. I am angry about issues I thought I had resolved, they all bubble up now at once. What a way to spend a Vision Quest, not holy at all. However, it is sacred because it is. My anger soon turns to sadness. This grief hurts profoundly. Yet, I also feel pleasure in its release. I am stretched out completely, body and belly writhing against the earth, tears pouring out of me and into her. I cry so hard I think I will not stop. Yet, I do.

I lie with my tear-drenched face muddied by the earth, her rich aroma filling me. My hands grab at grass tufts; my nails dig into the dirt. I feel the beating heart of this mother beneath me as I never have before in all my life. She claims me, "You are my daughter. I am your Mother." I belong here. The steed named Euphoria comes galloping back.

After some time, I get up in a bit of a delirium and notice the sun has come out. I grab my sun hat and lie on my back with my knees up and hat covering my face. I am exhausted, ready for a nap. Yet, upon closing my eyes I have a vision. Through a gateway I see deep into the valley at the heart of the canyon. A luminous figure, a man made of light, comes into view in the far distance. He walks toward me from the canyon's center. The closer he comes, the larger he appears. His gait is determined, confident. I feel his movement as if it is inside of me. Soon he is only a few feet in front of me, yet, does not stop. The man of light walks into me, I dissolve into him. The gateway disappears. I am in the center of the canyon's mystery, and my own. I hear singing. I am full. Nothing more needs to happen. Yet, it does.

The clouds have moved in, they are a solid, darkening mass. I put on the coat and hat and gloves and socks and shoes lying next to me. I look out to the cliffs in the distance across the river valley, then I search the sky; there is not a break in clouds. I get up and look behind me. I stand peering above the cliffs that were at my back and see a big, Blue Circle in the sky. I am looking through a portal to the blue sky beyond the clouds. There is no other break in the entire sky except for this faultless Blue Circle. A phenomenon; this is the miracle.

The clouds shift, the circle's edges drift counterclockwise like a slow spinning vortex. As the circle rotates and morphs, I think, "This is real, not a Vision." A cloud wisp moves down into the circle from the top center and the circle shape is changing. I wonder if it is forming a heart. "Yeah, right," I say. As the words spill out it happens right before my eyes. The canyon sky is a blanket of clouds except for where I look - a Blue Heart looms. The best of artists could not draw more perfect lines.

I look and cry and look and cry. The Blue Heart comes into me. I am it and it is me. The only way my own heart can open enough to take this in is by crying. I look and cry and look and cry. I feel like I will never stop. Yet, finally - I do.

I hear Euphoria's galloping hooves like prayer flags snapping in the wind.

The End Is Where We Begin

Indigenous shamanic peoples of diverse cultures say we and our world are an interconnected dream. We are one with everything and all is one with us. As is true of our sleeping dreams, this dream of who we are is malleable. We and our world can change. We can re-shape at anytime. Prophecies from all over the planet point to this time in human history as one of monumental shifting. The universal intelligence is ecstatic, its repertoire, infinite; and now the time is ripe to dream ourselves freshly. In doing so, we can realize our true potential and create a new world for our own, and all the earth's children.

May who we are, and how we live, benefit all of sentient life.

ABOUT THE AUTHOR

Llyn Roberts is a prominent teacher of healing and shamanism. She holds a master's degree in Tibetan Buddhist and Western Psychology, has undergone extensive training with traditional Andean healers, and has been initiated into shamanic circles by Quechua peoples in South America, and in Siberia. Llyn has facilitated sacred journeys to work alongside indigenous people living in remote regions of the Amazon basin, the Asian steppes, high Andes, and in ancient Maya lands of Central America. She teaches at highly regarded educational institutions, is a consultant to the University of Massachusetts/Dartmouth Sustainability Initiative and the non-profit organization, Earth Train. She served as adjunct faculty for Union Graduate School and has for many years directed the non-profit organization, Dream Change, dedicated to personal and global transformation. Llyn's books include *The Good Remembering, Shamanic Reiki* and *Shapeshifting into Higher Consciousness*. A modern day mystic and spiritual ecologist, her work inspires a deep sense of belonging with the natural world.

Llyn Roberts lives on an island in the Salish Sea in Washington State, USA. To find out more about Llyn and Dream Change visit www.dreamchange.org.

ACKNOWLEDGEMENTS

My profound gratitude goes to dear friend and inspirer, John Perkins - without John this book would not exist. The ever changing nature of our work together takes me deeper into my purpose.

These writings are possible because of many people. I offer sincere appreciation to the indigenous teachers, shamanic groups and *Shapeshifters* I have learned from, including: AiTchourek, Gerardo Barrios, Mercedes Barrios Longfellow, Tatyana Kobezhikova, Herrel and Aida and Nina, Kenin Lopsan, Ipupiara Makunainam, Maria Ernestina, Mario, Panamanian Kuna and Embera, Jose Joaquin Pineda, the Shor Mountain people, Don Esteban and Jorge and Jose Tamayo, Alberto Tatzo, Cleicha Toscano, Maria Juana and Antonio Yamberla, Diana Valesquez, Daniel Wachapa and so many others. I thank Dream Change and John Perkins, the Omega Institute, Bill Pfeiffer and The Sacred Earth Network, The Prophet's Conference (Robin and Cody Johnson), Julio Tot and Four Directions Travels in Guatemala, Michael Harner, Juan Gabriel Carrasco, Rollanda Kongar, Sasha and Luba Arbachakov, Boris Fomin, Valentina Glavcheva and Earth Train for making these connections possible.

I feel endless gratitude for the blessings and teachings of Tibetan Buddhism, especially those of Venerable Chogyam, Trunpga, Rinpoche, Tenzin Wangyal, Rinpoche, and recently of Kilung Jigme, Rinpoche (I so appreciate Kilung Rinpoche's supportive Sangha).

This book is inspired by countless colleagues and event participants, all of whom would be impossible to name. That said, I am indebted to Dr. Donald M. Epstein and Kathlyn Hendricks for opening me to the body's intelligence. I thank those teachers and students who make it possible for shamanism's earth-honoring message to flourish in the West. I extend heartfelt thanks to Dream Change, Inc. and my inspired partners who know how to play as hard as they work: Marilyn Dexter, Bob Southard, Moira Ashleigh, Vincent Santo Ferrau, Sean Adams, DiAnn Baxter, Mary Warejcka, Lynda Phelps and Sarah Stockwell-Arthen. I value the following people for their role in deepening my soul work: Bill Pfeiffer, Zacciah Blackburn, Joel Kaplan, Anne Hayden, Sheila Belanger and Mick Dodge.

I am grateful to John Hunt and all the dedicated people at O-Books who *Shapeshift* dreams into publications. I thank the folks at Useless Bay Coffee House where I wrote more than half of this manuscript.

I sincerely thank John Perkins, Caryn Markson, Marilyn Dexter and Bob Southard for traveling right along with me through the writing of this book. My undying gratitude goes to my husband, Dr. Joel Shrut, for being a great life partner, making me laugh and having bottomless patience while I write. I thank everyone in my family. I am grateful to Mira Steinbrecher and Gisela Timmermann who supported me through this book's final phases. I thank my children, Sayre and Eben Herrick, whose depth and creativity thrill me to no end.

I bow to the lands, waters, airs, the fires deep within the earth, and those within the heavens - and the spiritual fire within each of us. May these guide our way.

Llyn Roberts, Washington State, USA, February 28, 2011

SPECIAL ACKNOWLEDGEMENTS

I extend special thanks to the following people for their invaluable contributions during the editing process of *Shapeshifting into Higher Consciousness*.

Caryn Markson, Ph.D. is a Shamanic Reiki master teacher and practitioner. A licensed Clinical Psychologist and Consultant in Northampton, Massachusetts, Caryn has been in clinical practice since 1981, working with children, adolescents, adults and couples, specializing in the treatment of trauma. Her psychotherapy focuses on helping people heal through finding inner resources and strengths to guide them into the shift from past wounds to present capacity. Her therapeutic work is fully integrated with her long term spiritual practice and understanding that healing is a relationship that emerges from inner transformation. Caryn can be reached at (001) 413-585-1130.

Bob Southard is a Shamanic Reiki master practitioner, a Usui Reiki teacher and a certified hypnotherapist. He developed the Hypnojourney™ technique (see *HypnoJourney™ to the Amazon*, available on amazon.com) and is the author of *Ordinary Secrets ~ Notes for Your Spiritual Journey* and *Conscious Living Made Easy*. Bob co-produced, with Llyn Roberts, the Pathways to Inner Peace CD series (meditations, journeys and *Hypnojourney™)*. He has worked with the nonprofit, Dream Change, for many years and sits on its board of directors. To contact Bob for Reiki Distance Healing, and for more information: bob@boston-mystery.com and www.dreamchange.org or www.boston-mystery.com.

Mary Warejcka, M.A. is a Shamanic Reiki master teacher and practitioner offering individual sessions and classes in the

Dallas, Texas, area. A professional writer and editor, Mary also holds a master's degree in theological studies. She focuses on helping people connect with their inner wisdom, Spirit, and the healing forces of nature and the elements. She has led one-day workshops as well as 18-month-long Shamanic Reiki apprenticeship programs that help people go deeply into their essence to emerge with a new understanding of self and their place in the world. Mary can be reached at (001) 214-929-7902, or at mary@manypathsway.net and her website address is: www.manypathsway.net

RESOURCES AND REFERENCED MATERIAL

BOOKS

Adventures in Reincarnation (Jameison, Bryan)

Blink: The Power of Thinking Without Thinking (Gladwell, Malcolm)

Earthing (Ober, Sinatra & Zucker)

Confessions of an Economic Hit Man (Perkins, John)

Conscious Living Made Easy (Southard, Robert Y.)

In the Realm of Hungry Ghosts: Close Encounters with Addiction (Mate, Dr. Gabor)

Harry Potter Series (Rowling, J.K.)

Life After Life (Moody, Raymond)

Mantra: Sacred Words of Power (Ashley-Farrand, Thomas)

Ordinary Secrets: Notes for Your Spiritual Journey (Southard, Robert Y.)

Shaman, Healer, Sage and *Courageous Dreaming* (Villoldo Ph.D., Alberto)

Shamanic Reiki: Expanded Ways of Working with Universal Life Force Energy (Roberts & Levy)

The Shamanic Way of the Bee (Buxton, Simon)

Shapeshifting: Techniques for Global and Personal Transformation (Perkins, John)

Soul Companions (Sawyer, Karen)

Spirit Guides & Angel Guardians (Webster, Richard)

Spiritual Wisdom from the Altai Mountains (Shodoyev, Nikolai)

The Fellowship of the Ring (Tolkein, J.R.R.)

The Last of the Shor Shamans (Arbachakov, Alexander & Luba)

The Soul of Money (Twist, Lynne)

The World I Dream Of (Butz, Curt)

Weather Shamanism (Moss & Corbin)

Wittgenstein's Beetle and Other Classic Thought Experiments

(Cohen, Martin)

Yoga, Power, and Spirit (Villoldo Ph.D., Alberto)

FILM, MUSIC & PUBLICATIONS

Back Tuva Future – CD, Ondar

Dakshina – CD, Deva Premal

Gran Torino – Warner Bros

I Heart Huckabees - Fox Searchlight

New Dimensions Radio - newdimensions.org

Pathways to Inner Peace – CD, Roberts & Southard

Shamans' Healing – CD, Shastro

The Secret – Prime Time Productions

Yes! Magazine - Creative Commons Movement

INDIVIDUALS

Belanger, Sheila & Hayden, Anne: nwsoulquest.com

Blackburn, Zacciah: thecenteroflight.net

Carter, Majora: majoracartergroup.com

Dodge, Mick: barefootsensei.com or theearthgym.com

Ferrau, Vincent: dreamchange.org

Gerg Gegerenzer: mpib-berlin.mpg.de

Hand Clow, Barbara: handclow2012.com

Ingerman, Sandra: sandraingerman.com

Jenny, Hans: cymaticsource.com

Kaplan, Joel *International Clairaudient*: (001) 9878-470-1489

Wolf, Fred Alan: fredalanwolf.com

ORGANIZATIONS

Bioneers: bioneers.org

Dream Change: dreamchange.org

EarthTrain: earthtrain.org

Green Fests: greenfestivals.org

Heart Math Institute: heartmath.org

Junglewood: earthtrain.org

Roots and Shoots: rootsandshoots.org

The Omega Institute: eomega.org

The Pachamama Alliance: pachamama.org

B O O K S

O is a symbol of the world, of oneness and unity. In different cultures it also means the "eye," symbolizing knowledge and insight. We aim to publish books that are accessible, constructive and that challenge accepted opinion, both that of academia and the "moral majority."

Our books are available in all good English language bookstores worldwide. If you don't see the book on the shelves ask the bookstore to order it for you, quoting the ISBN number and title. Alternatively you can order online (all major online retail sites carry our titles) or contact the distributor in the relevant country, listed on the copyright page.

See our website www.o-books.net for a full list of over 500 titles, growing by 100 a year.

And tune in to myspiritradio.com for our book review radio show, hosted by June-Elleni Laine, where you can listen to the authors discussing their books.

mySpiritRadio